SOVIET STRATEGY

IN THE NUCLEAR AGE

SOVIET STRATEGY IN THE NUCLEAR AGE

Raymond L. Garthoff

GREENWOOD PRESS, PUBLISHERS
WESTPORT, CONNECTICUT

Library of Congress Cataloging in Publication Data

Garthoff, Raymond L
  Soviet strategy in the nuclear age.

    Reprint of the ed. published by Praeger, New York,
  which was issued as no. 71 of Praeger publications in
  Russian history and world communism.
    Includes bibliographies.
    1. Russia--Military policy. 2. Russia--Defenses.
  I. Title.
  [UA770.G3 1974]   355.03'3047   74-10015
  ISBN 0-8371-7658-1

This book is Number 71 of Praeger Publications in Russian History and World Communism

Originally published in 1958 by Frederick A. Praeger,
Publishers, New York

Reprinted with the permission of Praeger Publishers, Inc.

Reprinted in 1974 by Greenwood Press,
a division of Williamhouse-Regency Inc.

Library of Congress Catalog Card Number 74-10015

ISBN 0-8371-7658-1

Printed in the United States of America

355,033
G244

To

Margaret Frank Garthoff

My Mother

for her unceasing encouragement

CONTENTS

PREFACE

In order to establish the strategic thought and doctrine of an alien military culture, it is first necessary to escape the confines of one's own implicit and unconscious strategic concept. The ideas of others, when these are interpreted in terms of the military or political analyst's *own* strategic preconceptions, will appear distorted or, often, obsolete. And the comfort derived from a superficial assessment of differing views, in such a manner that these views seem to represent a simple "cultural lag" on the part of our opponent, may obscure the recognition of these views as manifestations of a different underlying doctrine and strategic concept.

Regrettably, such a condition colors much that has been written in the United States about current Soviet military thinking. Now, suddenly prompted by such spectacular technological achievements as *sputnik,* we tend to attribute all nature of superior concentration of skills to the Soviets. Yet, the idea of Soviet advance or advantage in the realm of military *thought* rarely, if ever, has been raised. It should be. For Soviet military doctrine figuratively has made a quantum jump from the bayonet age to the thermonuclear age.

The fundamental conclusion of this present analysis is that the Soviets continue, in the thermonuclear era, to adhere essentially to the classical military strategic concept that the path to victory lies in the decisive defeat of the enemy's armed forces. But far from representing a "lag," it will be seen that this approach has been retained and elaborated to meet the opportunities—and the equally important restraints—presented by the new and continuously developing military technology. The Soviets have prepared for the requirements of total thermonuclear warfare by attending both to the acquisition of new capabilities and to the revision of military doctrine.

The Soviet preparation—doctrinal and other—for general nuclear war does in no way *commit* them to this form of warfare. They retain diversified capabilities for nuclear and non-nuclear limited and local wars. Thus they secure flexibility for meeting any war contingency with whatever military forces are most expedient, without having their hands tied by an over-specialized capability which permits only a narrow choice or none at all. Soviet modernization of doctrine, weapons, and organization is distinguished not by replacement of the capacities for conventional war, but by the addition to them of capacities for either limited or total nuclear war.

That, in brief, is the main conclusion of this study of the challenge to the Free World of Soviet strategy in the nuclear age.

What is the Soviet image of future war? What military forces, organization, and doctrine do the Soviets consider necessary to wage such a future war? These problems are answered in some detail in this study, but it may be useful here to sketch in general outline the Soviet view of a future total war. Leaving aside for this purpose the important question of how the war is launched, we can begin with the reciprocal exchange of thermonuclear strikes. For in the Soviet view, while surprise of attack has now attained much increased importance with modern weapons, such an attack does *not* permit a quick victory.

The initial strategic strikes by modern jet bombers, intercontinental and intermediate range rockets and missiles, and

Preface

submarine-launched missiles, will wreak devastation upon both the United States and the Soviet Union, and upon their chief allies. But does mutual devastation spell mutual defeat? The Soviets answer: No. The priority strikes will destroy the enemy's strategic air and missile bases insofar as these are known. Major cities and industrial centers, on a lower level of priority, will also suffer heavily. Radiological and bacteriological weapons may be used. But this enormous mutual destruction will probably consume the major portion of the respective long-range air and missile forces. Thus the efforts of these forces would in a sense cancel each other out. This is a *crucial* phase of the war, one which a weak or ill-prepared power could lose. But it is not the *decisive* stage of a war between well-prepared major powers; it does not determine the final outcome of the war between them.

"Tactical" air power and rockets, those forces designated to attack the enemy's military forces up to roughly a 1,000-mile range from the starting borders, would similarly engage in mutual nuclear strikes. But here the Soviets do not see a mutual stalemate. The heart of such a capability is the ground forces —trained for nuclear war, armed with nuclear weapons—and here the war would begin with a serious imbalance: a preponderance of Soviet forces. Moreover, in the Soviet view, their mobilization and dispatch of ground forces would be much less critically disrupted than would ours by the nuclear exchange, due to their larger force-in-being and to its deployment. The surviving Soviet land armies are thus expected to be capable of defeating the proportionately weakened enemy forces on the ground. Thus the Soviets would strive to achieve at least a favorable "draw" by occupying the Eurasian continent, and exploiting such resources as might still be available to restore some of the Soviet Union's losses. The shrunken and devastated Free World would be entirely relegated to the Western Hemisphere.

In the major theater, Central-Western Europe, the Soviets would expect to defeat the NATO forces and to occupy the territory at least to the Channel and to the Pyrenees. Soviet intermediate and long-range air and missile forces would not only strive to knock out SAC and British Bomber Command strength in the United Kingdom, Spain, North Africa, and Turkey, but also effectively to interdict (with submarine action) any supply of men and materiel from the United States. Scandinavia and the Balkans would fall.

In the Middle East and Far East those countries allied with the West would be seized by exploiting local Soviet and Chinese superiorities in a situation where the mutual strategic exchange would have denied the United States the ability to bring in sufficient additional strength to prevent their advance. The "neutrals" would be left, at least for a time, on sufferance; local Communists would probably ride to power on the swell of victory.

This picture may seem to offer the Soviets more advantage than we would concede them. It does not mean that the Soviets are so certain of success, or so callous of costs, that they will favor launching a total war. But it does show the current Soviet blueprint for "winning" a total war if circumstances were to lead them to strike.

It is clear from this brief sketch that the Soviets recognize as absolutely essential the acquisition of tremendous intercontinental striking power, and its corollary of home defense to weaken the enemy's long-range attack. It is also clear that they consider as equally important the maintenance of large, modern "theater" land armies, with supporting air, missile, and naval forces. We shall in this book see many interrelated aspects of Soviet strategic thinking which underlie and contribute to these expectations and attitudes. They continue to believe in massive and extended land campaigns, even during total thermonuclear war. And here balanced forces—strong theater armies, as well as intercontinental offensive and defensive capabilities—are needed.

We shall not attempt in this introduction to deal even cursorily with the important Soviet views on other, limited wars. But it is clear that to preserve the flexibility needed to meet such contingencies the Soviets recognize the value of substantial dual capabilities for nuclear and non-nuclear warfare, and for speedy local commitment of forces in a geographically limited ("local" or "peripheral") war.

This glimpse of the Soviet image of future war points to but a few key aspects of Soviet strategy in the thermonuclear era. It is necessary to examine the role of military strategy in Soviet policy, and the roles of military considerations and military leadership in Soviet politics. Soviet military doctrine, as it now stands and as it has developed to meet the challenge of the nuclear age, occupies an obviously major place. The respective roles, missions, doctrines, and weapons of each of the major components of the Soviet armed forces—land, air, and sea—and of each of the missions—strategic offense and defense, theater offense, and deterrent—must be studied.

The chapters of this book investigate each of these questions. Finally, a speculative look into future trends of Soviet strategy, based upon a projection of current advanced thinking and weapons development, is also presented.

The author has one objective in making this study: to discover and interpret contemporary Soviet military strategic thinking so that we can better meet its challenge through better understanding its nature. It should, perhaps, be emphasized that the author is in no way concerned in this book with Soviet policy outside the field of military policy. The book is, therefore, confined strictly to the military aspects of the Soviet Union.

The author expresses his appreciation to those who have assisted him by their encouragement and suggestions, in particular Robert C. Tucker and Lewis Bohn. For the preparation of portions of this book the following journals have consented to the use, often in modified form, of material previously published by the author as articles:

Wehrwissenschaftliche Rundschau (for Chapter 3), *The Mili-*

tary Review (for Chapter 5), *Military Affairs* (for Chapter 6), *Army* (for Chapter 7), *The Air University Quarterly Review* (for Chapter 8), and *The United States Naval Institute Proceedings* (for Chapter 9).

The author assumes full responsibility for this study and its conclusions. He hopes that his work will serve its purpose: illuminating one important facet of the strategic challenge which we face.

RAYMOND L. GARTHOFF

WASHINGTON, D. C.
DECEMBER 29, 1957

I

CHAPTER 1

INTRODUCTION:

MILITARY STRATEGY AND SOVIET POLICY

"Strategy," as a term applied in analysis, and particularly in discussions of Soviet policy, is usually identified with "ends," in contradistinction to the equating of "tactics" with "means." This usage, while sometimes of value, may obscure the basic nature of strategy. *Strategies are themselves means to the attainment of objectives.* They are means of a higher order of generality, in scope and duration, than "tactical" measures, but they are not in themselves ultimate goals or objectives. Consequently, it is necessary to begin by attempting to identify the basic objectives of Soviet policy, in pursuit of which strategies, of both a political and military nature, are designed.

AIMS OF SOVIET POLICY

Soviet objectives in international affairs are at once obvious and obscure. It is assumed that their objectives of weakening and of attempting to destroy the power centers of the Free World—above all, the United States—and of expanding Soviet control and influence wherever feasible, do not require proof here. But the circumstances under which the Soviet Union would resort to war in order to accomplish these aims are by no means clear. The problem of determining precisely under what circumstances the Soviet Union might initiate hostilities, either to further its area of control or to defend its present position, is beyond the scope of the present discussion. Yet we must raise several aspects of this issue because these affect the basic Soviet strategic concept.

Does the Communist ideology determine Soviet policy? And, if so, does it require the Soviet leaders to launch military attack upon the "capitalist world" as soon as some given level of relative military power is achieved? The answer to the first question may be in dispute, although at the least there are presuppositions and influences of the ideology which distinguish Soviet foreign policy from that of a state merely seeking to increase power. But, paradoxically, the answer to the other question can be given definitely: The ideology does *not* require initiation of a war at any point. Whether or not the ideology determines Soviet policy, the prevailing balance of power—which is predominantly defined by the thermonuclear striking power of the United States and the Soviet Union—makes mandatory a most cautious calculation of risks and costs in any contemplated strategy. This being so, we cannot properly conclude that the Communist ideology "requires" the Soviet Union to launch a thermonuclear war to gain control of the world. Although Bolshevik ideology and Soviet history clearly bear witness to the fact that the Soviet Union drives toward world domination, it is nonetheless true that, again, both the ideology and practice of Communism require that this drive be carefully calculated in terms of costs and opportunities.[1] There may indeed be errors, as in the cases of the initial calculation to open the Finnish "Winter War" in November 1939, and the Korean War in June 1950; but no rational Communist leaders of the Soviet Union could ignore the terrible risks in an all-out military campaign against the United States. This is not to argue that the Soviet Union will never attack the West. Under various conceivable combinations of circumstances the Soviet Union may plunge the world into a thermonuclear holocaust. But in such a case the war will not be initiated as a consequence of a "requirement" of the ideology, but as a miscalculation on the

4

feasibility of gaining from such a move. In fact, the ideology not only does not *require* taking the great risks inevitable to launching a world war in the thermonuclear era; it *opposes* very strongly any measure smacking of "adventurism" or taking inadmissible risks. Soviet policy, whether in spite of or because of its ideological overtones, is predominantly based upon a calculation of power. What are its key objectives?

The paramount objective of any state is survival. No gain is meaningfully possible without self-preservation, and to carry this axiom one step further: No gain by attack is possible unless it exceeds the losses incurred in consequence of the attack. The primary Soviet objective, like our own, is survival.

Thus a cardinal Soviet objective is to deter the United States from launching a war. While *we* may be certain that the United States and NATO will never attack the Soviet Union, the Soviets are not so assured. It is often impossible to distinguish vituperous Soviet propaganda from indications of real Soviet fear of an attack, but it is apparent that the Soviet concern is real. In particular, while not necessarily expecting us to attack, they may fear that we *may* not be deterred when "rationally" we should be. This may be reflected in the Soviet statements which assert that the possession by both sides of powerful nuclear arsenals is no *guarantee* of peace.[2]

Soviet policy is also, however, distinguished by a powerful offensive aim: to weaken, and ultimately to annihilate and replace, the enemy. The "enemy" is defined as all who are not under Soviet control, with the most powerful and dangerous opponent—since the war, the United States—most strongly opposed. This objective of expanding power is dominant in Soviet political strategy, except insofar as it is restricted by the prescriptions of the cardinal objective, survival.

The fundamental Soviet objectives which determine political and military strategies may be concisely summarized in one: *Advance the power of the Soviet Union in whatever ways are most expedient so long as the survival of the Soviet power itself is not endangered.*

STRATEGY

"The objective of military strategy," a Soviet colonel has written in a General Staff organ, *"is the creation by military means of those conditions under which politics is in a position to achieve the aims which it sets for itself."*[3] Consequently, as Lt. General Krasil'nikov has pointed out: "Military strategy is directly dependent upon politics, to which it is subordinate. . . . Strategic war plans are worked out on the basis of objectives established by politics."[4] As Major General Pukhovsky has frankly declared: "The Soviet armed forces are a weapon of the policy of the Soviet state."[5] Thus we see the Soviet view that military strategy is a component *part* of political strategy. Acceptance of Clausewitz's conception that "war is the continuation of politics by other means" has long been carried to its logical conclusion by the Soviets. In the words of the late Marshal Shaposhnikov: "If war is a continuation of politics, only by other means, so also *peace is a continuation of conflict only by other means."*[6]

Political and military strategy are integral in the sense of identity of purpose: to further the basic objectives of Soviet policy. They are, in another sense, complementary; they coexist with one another at all times, the one dominant in peacetime, the other in war. Each is planned in a number of variants, to fit various conceivable contingencies. Ultimatum, cold war, peaceful coexistence, "Spirit of Geneva," united front —these are but illustrations of the span of familiar Soviet political strategies, designed to compel, confront, confuse, lull, and infiltrate, respectively. Military strategy likewise assumes a variety of forms: military demonstrations, little wars by proxy (as in Korea) or by internal dissidents (as in Malaya), local or peripheral wars (as with Japan in 1938-39), limited wars (without the use of nuclear weapons, for example), preventive wars, wars of conquest, and wars of annihilation.

For purposes of the present study, it is sufficient to bear in mind that military strategy is but one method for achieving the

6

basic Soviet objectives. Political strategies may be substituted, and these are already well-developed methods of expanding Soviet influence, control, and power. Indeed, Soviet policy probably envisages a long and continued avoidance of war, seeking to expand its influence and control by political measures. The success of such a strategy is uncertain, but it offers considerable promise at much less risk than resort to arms, even in local wars.

Khrushchev, in his first theoretical pronouncement (at the Twentieth Congress of the Communist Party, in February 1956), provided the ideological basis for a strategy of indefinite continuation of the substitution of political for military forms of conflict. The Marxist-Leninist precept on inevitability of war, he explained, had been correct for its time, but it no longer corresponded to contemporary conditions. The danger of war continues to exist and to require strong military defenses to deter war:

> *But war is not fatalistically inevitable.* Today there are mighty social and political forces possessing formidable means to prevent the imperialists from unleashing war....
> In connection with the radical changes in the world arena, *new prospects are also opening* in regard to the transition of countries and nations to socialism.[7]

This is the general political strategy presently envisaged: expansion of Soviet influence by means short of a major war. But regardless of whether the Soviet leaders are sincere in presently planning for indefinite reliance on political strategy, the importance of military strategy in Soviet policy remains of exceeding significance.

Military strategies are plans adopted to achieve particular objectives in specific actual or contemplated circumstances. Naturally, they are changed, or are discarded and superseded by new strategies, as key circumstances (political, technological, geostrategic, or other) are modified. Military doctrines represent codifications of views on the methods of conducting mili-

7

tary operations. They are guides to the employment of military forces in combat. Thus, while strategy relates to the attainment of objectives, doctrine relates to the employments of means.

Soviet military strategy is formulated by the Soviet military High Command and General Staff. But it must be accepted by the political leadership, and its particular requirements must be considered, and adopted or modified, in the course of Soviet national policy-making. The process of formulating and reconciling the sometimes conflicting requirements of military and political strategies occasioned no serious problems during Stalin's rule, since he was in fact the senior political and military decision-maker. The end of Stalin's personal dictatorship has created a more delicate situation in which the professional military leaders have acquired control over planning military strategy, although they must, of course, submit to its coordination by the political leaders. Thus the General Staff organ *Military Thought*, an authoritative journal restricted to senior Soviet officers, implicitly reflected the increased role of the military in the formulation of national policy when it stated in 1955: "The missions of [military] strategy, as is well known, are set by politics, *but political leaders must also know the potentialities of a strategy,* in order to set tasks before it skillfully at each concrete historical stage."[8] The rise of Marshal Zhukov to complete dominance within the military hierarchy and to full representation on the Presidium of the Party for a time simplified the mechanics of this national strategic integration. Since his ouster the problem has assumed a new form. The following chapter will review the role of the military in Soviet politics and note the relationship of this essentially technical and professional matter of strategic planning to the fortunes of internal maneuverings within the post-Stalin "collective leadership."

The scope of current Soviet military strategy is presented in some detail in a statement made in *Military Thought* in late 1954:

8

Contemporary strategy, as the science of directing military operations on the scale of military campaigns and the war as a whole, has as its main and immediate tasks:

—determining the basic means, methods and possible forms of *future* war, on the foundation of the objective laws of a concrete historical period;

—study of the strategic potentialities of the enemy as a whole and in each of the theaters of combat operations;

—determination of the concrete ways and means of armed struggle with the probable enemy;

—direction of the construction of the armed forces to correspond to the character and aims of presumed war;

—definition of the requirements for material preparation for future war and its campaigns;

—preparation in the theaters of military operations;

—selection of the direction of application of the main efforts in the war as a whole, and in its campaigns in particular;

—the disposition of forces and means by theater of combat operations and by strategic directions [areas];

—the accumulation and grouping of necessary reserves;

—the actions of military means on targets in the enemy's rear in the interests of undermining his morale and economic potentials;

—calculation and utilization of the results achieved by non-military ways and means of struggle in the interests of military operations;

—the organization and direction of military operations in war as a whole and in individual campaigns.

All these missions find their expression in the *war plan*, which expresses the practical functions of strategic leadership.[9]

Soviet military strategy has a series of tasks, which may be summed up in four parts: (1) evaluating the probable forms, means, and methods of future war to determine the strategic concept which will guide the employment of the armed forces in possible future wars so as to achieve victory and the objectives set for the given war most effectively; (2) elaboration of the doctrine, structure, organization, size and allocation of the armed forces to implement the requirements of the strategic concept for achievement of victory; (3) preparation of alternate war plans to meet various contingencies for possible future defensive or offensive wars against prospective enemies; and (4) the deployment of military forces and reserves in relation to the geostrategic priorities determined by the location of key objectives for neutralization by seizure or destruction, including the prospective enemy's armed forces and other strategic objectives specified in the war plans.

The present study, for readily apparent reasons, cannot attempt to duplicate Soviet war planning, nor to detail the Soviet "order of battle" deployment of forces. But on the basis of an extensive study of the available evidence—written Soviet sources and other materials concerning Soviet actions and weapons systems—it has been possible to establish the Soviet strategic concept, and to outline the doctrines and missions of the Soviet land, air, and sea forces in the nuclear era. These conclusions are presented in this book. To place them in the proper framework requires a brief summary of the "arena" or strategic context within which current strategy is formed.

THE ARENA

The strategic position of the Soviet Union which emerged from the Second World War was profoundly changed. The location of the new center of potentially opposing power across the sea has created for the Soviets new strategic requirements for intercontinental offensive and defensive capabilities, and doctrine to govern their employment. The major weapon of intercontinental warfare is presently air power, with the intercontinental ballistic missile (ICBM) soon to assume this role.

The Soviet Union was less well prepared by military tradition for this challenge than, for example, is the United States for the parallel challenge which Soviet aggressiveness poses for us. Russia has always been essentially a land power whose military interests, offensive and defensive, have been related to powers on adjacent territories. Even England was an opponent because the empires clashed on the rim of the Eurasian mainland. The endurance of this situation is attested to by the fact that over half a century ago Admiral Mahan correctly predicted that the United States, Great Britain, Germany, and Japan would find a common interest in containing Russia and China.[10] Geopolitical facts and historical tradition underlie and reinforce current views, providing deep roots for latter-day Soviet orientation toward land power.

Let us look first, briefly, at the situation in 1940, on the eve of the recent war. Soviet military doctrine had, after two decades of subsiding ferment, settled down into a basically determined conception. The aspect of most interest to our present discussion was the complete acceptance of the view that the ground forces, and in particular the infantry, are the element of military power which determines victory in war.[11] Sea and air power were explicitly designated to assist and support the ground forces in all their operations. The major potential enemy, Germany, was organized on similar lines and, most important, could be defeated by combined-arms forces focused on support to the ground forces.

In 1945, the same basic doctrine, modified in particulars, was on the whole even more firmly established by the experience of the war and wartime development. But the strategic situation was, as we have noted, drastically altered. The elimination of the former German and Japanese military power created a vacuum which the Soviets sought to fill. The dominating aspect of the arena in 1945 was, however, the location of the new major source of opposing power in North America. The United States was clearly unassailable by the weapons systems which the Soviets had previously developed and then employed in the Second World War. The strategic requirement to annihilate or to neutralize a power beyond the reach of Soviet infantry, tanks, artillery, and tactical air forces was completely unprecedented in Soviet experience. It is well to recall that the Soviets, unlike ourselves, have never engaged in war thousands of miles from their home base, across the seas.

In 1950, the strategic situation was very much the same, save that new opportunities were just appearing to the Soviet leadership. Mastery of the production of the atomic weapon and the introduction of tactical jet aircraft (fighters and light bombers) promised an important increase in Soviet capability. The ground forces had been substantially modernized for conventional warfare. But the basic need for intercontinental air and sea weapons was unfilled. And perhaps equally important, the basic *doctrinal* need had not been met. In all its essentials, Soviet military doctrine remained very much the same in 1950 as it had been in 1940. Efforts at innovation and originality in Soviet military thinking had appeared in the period from late 1945 to early 1947, but they were cut short by a new wave of internal censorship and "freezing" of thought. Whether as additional cause or as consequence of the intellectual autarchy born of the ban on discussion of new weapons and foreign military conceptions, "Stalinist" doctrine became, in fact, stagnant.

Now let us turn to the recent past, to 1955. We need note but a few recent developments affecting the "arena." The geographical-political contours of the arena in 1955 were on the whole similar to those of 1945. The major changes had been the accretion of Eastern Europe and China to the Soviet bloc on the one hand, and the creation of NATO, Middle Eastern and Southeast Asian alliances, and the integration of West Germany and Japan into the Western camp, on the other. But the military significance of the geographical arena had changed. First, there was the approach of nuclear "parity" between the two blocs, by which we mean the reciprocal ability to deal mutually incapacitating blows regardless of who strikes first. This, in turn, was largely the product of the development of thermonuclear weapons, long-range jet bombers, and long-range missiles, in both blocs. Even as of 1958, this may still be only an emerging situation, but nonetheless its effects are keenly felt.

Another important development was the end of "the period of Stalinist stagnation," which had stifled military thought from

12

1947 to 1953. To be sure, the legacy of this era is not yet entirely erased, but the death of the autocrat has permitted a renaissance of military thought, and revisions in the doctrine inherited from the prewar period and ingrained during the war.

By 1955, in other words, not only had the *means* of intercontinental warfare developed significantly, but also the way was open to a clearer understanding of the intermediate *objectives* required by the postwar changes in the geostrategic arena.

Before we turn to detailed analysis of current Soviet thought, it may be well to look briefly into the near future, let us say at 1960 and the years immediately following. The general political-geographical and weapons aspects of the arena by 1960 can perhaps be assumed by projections of current trends. Most important, if it is indeed not here already, nuclear parity, including strategic missile and aviation deliverability, will have arrived. This being so, what can we say about the Soviet strategic requirement *vis-à-vis* the United States? An important change will have occurred from the situation of 1945, 1950, or even 1955: namely, the acquisition of intercontinental capability by the Soviet Union may have led to a situation in which it is no longer necessary to *employ* such a capability in order to achieve its chief benefit. If the Soviet Union can stalemate the United States in the intercontinental arena, the way could be clear for gradual expansion of power through any of a variety of methods, military and non-military, in the entire Eurasian periphery. While the optimum Soviet aim of the *annihilation* of the major center of hostile power would be deterred and frustrated, the sub-optimum aim of improving the Soviet power position in peripheral areas would be greatly enhanced by the *neutralization* of the enemy power center. The emphasis will probably be on forceful political measures short of war.

In the concluding chapter of this work we shall return to a forecast of the outline of Soviet strategy in the period of 1970 and beyond.

POSSIBLE WARS: OBJECTIVES AND CONSTRAINTS

The varying political objectives which can be served by military action prescribe varying forms or types of wars. While there is no generally accepted set of categories, three main possible "types of war" of particular importance can be distinguished: (1) a general, "total" nuclear war, with no restriction either on weapons or on theaters of operations; (2) a major war with no geographical limitation but in which nuclear weapons either are not employed at all, or are used only "tactically" in the combat zone of ground armies, due to mutual restraint induced by the mutual ability to devastate; and (3) a local or "peripheral" war, waged within geographically defined limits, with or without the use of nuclear weapons.

Soviet views on wars of the second and third categories are rarely explicit. The questions of Soviet consideration of these possible wars are examined later (Chapter 5), but it is useful in this introductory discussion to clarify the relation of Soviet military doctrine and strategy as a whole to these varying possible types of wars.

In raising the question of possible wars, it is, of course, necessary to consider the different ways in which war might come about. The long-range calculations and objectives of each side would determine the conditions for aggressive wars consciously sought, but there also remain possibilities of wars precipitated through miscalculation or in response to sudden powerful shifts in the balance of power. Total nuclear war (although not necessarily other, limited forms of war) seems ever less likely as a rational tool for any state's advance of its power, but it remains only too likely a recourse in sudden reaction to an unforeseen and dangerous development. For example, if a serious revolt were to break out in the Caucasus or elsewhere in the Soviet Union itself, and if the United States were to attempt local military intervention with American forces in support of the insurrection, the Soviet Union would very likely resort to a massive retaliation against this very real threat to its existence. This hypothetical case is, of course, a politically extreme one, but it serves as an illustration.

"War by miscalculation" covers many possible cases. One which can be envisaged might arise from a situation in which one side instigates a local war and the other, misconstruing or overstepping the bounds of the theater of operations, opens a spiral of expansion which may lead to general war. Perhaps the most important of all causes of war by miscalculation would arise from the danger of incorrectly believing the enemy to be about to unleash a general attack and therefore launching a "pre-emptive" blow to seize the initiative and strike first. This, indeed, seems the most probable *casus belli* of general nuclear war for *either* side, though fortunately it appears to be a remote possibility. A general nuclear war may be launched in desperation if one side feels that its position is being so weakened by political, limited military, and other actions of the enemy (and growing internal weaknesses) that time is irrevocably running out, and that only a sudden powerful blow might permit recouping of the initiative and restoration of a precarious balance. These and other ways in which a general nuclear war might occur are all conceivable contingencies, but not even these few illustrative situations necessarily would lead to total war, or even to war at all. The mutual advantage in limitation might still lead to a major non-nuclear war, to a general war with tactical (theater) use of nuclear weapons only, or to a local war.

The objective behind all of the war situations discussed above is essentially defensive; even the pre-emptive (preventive) total nuclear war serves defensive aims. While the objectives of the West may be fully met by defensive measures, the Soviets' aggressive and expansionary goals might lead them to launch offensive wars. However, as earlier discussed, the primary motive of survival would probably deter the Soviets from launching a general nuclear war in favor of political and lim-

15

ited military actions, even if some militarily tempting political, technological, or other temporary advantage were to accrue to them.

The possible types of wars to serve the span of defensive and offensive political objectives alluded to in this discussion clearly require a substantial degree of flexibility in military strategic planning. The strategic concept for achievement of victory, and implementing doctrine on the employment of various forces, must be comprehensive. In fact, as we shall see, the Soviet strategic concept and military doctrine *are* comprehensive, in effect seeking to cover the requirements for all possible types of wars. Soviet military capabilities reflect and support these broad requirements.

In the period since 1953 the Soviets have increasingly prepared for the contingency of nuclear warfare, and doctrine has been modified accordingly. Specific tactical prescriptions are usually stated in terms of the *contingency* of nuclear warfare, while basic strategic thinking continues to be pitched in an over-all structure of military doctrine which the Soviets apparently consider applicable for nuclear and non-nuclear warfare. In practice, significant differences would, of course, characterize the strategy for the conduct of a general war with no limitation on use of nuclear weapons as opposed to one with restriction on or prohibition of that use. The Soviets do not, however, believe these differences require separate "doctrines." Instead, they believe that these require particular *applications* of their military doctrine to the concrete contingencies of nuclear or non-nuclear, general or local, wars.

Notes to Chapter 1

1. See R. L. Garthoff, "Ideological Conceptions in Soviet Foreign Policy," *Problems of Communism,* Vol. 2, No. 5, 1953, pp. 1-8; and Garthoff, "The Concept of the Balance of Power in Soviet Policy-Making," *World Politics,* Vol. VI, No. 1, October, 1951, pp. 85-111.

Introduction: Strategy and Policy

2. For example, see Marshal G. Zhukov, *Radio Moscow*, April 19, 1957, and *Pravda*, February 13, 1955; and see E. G. Panfilov, *Voprosy filosofii*, No. 1 March 7, 1957, p. 247.

3. Col. S. Kozlov, "Some Questions of the Theory of Strategy," *Voennaia mysl'* (Military Thought) , No. 11, November 1954, p. 23; italics in the original.

4. Lt. Gen. S. N. Krasil'nikov, "Military Strategy," in *Bol'shaia Sovetskaia Entsiklopediia* (The Great Soviet Encyclopedia) , 2nd ed., Moscow, Vol. 41, [April 21] 1956, p. 66.

Here, and throughout this study, italics are supplied by the present author except where otherwise indicated in the numbered footnote source reference.

5. Maj. Gen. Prof. N. V. Pukhovsky, *O sovetskoi voennoi nauke* (On Soviet Military Science) , Voenizdat, Moscow, [November 16] 1953, p. 26.

6. Boris M. Shaposhnikov, *Mozg armii* (The Brain of the Army) , Vol. 3, Moscow-Leningrad, 1929, p. 239. See also R. L. Garthoff, *Soviet Military Doctrine*, The Free Press, Glencoe, Ill., 1953, pp. 9-19, for a more extended discussion.

7. N. Khrushchev, Speech to the Twentieth Party Congress, February 14, 1956, in *Pravda*, February 15, 1956. This theoretical point was also endorsed by G. Malenkov (*Izvestiia*, February 19, 1956) and A. Mikoyan (*Pravda*, February 18, 1956) and later repeated by Khrushchev (*Pravda*, November 7, 1957).

8. "On Some Questions of Soviet Military Science," editorial, *Voennaia mysl'* No. 3, March, 1955, p. 6.

9. Col. S. Kozlov, *Voennaia mysl'*, No. 11, November, 1954, pp. 25-26; italics in the original. A number of these points are also made by Lt. Gen. S. Krasil'-nikov, "Military Strategy," *Bol'shaia Sovetskaia Entsiklopediia*, 2nd ed., Vol. 41 [April 21] 1956, pp. 65-66.

10. Captain (later Rear Admiral) A. T. Mahan, USN, *The Problem of Asia*, Little, Brown, Boston, 1900, pp. 63-65.

11.See Garthoff, *Soviet Military Doctrine, passim*, on the development of Soviet prewar, wartime and postwar (to 1953) doctrine.

CHAPTER 2

THE ROLE OF THE MILITARY IN SOVIET POLITICS

The Soviet military leadership in its relation to politics embraces two distinctive, if interrelated, roles. First, there is the inescapable requirement for coordination of military strategic planning, doctrine, and preparation with the national foreign policies. Second, there is the relationship of the military leaders to other Party and governmental leaders in terms of the internal distribution of power within the "collective" dictatorship.

The military have in recent years come to be an important political force in the Soviet Union. While the ouster of Marshal Zhukov in 1957 arrested, and indeed set back, a previous trend toward increasing political power of the military leadership, it also bore witness to the degree of political involvement and significance of the military. Why has the military become a political factor?

The mainspring of this crucial development was the death of the all-powerful autocrat, "Generalissimus" Stalin, in March 1953. The sharp decline in the role of the secret police in Soviet politics following Beria's fall was the second major step. And, finally, the very nature of the issues which arose between the factions of the Party leadership drew the military leaders into political action. The marshals, having contributed to the fall of Beria in June 1953, to the deposition of Malenkov in February 1955, and to the decisive defeat of the allied Malenkov

18

and Molotov factions in June 1957, had "known sin" in a way that had not been true for the military chiefs at least since the days of Marshal Tukhachevsky. In each of these three moments of political crisis the military decisively tipped the balance of decision. In effect, the disunity of the Party leaders in the period from mid-1953 to mid-1957 weakened the ability of the political leadership to maintain the military in a subordinate position. Instead, during those four years the military were wooed and, under the pressure of circumstances, virtually invited to become a political force.

The involvement of the military in politics was not achieved as the consequence of a deliberate desire on the part of the marshals to become politicians. Simply on the professional and seemingly non-political grounds of determining the security requirements and military posture of the Soviet Union, the marshals were led to endorse certain policies, and hence to support the factions favoring those policies. It is this involvement of the military leaders in political affairs, *as those responsible for framing Soviet military strategy,* which makes it important in this study to investigate the role of the military in Soviet "politics" and policy-making.

THE MILITARY IN THE LAST MONTHS OF STALIN'S RULE

Before tracing the progressive involvement of the marshals in the post-Stalin political struggle, it is useful to look into the unusual circumstances prevailing at the time of Stalin's death. A major purge of the secret police and Party was about to unfold, and a clear sign of this appeared in the so-called "Doctors' Plot" announced in January 1953. The prominent Kremlin physicians were accused of having plotted to kill "high government figures"—namely five military chiefs—and of having actually murdered Zhdanov and Shcherbakov (who died in 1948 and 1945). The secret police were specifically criticized for "lack of vigilance" in not discovering this plot earlier; Beria's days seemed

19

numbered. Khrushchev, in his famous secret speech of February 1956, devaluating Stalin, made reference to the danger from this purge felt by *all* the Soviet leaders. In these circumstances, Stalin's sudden death was suspiciously favorable for the surviving leaders—especially (if but temporarily) for Beria. But what of the military?

Two contradictory developments affecting the military occurred in late 1952 and early 1953. First, in preparation for the coming purge, Stalin wanted to ensure the passive acquiescence of the Army by presenting military leaders as the plot "victims," who were now saved. The selection of the "hero-victims-designate" in the plot was quite revealing. Marshal Vasilevsky (the Minister of War), Marshals Konev and Govorov, General Shtemenko (then Chief of the General Staff) and Admiral Levchenko (Deputy Minister of the Navy) were listed. Conspicuous by their *absence* were the names of Marshals Zhukov and Sokolovsky, and Admiral Kuznetsov.

But other forces were also at work, and late in 1952 Marshal Zhukov secretly returned to become Deputy Minister and Commander-in-Chief of the Ground Forces—resuming the position from which he had been removed by Stalin in 1946 to be sent to command a distant and secondary military district. And in late January or February of 1953, Marshal Sokolovsky (who had been Zhukov's wartime chief of staff) replaced General Shtemenko as a Deputy Minister of War and Chief of the General Staff. Vice Admiral Kuznetsov—wartime Admiral of the Fleet and Commander-in-Chief of the Navy, demoted and relieved of command by the ever suspicious Stalin in 1947—had also earlier been restored to the post of Minister of the Navy. Thus it would appear that Stalin had decided to name the best military leaders to responsible posts because of the danger of war, or possibly because of an intention to launch a war.

This restoration of some of the best military brains, as we have seen, was threatened by the implications of the "Doctors' Plot." In this context the naming of certain military chiefs as the hero-victims of the plot marked a clear attempt to capitalize upon existing rivalries among the marshals, and to assure certain ones that a purge would not affect *all* adversely. Specifically, Marshals Konev, Vasilevsky, and Govorov were being assured (while Zhukov and Sokolovsky were implicitly threatened).

Another key fact in the situation was the role of Khrushchev in these dark last days of Stalin's rule. Despite the inferences which Khrushchev intended his secret speech of February 1956 to convey, the evidence is strong that Khrushchev himself was a major driving force behind the Doctors' Plot announcement. Thus Khrushchev supported the fortunes of Konev at the obvious expense of Zhukov. Marshal Bulganin was also a supporter of this purge, and his associates Vasilevsky, Govorov, and Shtemenko were favored by it. This was not the first association of the fortunes of Konev with those of Khrushchev; during the war Khrushchev had served as political officer (with the rank of lieutenant general) with Marshal Konev's First Ukrainian Front. Nor would it be the last association, as we shall see presently.

Such was the stage at the time of Stalin's death in early March 1953.

POLITICAL INVOLVEMENT AND THE RISE OF THE MILITARY,
1953 TO 1957

With the death of Stalin, the purge, too, died stillborn. Beria consolidated his hold over the secret police, and he began to purge various supporters of Khrushchev. But Beria did not stop with a replacement of Khrushchev's supporters; he threatened *all* the other leaders by his tactics (including the shadowing of the other Politburo-Presidium members) and his policies. In this lay his undoing, for Malenkov and Molotov joined with Khrushchev and Bulganin (the latter now again head of a consolidated Ministry of Defense) in deciding that Beria was a threat to them all. The precise role played by the military leaders in this first crucial crisis is still partially obscure. Reportedly, Marshals Zhukov and Konev personally arrested Beria at a Central Committee meeting after his indictment by Malenkov. It is known that Army units from *outside* the Moscow Military District were alerted and secretly brought into the city the night of Beria's arrest. This was necessary because Colonel General Artemev, long the commander of the Moscow Military District, and Lieutenant Generals Sinilov and Spiridonov, Commandants of the Moscow Garrison and the Kremlin Guards, were deemed to be in league with Beria. Artemev was arrested.

Immediately after Beria's arrest several signs of the new role of the military leadership were evident. The same plenum of the Central Committee which sanctioned the arrest of Beria named Marshal Zhukov, since Stalin's death a First Deputy Minister of Defense, to assume the place on the Central Committee vacated by Beria's expulsion. Another indication of reward to the Army was the noticeable decline in the role of the political officers in the armed forces beginning in the summer of 1953. Finally, in the three months immediately following Beria's arrest the first postwar series of belated high-level promotions were bestowed on ten generals and admirals.

The decline of the political police which followed Beria's fall inevitably compelled the Party leaders to recognize the increased importance of the military as a decisive pillar of support for the regime. But this recognition led to political involvement of the marshals only when policy issues divided the Party leaders.

The "Malenkov era" lasted from the summer of 1953 until his resignation in February 1955. Four issues arose on which the military became dissatisfied with Malenkov's policies, and on which they found a common ground with Khrushchev. First was the policy of increased investment in consumer-goods industries. When, in late 1954, Khrushchev opened a campaign for renewed emphasis on heavy industry, the military press and leaders enthusiastically supported the campaign, *before* as well as after Malenkov's resignation.[1] The new Premier, Bulganin,

announced that "heavy industry is the foundation of the inde-
structible defense capability of the country."[2] A related issue
was Malenkov's use of state reserves (stockpiles) to accelerate
the consumer-goods program. Again, in his "acceptance speech"
Premier Bulganin reassured the marshals that "reserves comprise our might and strengthen the defense capability of the
country," and further promised that "to increase the state
reserves . . . is our most important task."[8]

This third issue which found the military (as well as the
Molotov group) in agreement with Khrushchev was opposition
to Malenkov's acceptance of the idea of "mutual deterrence."
Malenkov, perhaps prematurely, sounded this novel view in a
speech in March 1954, in which he said that a new world war
"would mean the end of world civilization."[4] The military
were chiefly concerned because it was premature to attribute to
themselves such thermonuclear strength as this view implied,
and especially because Malenkov used this issue to justify reduced military expenditures. Subsequent statements, while admitting great destruction, have been couched in terms of the
demise of capitalism and victory of Communism.

The fouth major issue which alarmed the marshals and
placed them firmly in the anti-Malenkov camp was the re-
trenchment in military appropriations. Budgetary allotments
and actual expenditures declined both in 1953 and 1954. Malenkov, and his associates Saburov and Pervukhin, pointedly
failed to include the usual call for strengthening the armed
forces in their March 1954 speeches. Again, in November 1954,
Saburov restated the "Malenkov line." On the very next day, in
response to this challenge, Bulganin called for strengthening
defense capability. And, in the Supreme Soviet session which
saw Malenkov's ouster, the military budget was increased by
over twelve per cent.

Marshal Bulganin, politician in uniform, and for many years
Stalin's "chaperon" of the marshals, had served as the link
between Stalin and the professional military leaders. He trans-
mitted orders down to the military chiefs and passed requests

up from them. In the period following Stalin's death he continued to serve as the link between the military and the various political factions. In late 1954 and early 1955 Bulganin probably played a major role in casting the support of the military to Khrushchev. This, however, reflected not the strength of Bulganin's position, but the fact that the views of the military professionals coincided with the policies advocated by Khrushchev.

Direct political action by the military was limited to their votes against Malenkov in the January 1955 Central Committee plenum (the first time that organ had played a politically significant role since 1934). But the importance of the military support was evident by the pains that Khrushchev and Bulganin took to meet the specific demands of the military for maintaining defense appropriations, military industry, and stockpiling of reserves, all departures from Malenkov's policies.

Soon after the victory of the Khrushchev-Bulganin group over Malenkov in February 1955, the military received a series of rewards. First, Marshal Zhukov replaced Bulganin as Minister of Defense, as the latter shed the use of the uniform and the title of a Marshal of the Soviet Union to become Premier. His selection as minister reflected both the growing political strength of the military as such and the personal popularity of Marshal Zhukov in the country. A month after Zhukov assumed the Defense Ministry in 1955, twelve marshals and generals were promoted, including six to the highest rank, Marshal of the Soviet Union. Among those promoted were a number of competent commanders and former associates of Zhukov; also among those promoted were several military supporters of the Khrushchev party faction. Later in the year six more professional generals with important field commands were raised to the rank of General of the Army.

Soon after the advent of the new regime, however, a period of intensive maneuvering began among certain of the military leaders. It is quite likely that Khrushchev himself wished to build up certain other military men to counterbalance Zhukov's new influence and prestige. If not, then at least some of the military men themselves sought to cultivate the favor of Khrushchev. The major figure in these maneuverings was Marshal Konev. He, together with Marshal Moskalenko and several senior political officers, aligned himself with Khrushchev. In contrast, Marshal Zhukov and most of the military leaders sought to remain aloof from factional political alignment in the period after Malenkov's deposition as Premier.

One element of maneuver was a bid by Khrushchev to have history so rewritten that he would be presented as a war hero. The campaign to emphasize the military role of Khrushchev (who had served as a military commissar with the rank of lieutenant general) was conducted by mentioning his name and that of a few other selected political figures as having been sent by the Party to the front in the war. In February 1955, with Khrushchev's victory over Malenkov, a flurry of such listings appeared, and the first senior professional officer, Marshal Konev, employed this theme.[5] Moreover, Konev significantly altered the previously standard listing to give precedence to the name of Khrushchev. Again in May 1955, in articles commemorating the tenth anniversary of victory in Europe, a number of these listings appeared. Again Konev and also Colonel General Zheltov (head of the Chief Political Administration) listed Khrushchev's name first.[6] But of the twenty key articles by military men on this occasion, only two other marshals, Bagramian and Chuikov, and two lesser political officers, mentioned the war role of political leaders at all. All of the other professional military chiefs (including Marshals Zhukov, Vasilevsky, Sokolovsky, Biriuzov, and Admiral of the Fleet Kuznetsov) studiously avoided reference to any living political figures.

Other signs of Khrushchev's attempt to be established retroactively as a war leader were references to his role at the Battle of Stalingrad and as one of "Lenin's associates" in the Civil War. In both cases history has been edited to raise his role and to exclude the role of certain others, in particular Malenkov. Again, the marshals *all* failed to contribute to this campaign.

In general, after mid-1955, Khrushchev's effort to gain retro-active achievement of military glory was not pursued vigor-ously. Since Zhukov's ouster there are signs that this campaign will be resumed on a large scale.

Another aspect of maneuvering among the military leaders is concerned with the attempts to restore the credit due to the military commanders for their wartime role. With the death of Stalin and the improvement of the status of the military, the restoration of due historic credit began. But precisely because it was a matter of history, it became one of politics. For, as has been observed, in the Soviet Union history is indeed the pro-jection of the present into the past. Marshals Zhukov (until his ouster in 1957), Konev, Vasilevsky, and Rokossovsky have gained most in prestige. Of particular interest was an abortive attempt in June 1955 to usurp the glory of the victorious Battle of Berlin for Konev, from its true hero, Zhukov.[7] The sensi-tivity of such matters and their political importance are evident from the bitter attack by Konev on Zhukov, after the latter's fall, for allegedly ascribing to himself greater credit than was his due for various wartime operations—including the battles of Moscow, Stalingrad, and Berlin.[8]

The Twentieth Congress of the Communist Party in Febru-ary 1956 is famous for Khrushchev's secret speech denouncing Stalin. In the course of this speech, not only did Khrushchev demolish the myth of Stalin's military "genius"; he also praised the military commanders. In particular, he presented himself as Zhukov's loyal friend and defender against Stalin's hints that Zhukov was not a good soldier. (Marshal Vasilevsky, subse-quently retired, and Malenkov, since purged, were on the con-trary presented as close to Stalin and unable or unwilling to argue with him.)

As early as the fall of 1953 the military sought a devaluation of the inflated image of Stalin's military role.[9] And, in 1955 and especially in 1956 and 1957, there occurred a revision of the military history of the last war which affected even current

26

military doctrine. The military leaders thus favored and sought this devaluation of Stalin's military role to facilitate certain developments in military thought, as well as to recover due prestige denied to them by Stalin. Similarly, the rehabilitation of military men who had been maligned and purged by Stalin was facilitated. But, while Khrushchev sought to please the military by including several thrusts at Stalin's military shadow, he has since made clear that this was a limited revision.

The Party Congress in February 1956 also saw Marshal Zhukov become the first professional officer to achieve the position of candidate membership in the Party Presidium (the old Politburo). Membership in the Central Committee of the Party also is a significant index of political standing among the senior military men. The Committe elected in 1956 included six full—and twelve candidate—members from the ranks of the professional military leaders. The full members were Marshals Zhukov, Konev, Malinovsky, Sokolovsky, Vasilevsky, and Moskalenko. Zhukov, in October 1957, was removed from the Central Committee as well as the Presidium. The absence of any senior officers of the political administration, even among candidate members, was unprecedented. This fact bore eloquent witness to the decline they suffered under Marshal Zhukov's administration of the Defense Ministry.

The most significant political implication of the military representation on the Central Committee was the apparent selection of men "acceptable" to Khrushchev, including several committed supporters of his faction. The most blatant example was the election, as a full member, of Marshal Moskalenko (who was only a colonel general and not even a candidate member in 1952). Moskalenko, promoted both in 1953 and 1955, has served ever since Beria's arrest as commander of the crucial Moscow Military District. He was associated with Khrushchev in the First Ukrainian Front in 1943-44, in the Ukraine from 1945 to 1949, and again in the Moscow Party Committee from 1949 to 1951. Finally, he—with Marshal Konev

27

—served on the military tribunal which sentenced Beria. The second case is Marshal Grechko, also promoted both in 1953 and 1955, who was from 1953 until 1957 Commander of the Soviet Forces in Germany, and has been since November 1957 First Deputy Minister of Defense and Commander-in-Chief of Ground Forces. On several occasions he has shown evidence of his strong support for Khrushchev's faction. A number of other marshals elected to candidate membership in 1956, while presumably not as committed to Khrushchev as Konev, Moskalenko, and Grechko, had past association with Khrushchev: Marshals Bagramian, Chuikov, Biriuzov, and Yeremenko (the latter two raised to this post for the first time). All of these men, too, had been promoted in 1955. It would not, however, be correct to consider these marshals as necessarily dedicated "Khrushchev men"—they are known quantities to him, and as such considered acceptable. Thus Khrushchev kept a hand in the selection of military representatives in higher Party organizations. "His" adherents among the military leaders, particularly Marshal Konev, bided their time for future changes in the High Command.

Marshal Zhukov had, nonetheless, concentrated his authority within and over the armed forces to an extent which was unparalleled in Soviet history at least since the purge of Tukhachevsky (who, it may be recalled, also had rivals who succeeded him upon his fall). The authority of the professional commanders was steadily reinforced. In late 1955 the position of political officer at the company level was quietly abolished. The role of the Party organizations was not clear. Then, in April 1957, a new Central Committee decree on "Instructions to the CPSU Organizations in the Soviet Army and Navy" laid down the basis of political work in the armed forces. This decree, and an accompanying Order of the Minister of Defense, represented a compromise between Zhukov's pressure for increasing the authority of the professional commanders and Party pressures to maintain the role of the political officers and the Party cells. During the period from April to October, 1957, there was considerable effort exerted *both* by the "Party-firsters" and the "Army-firsters" (in terms of relations *within* the military establishment; no one questioned the dominant role of the Party in national policy). The Central Committee "Instructions" embodied one very important point, at Zhukov's insistence: "Criticism of the orders and edicts of commanders will not be permitted at Party meetings."[10] Some articles stressed the commander's role; others the political officers and Party organizations. How much the situation changed after Zhukov's ouster is clear from the following tongue-in-cheek statement by *Red Star* immediately following his fall: "Trenchant principled criticism, far from undermining the authority of the commander, on the contrary enhances it and helps to achieve new success in military and political training."[11] Probably the April "Instructions" will remain in effect; but now there exists but one interpretation of them—the "Party-first" one. As *Soviet Fleet* has since stated: "Regardless of the rank or position of a Communist he not only can, but must, be subjected at Party meetings or conferences to criticism for shortcomings in his service."[12] The role which Zhukov had in fact played was criticized as "trying to diminish the importance of party-political work in the army and navy, to reduce it to abstract enlightenment, to carry it out apart from the tasks of military training."[13] At the same time, the Chief Political Administration was seeking to preserve its role as the directing party-political organ with a separate chain of command to the Central Committee and its Secretariat. Thus, in an article in June 1957, just prior to the June crisis with the Malenkov-Molotov group, it was reaffirmed that: "The Chief Political Administration of the Ministry of Defense works with the rights of a section of the Central Committee of the CPSU and simultaneously is a component part of the Ministry of Defense. . . . [It is] the directing and controlling organ on questions of party-political work in the Soviet Army and Navy."[14]

A crucial event occurred in June 1957: the attempt of the Malenkov-Molotov-Kaganovich alliance, joined by Khrushchev's erstwhile supporter, Shepilov, to depose Khrushchev as First Secretary of the Party. It is now known that this alliance succeeded in gaining a majority in the Party's Presidium.[15] But Khrushchev refused to accept this decision and, supported by Marshal Zhukov, insisted upon carrying the matter to the Central Committee (which he had "packed" with his supporters at the Twentieth Party Congress in February 1956). Zhukov is reliably reported to have announced to the Central Committee plenum itself that the Soviet armed forces would not "permit anyone to bid for power."[16] Zhukov, now elected to full membership in the Presidium, subsequently spoke "on behalf of the Armed Forces" in pledging continued support to the Party leadership under Khrushchev.[17] But Khrushchev was well aware that while Zhukov had extralegally pledged the Army to his support on this occasion, he could on some future occasion range this power against him, Khrushchev, if Zhukov was permitted to speak politically "on behalf of the armed forces."

Even prior to the June plenum of the Central Committee Zhukov had compelled Khrushchev to modify his ambitious plan for the abolition of economic ministries and decentralization of industrial administration. As a conspicious exception *not* originally included in Khrushchev's proposal, the military industries were in May even further centralized in the powerful Ministry of Defense Industry, and the Ministry of Aviation Industry was preserved. This was a concession to the military leadership—as confirmed, in part, by the fact that following soon after Zhukov's dismissal (in December 1957) the military production ministries were abolished and replaced by four "State Committees under the Council of Ministers," with less than ministerial responsibility. Following the June plenum and his promotion to full membership on the Presidium, Zhukov apparently sought three more concessions: (1) that the Chief Political Administration in the armed forces would cease to report directly to the Central Committee (in fact, to Khrushchev), and would report only to him as Minister; (2) that the military be represented in the secret police leadership, and (probably) that they assume responsibility for the Internal Troops and Border Guards; and (3) that Stalin's purges be formally denounced, including the purge of Marshal Tukhachevsky. These demands are inferred; the first listed has been strongly hinted at by official Soviet reports and "leaked" by Communist sources in Moscow,[18] the second was reportedly told by Khrushchev to Tito in August, 1957,[19] and the third can be surmised on the basis of tentative and unfulfilled steps in that direction.

As of this writing, and probably to continue, we do not know fully the precise grounds of conflict which precipitated the decision to oust Zhukov at the particular time that the event occurred. The charge that Zhukov attempted to place the Army outside the Party's sphere by interfering with the work of the political administration and the Party organizations has, as we have noted, some basis. It is, however, unlikely that this issue alone led to the decision by Krushchev to darken the Fortieth Anniversary of the Bolshevik Revolution by yet another strong sign of the dissension tearing the Party banner. But this was the issue which was most readily usable for general purposes of Party, and even popular, argument. Another underlying basis of the purge of Zhukov, though again not the sole or proximate cause, was Khrushchev's wariness of the marshal's rising power and popularity. Both of these considerations had become increasingly real in the period from June to October, 1957.

Thus it was that the progressive involvement of the military in Soviet politics led to their continuous rise to a position of such prominence that they then suffered a serious setback.

Marshal Zhukov's recent career illustrated well, and "not by accident" (as the Soviets would say), the changing role of the military. Immediately following Stalin's death, Zhukov was made a First Deputy Minister (one of three). Following Beria's arrest, he was elected to the Central Committee seat vacated by Beria, at the same plenary session which sanctioned Beria's expulsion and arrest. After Malenkov's deposition, Zhukov became Minister of Defense. Accompanying the denunciation of the Stalin myth, he became a candidate member of the Party's Presidium. Following the defeat of the Malenkov-Molotov factions, he rose to full membership on the Presidium. And, finally, in October 1957, he fell from power.

The question may well be raised whether this represented the rise, and fall, of Marshal Zhukov as representative and spokesman for "the military," or of Marshal Zhukov the individual, the popular hero and politician. There was clearly an important element of the latter, but there are good reasons for concluding that his rise and fall also have reflected the fluctuations in the role of the military. Most important, with each of the promotions in his status, the other military leaders, and the Army as an institution, were accorded more favors. And, in addition, since Marshal Zhukov himself acted in terms of the Army's needs and desires, their fortunes had to be parallel. And so it was that the *fall* of Marshal Zhukov also affected the role of the military.

Thus it is necessary to review the changing fortunes of the military as an institution.

THE MILITARY AS AN INSTITUTION

The institutional consequences of this recent history of political flux and involvement of the military are extremely important. The military establishment is technically but one of the several ministries of the Soviet government's executive branch. But it is a peculiar one in several respects. First, it is the repository of the ultimate political persuader—the tools of violence, weapons. Secondly, it is composed of a permanent caste of leaders and an annual slice of the population. Thirdly, this leadership caste has powerful rights of discipline and control over the armed portion of the total population which it disposes. Now these three features are, in general, not peculiar to the Soviet Army. But their political significance in a totali-

32

tarian society is quite different, and in Soviet society in particular there are still other distinctions. To begin with, the Army has its own traditions (including many antedating the Soviet regime) and "inbreeding," to a degree that has no other institution in Soviet society. In addition, the Army is generally and genuinely popular—again in a way and to a degree that the officially supreme institution, the Party, is not. Finally, changes in the political balance of Soviet institutions in the last five years have greatly altered the relative standing of the Army.

The first major development in this change, as we have noted, was the death of Stalin. *All* other major Soviet institutions automatically became more significant as the institution of the all-powerful autocrat disappeared. In the ensuing political readjustment, a second event strongly affected the balance: the secret police were drastically reduced in power and as a political institution in the aftermath of Beria's fall. The third event especially affecting the institutional balance of power was the abortive attempt of Malenkov, in the period from 1953 to 1955, to increase the power of the Government bureaucracy (including, of course, the entire economic managerial administration of the country), necessarily at the expense of the Party bureaucracy. Malenkov may have pursued this course as a last remaining expedient after losing the post of Party Secretary in mid-March 1953; but it is also possible that he would have acted in the same way even if he had retained his reins over the Party apparatus as well. In either event, the "charge" leveled at Malenkov (in 1955) that he had attempted to place the government over the Party was essentially true. And the defeat of Malenkov and his efforts led, of course, to a weakening of the government apparatus as a political force. The final defeat of the combined Malenkov and Molotov factions in June 1957 again underlined this point. The attempt in late 1956 and early 1957 to strengthen the managerial bureaucracy was succeeded by Khrushchev's decentralization of economic administration and consequent weakening of that institution. Thus *the Party* gained in stature as a political institution as Stalin died, the secret police were curtailed, and the government and managerial bureaucracy "put in its place."

But during this same period the Party itself was not only a *participant* in the political struggles and readjustments; it was also the *arena* of conflict. In the final analysis the leaders who "represented" the various institutions—Beria, Malenkov, Molotov, Zhukov, and Khrushchev—were all Party chiefs, and the formation and shifts of factional alignments within the Party organs (especially the Presidium, Secretariat, and the Central Committee) were the key maneuvers of the battle. The disunity of the professional Party leaders led them to seek whatever support could be rallied.

The Army was thus, almost by default, propelled into steadily increasing political importance as the dictator, the police, and the bureaucracy each declined, and the Party was divided. But this was by no means all that happened. For, as we have seen, the very nature of the issues which arose between the factions of the Party leadership drew the military into political action. And so it was that from early 1953 until mid-1957 the military as an institution increased in significance as a factor in current Soviet politics. Hence, too, the clash of this increasing role with the political leadership, and the consolidation of the Party in the hands of Khrushchev, led to the reassertion of the dominant role of the Party and, a serious reduction of the political status of the military.

The relief of Zhukov and his replacement by Marshal Malinovsky has ushered in a new era for the military as an institution. No longer is it given the opportunity to act as a political force. No longer are the marshals represented on the Party's Presidium by a professional soldier turned political figure as well. The military remains a powerful potential political force, and its voice in security matters is not stilled; but with the departure of Marshal Zhukov from the ministry, the military voice in Soviet policy-making has suffered a serious weakening.

The Role of the Military

The general implications of the new institutional status of the military since Zhukov's ouster are also supplemented by other aspects of the new role of the military. One of the main ones is simply: how and by whom is the remaining authority of the military leadership, within the Ministry of Defense, wielded?

The selection of Marshal Malinovsky to replace Zhukov was perhaps one way in which Khrushchev sought to separate Zhukov, as an individual, from "the military." If he had selected one of his factional adherents, such as Marshal Konev or especially Marshal Moskalenko, the military leadership as a whole might have taken this as a sign of impending general purge of their ranks, and might have been tempted to rally more steadfastly to support of Zhukov. By soliciting and obtaining support of Marshal Malinovsky (the third ranking military chief after Zhukov in the latter's administration) this danger was at least mitigated. In a sense Khrushchev, by this action, recognized the increased importance of the military as an institution and showed that he was not seeking to deny or assault it. But, of course, Marshal Zhukov's removal clearly meant that the Army was being restored to a position *below* the national policy-making level of the Presidium. The Ministry of Defense has resumed a role restricted to planning, advice, and implementation of military strategic preparations. The Presidium, now more than ever virtually equatable with the person of Khrushchev himself, has regained the final decision on military security matters which Marshal Zhukov had been assuming.

Marshal Konev remains the senior First Deputy Minister, and Commander-in-Chief of the Warsaw Pact Forces. It was doubtless a bitter pill for the ambitious man who had long ago "sold out" to Khrushchev, as we have noted earlier. But precisely because of this fact, he no longer had anything to "sell" when Zhukov was relieved. Konev had long been a rival of

Marshal Zhukov—in the Far East in 1939, at Moscow in 1941, and at Berlin in 1945. When Zhukov was banished in 1946, it was Konev who succeeded him as Deputy Minister and Commander-in-Chief of Ground Forces. When Zhukov returned in late 1952, he replaced Konev in this very post, and sent him in turn to command a minor military district. But Konev's growing political connections with Khrushchev stood him in good stead. His services were varied. In December 1953 Konev served as chairman of the military tribunal which sentenced Beria to death, and at which Khrushchev's associate Mikhailov returned the indictment. And, as we have seen, in 1955 Marshal Konev—alone among the senior marshals—assisted a drive by the ambitious Khrushchev to refashion history by crediting himself as a war hero. What his role was in preparing the ground to unseat Zhukov is not known. But he was given the opportunity to indulge himself—and, incidentally, probably to lower his prestige with the Army and the people—by a bitter partisan attack in *Pravda* on the fallen Zhukov.[20] Another reason for Konev's long-standing support of Khrushchev is that Konev has always been more "Party-minded" than Zhukov. His tenure on the Central Committee, since 1939, antedates Zhukov's, and although he is a professional marshal with extensive field command, he (unlike Zhukov, Malinovsky, and the other senior marshals) was once a military commissar, a political officer.

Marshal Malinovsky has been less politically involved than Zhukov had become, or than Konev. As commander in the Far East during virtually the whole of the postwar period until mid-1956, he was apart from the intrigues of the Kremlin. As the leading representative of the military he will doubtless strive to do his best in preparing the armed forces—but without the dynamic initiative of Zhukov. In short, he will implement the decisions of the Presidium rather than participating in the deliberations of that body as they relate to foreign political and strategic decision-making.

On the whole, the military leaders are, to the extent their advice is solicited, likely to continue to display the same general conservatism as did Zhukov. This conservatism has meant an opposition to moves of accomodation or partial withdrawal (as in their favoring armed intervention to preserve the Hungarian base). It also has meant an opposition to "adventuristic" aggressiveness which threatens unnecessarily to risk a general war. Regrettably, Malinovsky and Konev personally are likely to be less of a moderating influence in this latter respect than was Zhukov (not as a humanitarian or friend of the West, but as a coldly calculting military planner).

The general organization and function of the Ministry of Defense and the armed forces remain unchanged. (They are reviewed in the following chapter.) The role of the military in Soviet politics, though it doubtless has not reached a final definition, has thus made an initial transition from its recent rise to a tentative stabilization under Khrushchev's Party.

THE ROLE OF THE MILITARY AS STRATEGIC ADVISERS

One remarkable and extremely significant fact in the long path of rise and partial decline of the military as a political factor has been the *absence* of conflict over military strategic thinking or concepts. To be sure, the military opposition to Malenkov was inspired largely by military considerations relating to appropriations, and to the implications of "mutual deterrence." But even this was not a direct clash on strategic views, and the subsequent involvement of the military has avoided doctrinal or strategic conceptual conflict.

There have been a few possible exceptions. Most notably, Admiral of the Fleet Kuznetsov was dismissed in 1955 for favoring a conventional surface navy as well as missile-launching submarines. He may have favored the construction of aircraft carriers, and certainly of cruisers. But this whole view of the role of a surface fleet was opposed, presumably by Zhukov and the

37

military leaders, and definitely by Khrushchev. There may also
have been other naval considerations in dispute, but in any case
Kuznetsov was relieved and dropped from the Central Committee of the Party (in which he had been a full member from
1939 to 1947, and again from 1952 to his dismissal). But aside
from such relative details, there has been no clear politically-
related doctrinal controversy.

The major Soviet strategic-political involvement has been
non-controversial, so far as we know. This is the significant
role which Marshal Zhukov played, particularly from the beginning of his ministerial tenure in early 1955, in reinvigorat-
ing Soviet military thinking. There had been earlier theoretical
debates, but Zhukov gave real momentum to a movement for
revision of military science and for adaptation to the new strategic requirements of the nuclear age.* The year 1955 marked
the key turning-point in revision of military doctrine, and 1956
and 1957 were largely marked by consolidation both of doctrine
and of training.

In the light of Zhukov's important role in this doctrinal
development, it is pertinent to raise the question of changes
which may have occurred—or may yet occur—as a consequence
of his fall. On the whole, no change of importance has yet
occurred, nor is it likely to as a direct result of Zhukov's departure. The main reason for this is, of course, that military
doctrinal and strategic questions were not at issue between
Zhukov and Khrushchev, or between Zhukov and Konev or
Malinovsky. In his "obituary" article, Marshal Konev did
charge: "The mistakes of Comrade Zhukov in the guidance
of the armed forces were aggravated by some of his unfounded
utterances on questions of Soviet military science and the construction of the armed forces."[21] But other than a tortured and
ambiguous claim that Zhukov belittled the military regulations,
he cites only alleged errors of Zhukov in the period from 1940
to 1945.

---

* See Chapter 4 for a comprehensive review of this revision of doctrine.

38

The Role of the Military

In one respect the reassertion of the role of the Party in achieving victory in the recent war may serve to retard or lead into retrogression the "de-idealization" of the Soviet military experience in the war. This, in turn, may increase the already strong conservatism in Soviet military thought.

There remains one possible and important area of potential conflict between the professional military leaders and the political leadership. It is not particularly related to Zhukov, as it reflects a commonly held military view on the one hand, and the intuitive view of Khrushchev on the other hand. What is the area of possible controversy? It is the evaluation of the *military* effectiveness of the emerging temporary Soviet advantage in intercontinental ballistic missiles. If Khrushchev really believes that the new missiles immediately make bombers "obsolete," he is diverging from the views of his military experts and the tenets of Soviet military doctrine. An issue would arise if he wished to act on the basis of his expressed view either to reduce prematurely the Soviet long-range air force, or to conclude that the time was ripe to attack the West. But these contingencies are not probable, and though Khrushchev's impetuous nature may make him unduly exuberant in his own evaluation, his statements are doubtless guided in part by his recognition of their effective propaganda value. It is, therefore, not likely—although not inconceivable—that the political leadership would minimize the strong Soviet military doctrinal consideration of the non-*reliance* on any particular weapons system, including the ICBM with thermonuclear warheads.

Thus the marshals continue to serve as professional-specialist advisers on military matters, but they are now denied the role of participants in national policy-making.

Notes to Chapter 2

1. See, in particular, the editorials in *Krasnaia zvezda*, December 30 and 31, 1954; Lt. Col. I. Sidelnikov, *Krasnaia zvezda*, January 15, 1955; the editorial,

Krasnaia zvezda, February 15, 1955; Marshal G. Zhukov, *Pravda,* February 23, 1955; Marshal V. Sokolovsky *Izvestiia,* February 23, 1955; and General of the Army V. Kurasov, *Radio Moscow,* February 21, 1955.

2. N. Bulganin, *Pravda,* February 10, 1955.

3. *Ibid.*

4. G. Malenkov, *Pravda,* March 13, 1954.

5. Marshal I. Konev, *Pravda,* February 23, 1955.

6. Marshal I. Konev, *Pravda,* May 9, 1955; and Col. Gen. A. Zheltov, *Kommunist,* No. 7, May, 1955, p. 49.

7. "Marshal I. S. Konev," *News,* No. 11, June, 1955, p. 5.

8. Marshal I. Konev, *Pravda,* November 3, 1957.

9. See the discussion in Chapter 4. The earliest reference was by Maj. Gen. N. Pukhovsky, *O sovetskoi voennoi nauke* (On Soviet Military Science), Voenizdat, Moscow, [November 16] 1953, pp. 84 and 85.

10. The "Instructions" have never been published in full, but they have been liberally quoted. This sentence, directly quoted from them, was included in the initial main article, titled "For Concreteness and Expediency in the Work of Party Organizations," in *Krasnaia zvezda,* May 12, 1957.

11. *Krasnaia zvezda,* November 5, 1957.

12. *Sovetskii flot,* November 1, 1957.

13. *Ibid.*

14. Capts. 2nd Rank B. Demidov and P. Domrin, "The Political Organs of the USSR Armed Forces," *Sovetskii flot,* June 13, 1957.

15. This crucial fact was virtually admitted in the authoritative Party organ *Partiinaia zhizn',* No. 13, July 1957, p. 13.

16. See the well-informed accounts by Harrison Salisbury, "Key Moscow Role Played by Zhukov," and Sydney Gruson, "Zhukov Pledge Described," in the New York *Times,* July 9, 1957; and "Party Presidium Soviet Power Key," the New York *Times,* November 3, 1957.

17. See Zhukov's Leningrad speeches, esp. on *Radio Moscow,* July 16, 1957; and see "Communists of the Ministry of Defense and the Moscow Garrison Unanimously Welcome and Support the Decision of the June Plenum of the CC CPSU," *Krasnaia zvezda,* July 5, 1957.

18. See the official announcement, *Pravda,* November 3, 1957; and see the well-informed report of the London *Daily Worker's* Moscow correspondent, cited in the Washington *Post-Times-Herald,* October 29, 1957.

19. The report of Marshal Tito's was obtained in Warsaw by Joseph Alsop; see his column in the New York *Herald Tribune,* October 25 and November 3, 1957.

20. Marshal I. S. Konev, *Pravda,* November 3, 1957.

21. *Ibid.*

CHAPTER 3

THE ORGANIZATION AND POSTURE

OF THE ARMED FORCES

The organization of the Soviet armed forces reflects the basic Soviet strategic concept and military doctrines. As Marshal Zhukov put it (in 1957): "In the postwar construction of the armed forces we are proceeding from the fact that victory in future war will be achieved only by the combined efforts of all arms of the armed forces and on the basis of their coordinated employment in war."[1] This continues to be the Soviet view.

THE UNIFIED DEFENSE MINISTRY

The basic characteristic of the organizational structure of the Soviet armed forces is, therefore, their unity in a single powerful Ministry of Defense. This has not, however, always been true. Throughout the period of Soviet rule, the Army and Navy have alternately existed under independent ministries (formerly "Peoples' Comissariats") and under combined administration. During the Second World War they were separate; from 1946 to 1950, unified; from 1950 to 1953, independent; and they have been unified since the governmental reorganization which immediately followed the death of Stalin. At no time has the Air Force been represented by a ministry.

Before we examine further the organization of the Ministry and High Command, it is useful to note the role of the Ministry in the Soviet political system. The general functions are

41

obvious and need little attention: to administer the various components of the armed forces, to provide for their proper supply and maintenance, to direct the training and preparation of the military arms and services for war, to plan for the employment of the armed forces in war, to deploy and station the military units, and finally to advise the Government (including the formal government, the Council of Ministers, and the real policy-making body, the Presidium of the Party's Central Committee) on the requirements of the military establishment.

THE HIGH COMMAND

The Minister of Defense, presently Marshal of the Soviet Union R. Ya. Malinovsky, is in fact the Commander-in-Chief of the Armed Forces. The importance of the post is evident in the fact that no professional military officer had ever been given the responsibility for all the armed forces until Marshal Zhukov's accession in February 1955. Marshal Malinovsky, since his assumption of the post in October 1957, has continued to have the same general responsibility, though not, of course, the political power which Zhukov had in the post.

After the Minister come the senior deputies who sit on the Military Council of the Ministry. Foremost is the First Deputy Minister for General Affairs, currently Marshal I. S. Konev (who also holds the important field command of Commander-in-Chief of the Warsaw Pact Forces). Marshal Konev is an able and ambitious man, and it is no secret that he aspires to the post of Minister. Whether for this reason or for other political convictions, as we have seen, Marshal Konev—alone among the senior marshals in the High Command—has committed himself politically to the support of the Khrushchev Party faction in a way that Zhukov had not, and in a way that even Malinovsky and their other chief associates have not done. But it is useful to recognize that, while Marshal Malinovsky has full authority in the armed forces, his senior deputy is a rival officer. Marshal

The Armed Forces

Konev originally fell in standing (in 1952 and 1953) as Marshal Zhukov staged his comeback from the oblivion to which Stalin had relegated the popular war hero. Since early 1955 Konev has risen, acquiring his present post in mid-1956 as it was vacated by Marshal Vasilevsky, but he failed to succeed Zhukov on the latter's ouster.

The third ranking military leader is First Deputy Minister and Chief of the General Staff, Marshal V. D. Sokolovsky. In this post since early 1953, Sokolovsky shared with Marshal Zhukov the chief role in overcoming the legacy of "Stalinist stagnation" in military thought, and the vigorous if belated reorientation of the Soviet armed forces to the atomic age. The general staff itself, formerly in fact the Army's staff, has now become the "General Staff of the Armed Forces," superior over all arms and directly under the Minister of Defense and his Military Council. The General Staff comprises six sections or administrations, of which two are "chief administrations":

The Chief Administration for Operations
The Chief Administration for Intelligence
The Signal Communications Administration
The Organization and Mobilization Administration
The Topographical Administration
The Historical Administration

The various commands, arms, and services are represented by liaison on the General Staff. The ground forces, Navy, air defense forces, and the air forces each maintain a "main staff" which largely mirrors the functions and organization of the General Staff, with such peculiarities as the natures of the respective services require.

The fourth senior military chief is Marshal A. A. Grechko, First Deputy Minister and Commander-in-Chief of the Ground Forces. Grechko is known as a personal supporter of Khrushchev.

Until mid-1956 Marshal A. M. Vasilevsky was the senior first deputy, but since that time he has been retired from an active position in the High Command and largely engaged in such duties as guiding the work of the recently formed Soviet War Veterans Association, and contributing occasional articles to the press.

There are an additional dozen or more deputy ministers and even junior *ex officio* first deputy ministers. They include the Commander-in-Chief of the Air Defense Forces, Marshal S. S. Biriuzov; the Commander-in-Chief of the Naval Forces, Admiral S. G. Gorshkov; and the Commander-in-Chief of the Air Forces, Marshal of Aviation K. A. Vershinin. The naval chief has recently been identified officially as a first deputy, and the air chief presumably is also a first deputy (although his status has never been so identified publicly), but they currently stand in about thirteenth and fourteenth places—after the dozen senior Army marshals.

Before discussing further the key agencies of the High Command, it is useful to visualize the organizational framework of the Ministry of Defense. The chart on page 45, simplified by the omission of a number of minor administrative units, presents the essential structure of the Soviet High Comand.

The Commander-in-Chief of the Ground Forces does not exercise operational command of field forces. As head of the Chief Administration for the Ground Forces he is responsible for the preparation of tactical doctrine for the infantry, and for the development of ordnance, weapons, and equipment for the ground forces (except for tanks and artillery) . Subordinate to his chief administration are administrations for the signal troops, engineers, chemical warfare units, and the cavalry. The heads of the chief administrations for artillery, tank troops, and airborne troops are similarly responsible for preparation of tactical doctrine, technical training, and development of weapons ordnance for their respective arms.

The Commander-in-Chief of the Air Defense Forces has risen to become a figure of importance only since 1954 or 1955, at which time command was given to Marshal Biriuzov. He has operational command and control over all the components of

44

THE SOVIET HIGH COMMAND

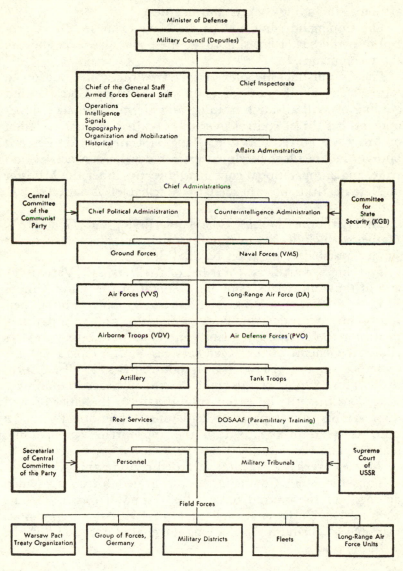

Minister of Defense

Military Council (Deputies)

Chief of the General Staff
Armed Forces General Staff

Operations
Intelligence
Signals
Topography
Organization and Mobilization
Historical

Chief Inspectorate

Affairs Administration

Chief Administrations

Central Committee of the Communist Party

Chief Political Administration

Counterintelligence Administration

Committee for State Security (KGB)

Ground Forces

Naval Forces (VMS)

Air Forces (VVS)

Long-Range Air Force (DA)

Airborne Troops (VDV)

Air Defense Forces (PVO)

Artillery

Tank Troops

Rear Services

DOSAAF (Paramilitary Training)

Secretariat of Central Committee of the Party

Personnel

Military Tribunals

Supreme Court of USSR

Field Forces

Warsaw Pact Treaty Organization

Group of Forces, Germany

Military Districts

Fleets

Long-Range Air Force Units

the active air defense system: the radar and other warning systems, the fighter aviation component, and the anti-aircraft artillery (including rockets and missiles).

The Commander-in-Chief of the Navy exercises direct control over the Soviet fleets, flotillas, the naval air force, and the shore commands.

The Commander-in-Chief of the Air Forces, in addition to representing all the air forces in the Military Council, and guiding over-all air-force training and aircraft ordnance development, has direct control over the so-called Frontal Aviation or Army Air Force. The Long-Range (Strategic) Air Force is both an independent headquarters for developing tactical doctrine, and an operational command directly under the Minister of Defense. It is now headed by Marshal of Aviation V. A. Sudets.

The Airborne Troops Command, under Lt. General V. Margelov, includes its own substantial air transport element (under Marshal of Aviation N. S. Skripko).

The chiefs of artillery (Marshal of Artillery S. S. Varentsov) and of the tank troops (Colonel General of the Tank Troops P. P. Poluboiarov) are occupied essentially with training, perfection of tactical doctrine, and guidance of ordnance development, for their respective arms. The chief of the rear services (Colonel General of the Rear Services V. I. Vinogradov) has an important and wide span of responsibilities for all logistical support and supply of the combat arms in peacetime and for war. Consequently, he is not subordinate to the chief of staff (nor are his counterparts in field units), but directly to the minister (and in the field to the appropriate commanding officer). The Chief Inspector (now believed to be Marshal K. A. Meretskov) has a position accorded considerable weight.

Thus the High Command of the armed forces is divided among: (1) the ground forces, (2) the naval forces, (3) the air forces, and (4) the air defense forces, with two autonomous excepted commands, (5) the long-range air force, and (6) the airborne troops.

46

The Armed Forces

POLITICAL CONTROLS

The Chief Political Administration is directly subordinate to the Military Section of the Central Committee of the Communist Party. Simultaneously it is in the chain of command below the Minister of Defense. From mid-1953 until the end of 1957 the head of the administration was Colonel General A. S. Zheltov. Apparently for failing to meet the new demands since Zhukov's fall, he was replaced by Colonel General F. I. Golikov. As head of the Chief Political Administration, he controls a complete system of political officers from ministry to battalion level (the post of political officer at company level was abolished in 1955). These political officers, formerly notorious as "military commissars," are now "deputy commanders for political affairs" in all units down through regimental level. No longer must the political officer countersign every operational order, as was required until late 1942. The importance of the political administration has declined since 1953, and its functions have in part been accorded to the command personnel, and in part to the unit Party and Komsomol organizations. Marshal Zhukov played a major part in achieving this reduction in the role of the political officers. Their primary function now, shared with the Party organizations, is that of indoctrination. Officers and enlisted men are required to study ideological texts and to attend numerous lectures on political themes; the political officers organize and conduct this indoctrination. Also, the political officers have general responsibility for maintenance of morale, and they submit (through their own channels) periodic reports on the state of morale of their units and their officers. But the guiding "Instructions to the CPSU Organizations in the Soviet Army and Navy," issued in April, 1957, emphasize anew that "the *commander* guides the entire military *and political* training of the personnel."[2] The role of the political officer has, thus, been significantly reduced. But this also imposes duties upon the commanders, which have been stressed since Zhukov's fall. However, this is not the only, nor indeed the most important, external "control" element in the armed forces.

Since the ouster of Zhukov, the political officers have assumed a more important role in the military councils. Whether it is true, as charged, or not, that Zhukov sought the abolition of the councils, these have considerably increased in significance. The local civilian Party apparatus may also now have representation on the military councils of the Military Districts.

The secret police counterintelligence officers in the armed forces are an institution separate both from the professional military and the Party. They are under the KGB or Committee for State Security (which is not a part of the Ministry of Defense). Counterintelligence, in the Soviet conception, is directed primarily against the personnel of the Soviet armed forces, as well as to a lesser extent against actual or potential enemy penetrations. We have characterized the chief function of the Party organs and the political officers as indoctrination; the chief mission of the counterintelligence officers is surveillance, and their second mission is liquidation of any anti-Soviet tendencies uncovered in the course of this surveillance.

Thus there are three separate organizations paralleling the normal military chain of command: the Communist Party and Komsomol cells to maintain ties with members of the Party; the Chief Political Administration to indoctrinate the armed forces as a whole; and the Chief Administration for Counterintelligence to uncover and eliminate questionable persons in the armed forces. All report at their highest levels to agencies outside the Ministry of Defense, despite their nominal subordination to it.

THE MILITARY DISTRICTS

The forces in the field, as we have seen, are directly under the command of the Minister of Defense. The major peacetime organization for directing military formations is the system of "military districts." At present there are eighteen districts.

48

The military districts are geographical commands embracing all military units and installations within their defined areas, excepting only the political police (border guards and internal-security units) and special military bases (such as units of the Long-Range Air Force and of the Air Defense Forces). The peacetime frontier military districts are the nuclei of wartime "fronts" (Army Groups). The interior military districts may become fronts or armies, or may continue to serve as training centers, depending upon their individual mobilization orders and the character of the war. The military districts are directly subordinate to the Minister of Defense. Only in the Far East may a special area command embrace two military districts for operational purposes.

The commander of each military district is a senior officer with extensive experience in command. Until recently, most of the military districts were commanded by marshals, but with reshuffling of the High Command and some retirements in 1954, 1955, and early 1956 the "second generation" of wartime generals has come to occupy many district posts. But these generals of the army and senior colonel generals were also high-level field commanders in the last war.

The key military districts (the Leningrad, Baltic, Belorussian, Transcarpathian, Kiev, Moscow, North Caucasus, Transcaucasus, and Far East), for the most part districts near the periphery, are virtually on a war-ready basis at all times.

The commander of each military district is "the supreme commander of all troops and military installations located in the district," with certain limitations we shall note presently. The commander's staff is composed of a Chief of Staff (who is the senior deputy commander), a "Deputy Commander for Political Affairs," a "Deputy Commander for the Rear Services," and air force, artillery, and tank commanders. The commander, chief of staff, and political deputy form the military council of the district. The staff sections are not in a line of command from their counterparts in the General Staff and Ministry of Defense, but are directly under the commander of the district. Nonetheless, much of their business is handled directly with the corresponding chief administrations of the ministry.

Units of the Air Defense Forces and the Long-Range (Strategic) Air Force are not operationally subordinate to the commander of the military district, but only administratively and logistically so. Other units, including the Army Air Force (tactical aviation), are operationally subordinate as well.

The primary peacetime duty of the military districts, groups of forces, and fleets is, of course, training.

In addition to the military districts within the U.S.S.R., the "Group of Soviet Forces, Germany" represents a powerful army group. It now numbers twenty combat-ready divisions, of which eighteen are tank and mechanized divisions, providing a powerful offensive capability.

The Army field forces continue to be organized in conventional armies, corps, divisions, regiments, battalions, companies, platoons, and squads. The three basic divisional types are the tank, mechanized, and infantry (motorized). Armies are either "rifle" (if predominantly infantry) or "mechanized" (if largely armored forces).

The Navy

The Soviet Navy is organized around four major fleet commands corresponding to the four separate major seas which surround the Soviet Union. The Black Sea and Baltic Fleets are on seas, the access to which is held by potential enemies, but these seas are also so located in proximity to key areas of the Soviet Union that they receive considerable attention, particularly the Baltic. The Northern Fleet is remote, but still the most easy Soviet access to the Atlantic. The Pacific or Far Eastern Fleet is isolated, but the necessary bulwark for offensive and defensive operations in that area. Each command controls the shore defenses and installations, naval air units, and the numbered surface fleets (two in the Baltic and one each in the Pacific, the Black Sea, and the Northern areas). These commands are the naval equivalent of military districts.

The Commander-in-Chief of the Navy, Admiral S. G. Gorshkov, replaced Admiral of the Fleet N. G. Kuznetsov in late 1955. His senior first deputy is Admiral A. G. Golovko. The chief of the Naval Main Staff, and also a deputy C-in-C, is Admiral V. A. Fokin. Naval aviation is under the command of Colonel General of Aviation Ye. N. Preobrazhensky (who, as a naval colonel, led the first successful Soviet air raid on Berlin, in August 1941). Each fleet has its own corresponding air component.

The Baltic Fleet is commanded by Admiral N. M. Kharlamov. The largest of the Soviet sea forces, this fleet has about eight modern light cruisers of the *Sverdlov* class, and a proportionately substantial share of all the other naval components, including submarines. The purposes of the fleet are: first, to protect and extend Soviet control of the Baltic; secondly, to assist the Soviet Army and air forces to open the Danish straits; and finally, to participate in subjecting the Allied areas bordering the Eastern North Atlantic.

The Northern Fleet, commanded by Admiral A. T. Chabanenko, has about six modern light cruisers of the *Chapaev* and *Sverdlov* classes, a score of modern destroyers, and a substantial submarine force. It is the only force able to achieve access to the open seas of the Atlantic hemisphere without running the gauntlet of hostile closed waters. After an assault on Norway and Spitzbergen, at least its submarines would be committed to the Norwegian Sea and North Atlantic.

The Black Sea Fleet, formerly commanded by Admiral Gorshkov himself, is now under Admiral V. A. Kasatonov. The mainstay of the fleet is a force of about half a dozen *Sverdlov* and modernized *Kirov* class cruisers, and there are (as in the Baltic) large numbers of smaller combat vessels. The command of the Black Sea, first priority, is no great challenge, but the possibility of contesting the Eastern Mediterranean is severely constrained both by the Turkish straits and the American Sixth Fleet in the Mediterranean.

The Pacific Fleet, under Vice Admiral V. A. Chekurov, has in recent years been strengthened. It now possesses about six modern cruisers of the *Sverdlov* and *Kalinin* classes, a number of destroyers, and a large submarine arm. It is a potent local defensive force, and the submarine forces could easily fan into the Pacific, but its strength is not up to the American Far Eastern naval forces, to say nothing of the whole American Pacific Fleet. The surface fleet would probably assume the strategic defensive in the Seas of Okhotsk and Japan, save only to support any attempted invasion of Japan.

There are presently no aircraft carriers in the Soviet Navy, and no battleships (two old ones recently retired), nor are any capital ships planned.

The Soviet Navy has general responsibility for coastal defense (including anti-aircraft artillery and rockets).

Much of the Soviet "Naval Infantry" or marines are organized in brigades for amphibious operations, and in recent years some progress has been made in filling the gap in landing-craft. But at present there is no significant amphibious capability.

The Soviet Navy as a whole is autonomous within the Ministry of Defense.

THE AIR FORCES

Marshal of Aviation K. A. Vershinin, as a First Deputy Minister of Defense, "represents" all of the Soviet military air forces in the Military Council of the ministry. His title is at present given variously, even in official Soviet identifications, either as Commander-in-Chief of the Air Forces of the Soviet Army (VVS-SA), or as Commander-in-Chief of the Air Forces of the Armed Forces (VVS-VS). His First Deputy Commander-in-Chief is Marshal of Aviation S. I. Rudenko, who also serves as Chief of Staff of the Main Staff or General Staff of the Air Forces (again, inconsistency marks the Soviet published identification of the staff designation itself). The Commander of the Long-Range Air Force (DA), Marshal of Aviation V. A. Sudets; the Commander of Fighter Aviation of the Air Defense Forces (IA-PVO), Colonel General of Aviation I. D. Klimov; the Commander of the Aviation of the Airborne Troops (A-VDV), Marshal of Aviation N. S. Skripko; and the Commander of Naval Aviation (A-VMF), Colonel General of Aviation Ye. N. Preobrazhensky, are all "deputies" to Vershinin. But each of the four air forces identified above is *operationally* independent of Marshal Vershinin and his staff. Only the important tactical or "army" air force, termed Frontal Aviation of the Air Forces (FA-VVS) is directly under Vershinin's command.

The combat air forces are divided into four categories. The major one, in numbers of aircraft, is the tactical army air force, organized in Frontal (Tactical) Air Armies (FVA). Ordinarily, a tactical air army includes a number (perhaps nine) of fighter, ground support or fighter bomber, and of tactical light-medium bomber, air divisions. One such tactical air army is usually assigned to each Army Group of the ground forces to provide cover, support, interdiction, and reconnaissance for the appropriate sector of the front. Those military districts designated for activation as fronts (Army Groups) in wartime are each generally assigned a tactical air army in peacetime. (Other military districts have an "Aviation of the —— Military District" to administer such tactical and training air forces as are within the district.) All tactical air armies are subordinate to the senior ground force commander (of the front, group of forces, or military district).

The Air Armies of the Long Range Air Force (VA-DA), of which there are three or four, are directly under the commander of the DA, and he in turn under the Minister of Defense.

The Fighter Air Armies (IVA-PVO) form the interceptor force of the air defense system, and are assigned to the established air defense districts. The commanders of these districts (which overlap the military districts and cover only particularly key and defended areas) are the superior level for all air defense forces and installations in their districts. They, in turn, are directly under the Commander-in-Chief of Air Defense Forces in Moscow, who is again directly subordinate operationally to the Minister of Defense.

RANKS, STATUS, AND STANDING

It is useful to examine the standings of the senior officers of the armed services because this further reveals the relative status of the various armed-force components in the Soviet military establishment.

The Soviet hierarchy of military ranks is complex and frequently misunderstood. It is an amalgam of Imperial Russian, German, and new ranks and equivalent standings.

The highest military rank is Marshal of the Soviet Union, and its naval equivalent, Admiral of the Fleet of the Soviet Union. There is no corresponding Air Force rank. Thus, by current regulation and law, no Air Force officer in the Soviet Union can reach the highest level of military rank! On a slightly lower level are Chief Marshals of the main arms—Aviation, Artillery, Tank Troops, Engineers or Signal Troops. Below this level are Marshals of an arm. There are no naval or infantry equivalents for these two levels of rank. The fourth level grade is General of the Army, exclusively for ground force generals (with but two exceptions: I. I. Maslennikov, chief of the Internal Troops, and I. A. Serov, chief of the Committee of State Security [KGB] hold this rank). The fifth level of rank is: Colonel General (Infantry) ; Colonel General of an arm or service (Aviation, Artillery, Tank Troops, Signal Troops, Engineers, Rear Services, Medical Service, Veterinary Service, Technical Services, Aviation Technical Services, Engineering Technical Services, Shore Services, Intendance, or Justice) ; and

Admiral or Engineer Admiral. The sixth level is equivalent for Lieutenant Generals and Vice Admirals; and the lowest level of general or flag grade officer is Major General or Rear Admiral.[3]

In December 1957 there were seventeen living Marshals of the Soviet Union (including the political figures Voroshilov and Bulganin, and the retired Budenny). Four others had been executed (including Beria); one (Kulik) was demoted; and four had died presumably natural deaths (including Stalin). The two Admirals of the Fleet of the Soviet Union were both retired (N. G. Kuznetsov and I. S. Isakov). There were three Chief Marshals of Aviation, two retired (A. Ye. Golovanov and A. A. Novikov), and the other head of the Civil Air Fleet (P. F. Zhigarev). The one Chief Marshal of Artillery (N. N. Voronov) was in semi-retirement in a research position. There were eight living Marshals of Aviation (including three retired and one in civil aviation), five Marshals of Artillery (including one probably retired), two Marshals of the Tank Troops (one retired), and one Marshal of the Signal Troops (retired). Thus we see that there are presently on active military duty: 14 Marshals of the Soviet Union (all infantrymen except for 1 artillerist), 4 Marshals of Aviation, 4 Marshals of Artillery, and 1 Marshal of Tank Troops. There are 17 living Generals of the Army (not including the two senior police generals), of whom 4 are probably retired. Below this level, there are approximately 120 Colonel Generals of all arms (not including police generals), and 27 Admirals.

It is interesting to note the respective numbers of senior officers of the ground forces, air forces, and Navy. And it is revealing to compare these figures with the relative distribution in 1940, to gauge the degree of change or continuity.

In June 1940 there were a total of 1,064 generals and admirals in the Soviet military establishment. Of this total, ten per cent (101) were Air Force officers. But of the senior grades (marshals, admirals, and colonel generals) there were 15 ground force, 3 naval, and *no* Air Force officers. In December

1957, if allowance is made for the change in meaning in rank designation, and only marshals on active duty are counted, there were, as we have seen, 20 ground force, 4 air force, and *no* naval officers. If the next level is included (through lieutenant generals in 1940, and through colonel generals and admirals in 1957) , we see: in 1940, 103 ground force, 15 Navy, and 13 air force officers; in 1957, there were approximately 100 ground force, 32 Navy (including two naval aviation), and 24 Air Force officers—a surprising continuity.*

We have observed earlier that the Minister of Defense and his dozen senior first deputies and deputies are ground force marshals. Similarly, in the Supreme Soviet of the U.S.S.R. elected in 1955, of the 26 senior military marshals and admirals elected, 21 were ground force, 3 Navy, and only 2 Air Force officers. In the important Central Committee of the Communist Party, the membership elected in 1956 included 6 full members—all ground force marshals (Zhukov, since ousted, Malinovsky, Konev, Sokolovsky, Vasilevsky, and Moskalenko) ; and of the 12 military candidate members 10 are Army, and only the then senior airman (Zhigarev) and the senior naval man (Gorshkov) were included from their services.

MILITARY STRENGTH

It is only necessary to outline in general the strength of the Soviet ground, air, and sea forces. The figures below represent the best available *estimates;* they may be subject to some error in detail, but in general they are believed to be accurate.[4]

---

* By contrast, in the United States there are in the senior grades (three- and four-star generals and admirals) 38 Army, 37 Navy, 30 Air Force, and 8 Marine generals; this includes 29 four-star generals on active duty: 9 Army, 9 Navy, 9 Air Force, and 2 Marine. The continuing heavy predominance of ground force officers in the Soviet military establishment thus stands in marked contrast to the near equality of representation of the three arms in the senior grades in the United States.

The Armed Forces

Army
> 140 divisions, including:
>> 70 tank and mechanized
>> 70 infantry
>
> 130 cadre divisions, including units both designated "divisions" and "independent brigades"
> 40 "artillery divisions"
> 25,000 tanks (plus reserves stockpiles)

Air Forces
> 400 regiments (equivalent to USAF wings)
> 19,000 aircraft, including:
>> 10,000 tactical air armies
>> 3,500 air defense
>> 3,500 naval air force
>> 500 airborne forces
>> 1,500 long-range forces

Navy
> 27 modern cruisers (including at least 16 postwar)
> 150 destroyers, sea-going (including 125 postwar)
> 250 modern long-range submarines
> 150 older sea-going submarines
> 100 coastal submarines, mostly old
> 500 patrol and minesweeping vessels
> (In "reserve": 2 obsolete battleships, 3 old cruisers, and 1 monitor).

In terms of manpower, with estimates of actual but partial fulfillment of the announced reduction in forces, the figures are:

Army	2,250,000
Air Forces	800,000
Navy	650,000
Marines	50,000
Total	3,750,000

Not included in these figures are the Internal (Security) Troops of the KGB, numbering approximately 400,000 men and organized in a dozen divisions, nor the many thousands of Border Guards of the MVD. Thus the total exceeds four million men, *after* reductions of a little over a half-million men since 1955.

IMPLICATIONS

In concluding our discussion of the organization of the Soviet armed forces it is desirable to reflect upon the major implications of this organizational picture. As we noted at the outset, the structure of the military forces embodies the basic Soviet strategic concept and military doctrines. The Soviets have, if belatedly nonetheless intensively, prepared in recent years for warfare in the nuclear age. Literally each component of the military establishment has tremendously increased its capabilities in the period of postwar modernization. It is significant and important that the Soviets have greatly increased their long-range air and sea offensive capabilities, and their air defense, without slackening attention to the improvement and maintenance of a large modernized ground force and supporting tactical aviation.

Notes to Chapter 3

1. Marshal G. Zhukov in *Krasnaia zvezda*, March 23, 1957.

2. The Decree itself has not been published, but direct excerpts have been printed in the many articles devoted to its role in political indoctrination. This quotation appears in *Krasnaia zvezda*, May 12, 1957. It is believed to have remained in effect since Zhukov's ouster.

3. All data on ranks are taken from the current official *Ustav vnutrennyi sluzhby Vooruzhennykh Sil Soiuza SSR* (Internal Service Regulations of the Armed Forces of the USSR), Ministry of Defense, Voenizdat, Moscow, 1957, pp. 8-9 and 189-190.

4. These data are all the author's estimates, since official Soviet information and Western intelligence estimates are not available. They are based upon indirect Soviet references and incomplete official Western releases.

II

CHAPTER 4

STRATEGIC CONCEPTS AND DOCTRINE

FOR THE NUCLEAR ERA

The path of development of Soviet military doctrine and strategic thinking was steady and slow from 1945 to 1953. Then, beginning in mid- to late-1953, and achieving its greatest momentum in 1955, a new belated adjustment was made to meet the requirements of the nuclear era. Why this tardiness?

THE LEGACY OF STALINIST STAGNATION

The death of "the greatest military genius of modern times," the "inspirer and organizer of all victories," could not fail to make an imprint upon Soviet military development. But Stalin's death made a crucial difference because it marked a turning point away from the rigid autocracy of his personal dictatorship. Military affairs again became (though not immediately nor all at one time) the province of the professional military leaders, just as the Party again became the dominant political force replacing the Autocrat.

As early as November 1953, Major General Pukhovsky said that "the cult of the individual" had adversely affected "questions of military science," and that sterile repetitious quotations of authority (Stalin was not yet named) "voluntarily or involuntarily have hindered the development of military-theoretical thought."[1] The authoritative limited-circulation General Staff organ, *Military Thought,* said in early 1955, almost a full year before Khrushchev's famous secret speech: "It is necessary to say frankly that in connection with the cult of the individual, no science sinned so much as did military science."[2] Stalin, at that time, was still praised and credited with "an enormous role in the development of military science" (a tribute never restated since 1955), but he was also obliquely criticized for having permitted doctrinal development to have become sluggish. "One must not consider it normal when books and articles . . . mostly boil down to a repetition of things said at various times by J. V. Stalin, instead of objective research on military theory and historical facts. . . . Such copying, freeing one from the necessity to think about serious problems, holds back creative thought, and clearly brings *harm* to our military science."[3] This statement was published following two important events: a debate on "the laws of military science" which appeared in the sheltered pages of *Military Thought* from late 1953 until late 1954, and the accession of Marshal Zhukov to the post of Minister of Defense in February 1955. We shall return to consider both, after briefly noting the antecedent state of affairs under Stalin.

The dominant feature of Soviet military doctrine in the period from 1947 to 1953 was the virtual canonization of the basic "Stalinist" military science as it existed in 1945. Thought was reduced to silence, and genius reduced to Stalin. This was the period of Stalinist stagnation in Soviet military doctrine.[4] The only accepted foundation for the development of doctrine was the one laid down by Stalin in an Order in February 1946, which declared that "the whole preparation of the army" and "the further development of Soviet military science" in the future "must be conducted on the basis of a skillful mastering of the experience of the recent war."[5] And, indeed, Soviet experience in the war did become the basis for postwar development until 1953. This meant not merely an intensification of the universal attention to recent military experience; it meant a prohibition upon anything else. Oppressive censorship led to virtual absence of discussion, almost of mention, in the military press of atomic weapons, guided missiles, and other new weapons. The few discussions which appeared in the early postwar months were entirely cut off by 1947. This atmosphere was hardly conducive to innovation in military thought or to interpretation of the doctrinal implications of new weapons. Stalin's injunction to study the Soviet experience in the war was also used to sanctify the military genius of the Generalissimus, extending into military history retroactive exaltation of Stalin's alleged roles in strategic planning, command, and doctrinal achievement. Who would dare to become "creative" by meddling with "Stalinist military science"? Moreover, lest it be thought that some matters were beyond or beneath Stalin's interest, as early as 1947 it was held that: "There is not a single aspect, not a single problem, of military art which has not received its further development from Comrade Stalin." [6]

Soviet military doctrine of early 1953 represented a formulation, an elaboration, a canonization of Soviet military doctrine of 1945. But there was this critical difference: while this doctrine had perhaps still been applicable to the geostrategic and technological world of 1945, to what extent was it applicable to the world of 1953 and to the future? This question, rather than an answer, was the legacy of the period of Stalinist stagnation.

NEW DOCTRINAL FOUNDATIONS

The post-Stalin era in Soviet military thought was opened by this laconic statement by Admiral of the Fleet Kuznetsov in July 1953: "The experience of the Great Fatherland War alone is no longer sufficient." [7] It is significant that this, the first sign of revision, dealt with the inadequacies of the former theoretical foundation for developing doctrine. By November 1953 *Military Thought* editorially admitted by implication that a number of factors which *should* influence doctrine had remained in neglect in the previous years: "The military art of the Soviet Army must take account of a whole series of new phenomena which have arisen in the postwar period."[8] From this time on, it became usual for Soviet statements, reflecting a new attitude in practice, to devote serious attention to the progress and potentialities of military technology, as well as to the study of military history (which continues to be a subject of greater importance in the U.S.S.R. than here). Beginning in 1954, there has been a systematic effort to inform Soviet officers of the nature and effects of new weapons and military technology, and a parallel intensified effort to stimulate thinking on the problems and potentialities for military science created by the introduction of new weapons systems. For example, breaking seven years' silence, in *Red Star* alone approximately fifty articles on atomic energy and nuclear weapons appeared in the two years 1954 and 1955. Similar articles on atomic weapons, jet and nuclear propulsion, missiles and rockets, radar, military uses of television, earth satellites, and the like, have appeared throughout the military press. To be sure, these discussions are all screened for military security, and are often quite elementary in comparison to what is published openly in this country. But in contrast to the period of Stalinist stagnation the significance of these discussions as a stimulus to doctrinal development is very great. To take the single prominent example of atomic energy and weapons: although three articles had appeared in the Soviet military periodical press in late 1945 and in 1946, not a single article on atomic energy or atomic weapons is known to have appeared in the period from 1947 through 1953 in the Soviet military daily and periodical press, open or restricted in circulation. The importance of the long delay in informing Soviet officers about the nature, effects, possibilities, and limitations of these and other new weapons was substantial. Nonetheless, the belatedness may even have had certain advantages: the Soviets, for example, did not delay their efforts to obtain long-range ballistic missiles because of Service commitments to bombers (piloted and pilotless) or aircraft carriers. For even in the Stalinist period, new weapons were added to the arsenal of arms; it was only the arsenal of Stalinist military science which was fully stocked. And so, along with the new informational program, efforts were made beginning in 1954 and 1955 to elicit creative enrichment (not, be it noted, disestablishment) of Soviet military doctrine.

Major General Pokrovsky, an eminent military technologist, summed up the basis for the new emphasis on developments in means of warfare in the following passage, in 1956, in a way that would have been impossible in Stalin's Russia four years earlier:

> The appearance of the atomic weapons, long-range rockets, guided missiles, supersonic aircraft, helicopters, nuclear propelled warships, radar for reconnaissance and for bombing, and many other things has so strongly affected the possible means of combat that contemporary military affairs are completely dissimilar to what they were in the period of the Great Fatherland War of 1941-1945, or to what they were in recent times in military operations in Korea. Therefore, at the present time the practical experience of the wars of the past can be regarded only as important historical landmarks of the past, and not as an unchanging dogma determining military affairs of today and tomorrow.[9]

The continuing revolution in military technology and weapons development has thus been belatedly recognized as an important basis for doctrinal evolution. The legacy of Stalinist stagnation, while perhaps not fully dispelled, has at least been recognized as insufficient. In contrast to the postwar Stalinist period, information on weapons progress is being made available as a source of ideas for military thought. Efforts are definitely being made to stimulate creative military thinking as a step toward doctrinal modification and evolution to accord more fully with the new world of weapons. At the same time considerable attention continues to be directed to the interpretation of past military experience in the light of these new developments.[10]

"The Laws of Military Science" Debated

A debate over "the laws of military science" began in late 1953, ending almost three decades of absence of open discussion among Soviet military men on basic military theory. Curiously, it was similar in many respects to its distant predecessor of the mid-1920's; both concerned definitions of the "laws" of military science and the content of military science (i.e., of the scope of competence of the professional military). Both were highly abstract and theoretical, and yet related to concrete and current issues of practical significance. But there were important differences, too. The debate of the 1920's involved a political and personal rivalry between two factions; the recent debate did not. And while the earlier conflict resolved formulation of a new doctrine, the latter one merely modified and adapted a basically unchanged doctrine.

The wide spontaneous interest in "the character of the laws of military science" was evident in the fact that *Military Thought* received forty articles and letters on the subject in the year following the original article by Major General Talensky in September 1953.* (General Talensky was then chief editor of the journal; he was replaced in this post in June 1954, in the middle of the discussion, but he continues to occupy important positions.) The main issue in the debate was whether military science broadly covers "in addition to military questions a whole complex of questions on war as a social-historical process," or, on the other hand, should military science, while

---

* Another sign of interest in this subject was the establishment in 1953 and 1954 of a number of "Military Science Societies," probably similar to those existing in the 1920's and 1930's. Little is known of their work, but they are voluntary groups open to officers on active duty, reserve, or retired, and some of their work is occasionally published in the military journals. In 1956 commanders of "all units, staffs, commands, institutions, and enterprises of the Soviet Army" were enjoined to organize such societies in an order by Defense Minister Zhukov. (See the editorial, *Krasnaia zvezda,* December 2, 1956; and the editorial "Military Science Societies," *Voennyi vestnik,* No. 1, January 1957, pp. 2-7.)

"basing itself on Marxist-Leninist teachings on war and the armed forces," but not including them in its scope, study "the laws of war as armed conflict"? The conclusion officially accepted was the latter. "A wider interpretation of the subject of military science leads it away from the resolution of its specific tasks. . . . Therefore to include in military science questions beyond its competence means to ruin military science as a specific branch of knowledge."[11] Of course, the new view does not deny in any way the basic importance of Marxist-Leninist views on the nature of war. What it does do is *to exclude from the competence of Soviet military scientists the basic issue of peace and war,* and at the same time by implication *to exclude from the competence of the Soviet political leadership the questions of military doctrine, of how to wage a war.* Similarly, the innate "professionalism" of military art was reaffirmed in the second issue of the debate: Do the laws of military science apply equally to *both* sides in a war between states with different social systems (e.g., between the Soviet Union and the United States)? The conclusions were that the same laws *do* apply, although "the potentialities for understanding and utilizing the objective laws . . . are different."[12] Superiority is still attributed to the Soviet Union, but now on a more realistic (even if incorrect) basis. The CEP accuracy of a hydrogen bomb is recognized to be the same for a socialist target as for a capitalist target. Finally, in concluding the debate, the door was left open for further revisions. "The editors deem that it is still not possible to establish conclusively any definitive formulation of the general law."[13] Having marked a liberation from the stagnancy of Stalinist formulations, the Soviet military theoreticians were not anxious to establish a new stereotyped "general law of victory in war."

Almost coincidental with the end of the debate on the laws of military science, a secret meeting of "the leading personnel of the armed forces," addressed by Marshal Zhukov, was told there was "need for further systematic perfection of their knowledge on the basis of a deep study of contemporary military technology and advanced military theory."[14] The editorial in *Military Thought* which reported this meeting went on to acknowledge frankly for the first time that: "Work on military science in the armed forces still lags behind those requirements which the contemporary development of military affairs and the *missions* standing before the Soviet Army and Navy establish for it. *Soviet military science is working out [too] slowly many important theoretical problems of the present time.*" Consequently, "in planning work on military science it is necessary to obtain formulations of sharp, burning issues having exceptionally great significance *for practical actions*," and "to publish only fresh, original articles advancing new scientifically based questions or containing valuable generalizations and conclusions."[15] The meaning and significance of this admission is found in certain criticisms which *Military Thought* mentioned, summing up some of them as "the fear to say something new" and "lingering too long on the repetition of already long-known facts."* Most specifically, in self-criticism, the editors admitted that they had "held up, without basis, the publication of the article by Marshal of the Tank Troops P. A. Rotmistrov, 'On the Role of Surprise in Contemporary War,' thus displaying a lack of the necessary boldness in raising *a new and timely question having important significance* for a correct understanding of the character of contemporary war."[16] Indeed, as we shall see later, the revision of views to recognize the increased role of surprise was one of the most important modifications made in Soviet military doctrine. It is not certain, but it is quite probable, that Marshal Zhukov's secret address on the eve of his assumption of the Ministry of Defense used the withholding of Rotmistrov's article as an example of the ill practices in need of change, and the article itself as an illustra-

---

* The recognition of this problem did not, of course, mean its solution. Nearly two years later *The Military Herald* still had to state: "The fear of saying anything new, or other than had already been said by one or another authority has not been entirely overcome," and this "puts a brake on the development of military science." (Editorial, *Voennyi vestnik*, No. 1, January, 1957, p. 7.)

tion of the creative thought needed. As we have earlier observed, the "cult of Stalin" was also attacked at this same time for its harmful effects on the development of military thought.

The editorial in *Military Thought* in March 1955, calling for creativity and original thought in the study of military science, also criticized those who failed to write, as well as those who had merely memorized Stalin's writings. In particular, high-level military field commanders—military district, fleet, and army commanders—rarely publish; and, "as a result, valuable individual experience is lost to military theory without purpose...." And, also: "The experience of training and maneuvers is used weakly in the development of military theory." Finally, criticism is also leveled at the state of the study of strategy. "Our military science institutions, in essence, don't study the theory of strategy, considering it to be a sphere of creative activity only of the Supreme High Command, and do not prepare qualified scientific cadres for this purpose." [17]

Whether Marshal Zhukov's secret address in January 1955 covered all the major points raised in the *Military Thought* editorial of March 1955 is not known. It is, however, probable that he was responsible for these views. The timing would suggest that the critical examination of the state of Soviet writings on military science might have been related to Zhukov's assumption of the Ministry of Defense. While there is no evidence to substantiate this view conclusively, it is likely that Zhukov displayed the initiative in opening the question of revitalizing Soviet military thought.

FOREIGN AND SOVIET VIEWS REASSESSED

Since "Stalinist military science" was superior to all others, why bother to study foreign military views and developments? To be sure, there appeared in the Stalinist years a number of articles on specific aspects of tactical doctrine (especially of the American armed forces). But articles on subjects such as "The

U. S. Infantry Battalion in Defense on a River Line" were in the nature of information on tactical "doctrinal terrain" similar to articles providing information on the physical terrain of possible theaters of combat. On the whole, from 1946 until 1954 non-Soviet military thought was considered below discussion, save for occasional propagandistic ideological diatribes.

During 1954 and 1955, and continuing since, a number of articles have reflected the new Soviet view that it is important and useful to study the military views of foreign countries, and especially of the main "imperialist" powers.[18] The main reason is to understand more accurately the strengths and weaknesses of the enemy. In addition, some discussions have implied that the Soviets themselves might pick up a few new useful ideas.

The realization (or, probably, admission) that Soviet military science is not unique and inherently superior in all respects implicitly raised an important question: Had Soviet military science and experience really been infallible?

Since Stalinist military history reflected the application of all-perfect Stalinist military science by the greatest strategic genius, Stalin, it admitted to no failures or flaws. Since 1955 Soviet military history has finally been admitted to have known its failures, and the Red Army its reverses (if still not "defeats"). The war record, while hardly candid, is no longer completely idealized. Again, the *Military Thought* article in March 1955, reflecting at least in part the views expressed by Zhukov in his secret address, marked the significant step in this "de-idealization" of Soviet military history. In particular, both this article and the many subsequent ones have pointed to the failures and reverses of 1941. And *Military Thought*, unlike the public sources which have followed, explained *why* it was necessary to set history aright. "Singing praises to active defense, to its incorrect interpretation as pre-planned, leads not only to distortion of the factual military events of 1941, but also to idealization of this form of struggle, *to incorrect orientation of our military cadres on the possibility of its repetition in future war.*"[19] Some articles have even gone so far as to

70

admit that the Soviet Army had known "blunders and failures" during the war, and "some insufficiently worked-out theses of our military science, individual erroneous views and tendencies."[20] On the whole, however, the Soviet war record is still grossly inflated and non-objective. Despite these recognitions of Soviet fallibility, and partial modification of the former idealized military history of the recent war, Soviet writers continue to claim that: "The progressive character of Soviet military science demonstrated itself with particular force in the Great Fatherland War . . . it was a victory of Soviet military science over contemporary bourgeois military science."[21] Both the partial changes, and the limits to such modifications, are significant simply in view of the continuing Soviet attention to military history as a source for doctrinal development. This historical revision, together with the recognition of the need to study imperialist military views, the newly defined scope of military science, and the belated recognition of the influence of new weapons development on doctrine, are the ways so far used to revive Soviet military thinking. Now we can review the effect these changes have had on current Soviet military doctrine. What has changed, and what has not changed—above all, what is the pattern of continuity *and* change? What is the doctrine *today*?

THE SOVIET STRATEGIC CONCEPT

A strategic concept underlies and welds together into a coherent and inter-related pattern all aspects of doctrine, organization of the military establishment, weapons systems and other components of any military structure. The Soviet strategic concept, in the thermonuclear era as before, is founded on the belief that the primary objective of military operations is the destruction of hostile military forces, and not the annihilation of the economic and population resources of the enemy. Thus the Soviets continue to adhere to the classical military strategic

71

concept, while contemporary American views often diverge sharply from this traditional stand. The dominant view in the United States is that war, if not deterred, can be won by disrupting the enemy's capacity for war and undermining his will to fight—that is, by attacking primarily his economic and population resources. The technological revolution of the twentieth century could not fail to pose the question of whether the military forces of the enemy should necessarily continue to be the priority objective of military action. The advent of nuclear and thermonuclear weapons, in particular, conferred a powerful advantage in efficiency to a strategy of annihilation. But the existence of two powerful opponents able to deal mutually devastating strategic blows may well serve mutually to deter each side, in the inherently dominant interests of self-preservation, from implementing such a strategy. It was in recognition of this that the Soviets were able to effect an advantage from their belated doctrinal recognition of the effects of nuclear weapons. For they plunged directly into the emerging era of thermonuclear weapons and "nuclear parity," and were never attracted to reliance on a weapon that they might later find inexpedient.

It is doubtful if such considerations suddenly occurred to the newly liberated Soviet military theoreticians and leaders. It is uncertain if these are the main considerations even today. But it is clear that the Soviets have held fast to the strategic concept of destroying the enemy's armed forces. For example, the authoritative *Military Thought,* in officially closing the theoretical discussion we have reviewed, declared that *"the defeat of the enemy will be achieved above all by means of the annihilation of his armed forces . . . "* [22] Lt. General Tsvetkov, also in the same journal in 1955, defined the objective of armed conflict as "the complete defeat of the armed forces of the enemy." [23] More recently, in 1957, Major General Mil'shtein and Colonel Slobodenko have reiterated: "Wars are won only when the enemy's will to resist is broken and that can only be broken, as the experience of history shows, when the armed forces of the enemy are destroyed. Therefore *the objective of combat operations must be the destruction of the armed forces, and not strategic bombing of targets in the rear.*" [24]

The Soviet adherence to a strategy of destroying the enemy's military forces may persist for other reasons, as well as for purely military ones. Once the obstacle of the enemy's instruments of warfare was overcome, other Soviet political and police measures would be prepared to refashion the will of the population and to exploit conquered economic resources. There are indications in Soviet military writing supporting the view that for offensive wars, at least, Soviet strategy is consciously influenced (if not shaped) by the acquisitive aims of Communist imperialism. In particular, various articles have, at least since 1949, discussed the idea that "the seizure of important economic or industrial areas . . . has become a significant factor in strategic war planning." [25] The article in the *Great Soviet Encyclopedia* (1956) on "Strategic Objective" *defines* such an objective, without any reference to destruction of such targets by bombing, as: "an important political or economic region or center (a city, industrial center, military or naval base, etc.) *the seizure of which* influences the course of the war as a whole. . . ." [26] Of course, Soviet aims and opportunities in any given war would have an important effect on whether "seizure" or destruction were the operational means best suited to the neutralization of enemy strategic objectives.

The Soviets have often reiterated, in serious writings intended only for Soviet officers, their view that reliance on strategic bombing of the enemy's economy is a strategy "defective in its foundation," and that American strategic bombing experience in the war bore witness to "the complete failure of the theory of winning the war by means of economic exhaustion of the enemy by aerial bombing." [27] Soviet rejection of *reliance* on a strategy of economic-industrial bombing, even in the thermonuclear era, does not, of course, mean a failure to recognize the military value of nuclear bombing of the enemy's economy. *Within* the strategic concept of destroying the enemy's military forces there is recognition of the value of supplementary operations to disrupt the economy. Colonel Denisov, an air officer, put it in the following terms: "Our air thought *considers necessary the action of air power against military-industrial centers and communications* of the enemy, evaluating this action *as a means supplementing but by no means replacing* operations conducted by the combined efforts of all the armed forces."[28] And Lt. General Krasil'nikov spelled this out clearly (in 1956):

> Powerful blows against the armed forces—land, air and sea—will clearly be combined with intensive and determined operations against the rear of the enemy country, against its economy, since only such a combination of attacks can speed victory. . . . Thus intensive and determined operations of the ground forces with the aim of defeating the armed forces of the enemy, and operations of the air forces to gain air supremacy, must have combined with them powerful systematic strategic air attacks on the basic military-economic centers and communications centers of the hostile countries, constant intensive submarine surface and air combat against his sea communications, and other forms of combat aimed at undermining the economic might of the enemy and weakening his will for resistance.[29]

But Soviet strategy does not subscribe to the concept that disruption of the war-making capacity of the enemy is the most effective primary means to achieve victory. Thus General Krasil'nikov, in the discussion quoted above, endorses the conclusion that the correct *strategy* must be "the conduct of armed conflict *with the aim of decisive destruction of the enemy's armed forces* by means of a series of consecutive powerful blows. . . ."[30]

Strategic bombing seeks to undermine the economic foundation of the enemy's ability to fight. In addition to weakening the physical capacity to resist, strategic bombing also seeks to undermine the will to fight of the enemy. And the chief means is direct attack on the collective seat of the will power of

74

the enemy nation: the population. But again, Soviet military thinkers state that military action against population targets cannot form the basis of a war-winning strategy: the enemy armed forces must be destroyed. Soviet military planners doubtless take into account the "bonus" effects of population losses to the enemy resulting from Soviet nuclear attacks on the enemy military forces (particularly SAC air bases) and selected military-industrial and interdiction objectives.[31] It is possible that they may plan strikes on military objectives to maximize population casualities. And in reply to American city-bombing in a total war the Soviets might retaliate in kind for purposes both of home morale and of lowering American morale. But even if the number of casualties is many millions, the Soviets do not regard population attacks and the morale effects of population decimation as the key strategic objectives. Thus the Soviets consistently reject a strategy built primarily on direct action against the enemy population as a target.

The fact that the Soviet Army maintains over one hundred combat-ready ground divisions, and dozens of additional under-strength divisions and cadre divisions (termed "independent brigades") is a reflection of the Soviet strategic concept. These powerful forces, and the more than two-thirds of Soviet military aircraft strength assigned to support of the surface forces, clearly are intended for combat with enemy military forces. The maintenance of these massive forces underlines the relevancy of the written expressions of Soviet doctrine developed under the strategic concept of destroying the enemy's military forces. The one arm which has other potentialities is the Long-Range Air Force (and in the near future, also the intercontinental ballistic missile force and submarine-launched missiles). Here, too, the emphasis is on destroying the enemy's strategic air and missile forces on their bases. "It is essential to select most carefully the targets for strategic air strikes *so that the enemy cannot deal a retaliatory blow.*"[32] Thus we see that this intercontinental striking force also is designed primarily to

75

implement the fundamental strategic concept, destroying the enemy's military forces which lie beyond the range of theater air and ground forces.

Balanced Forces and Rejection of "Ultimate Weapon" Strategies

In keeping with the strategic concept, Soviet military doctrine has consistently rejected any strategy based upon predominant *reliance* on *any* particular weapons system. The Soviet opposition to the idea of any "absolute weapon" is a long-standing characteristic of their doctrine. But the Soviet condemnation of one-weapon strategies as "adventuristic," "bankrupt," and "false" is not only in keeping with their resolve to utilize all means for advancing their aims rather than "gambling" on any one. For it also reflects their military evaluation of the forces needed to meet the requirements of their strategic concept for achieving victory through the defeat of the enemy's armed forces. This concept requires forces to neutralize or destroy enemy missiles and bombers thousands of miles away, and also to overcome infantrymen and tanks at close quarters. The doctrine has therefore continued through Soviet acquisition of the atomic bomb (in 1949), the thermonuclear weapon (in 1953), the intercontinental jet bomber (in 1954), and the intercontinental ballistic missile (in 1957). This author's survey of all available Soviet military periodical and other publications reveals at least eighty specific Soviet reaffirmations of the rejection of reliance on one-weapon strategies in the period 1953 through 1957, and *none* diverging from it. To cite but one illustration, Marshal Moskalenko expressed this principle of Soviet military doctrine in the following terms:

> *Soviet military science decisively rejects* any arbitrary fabrications of bourgeois military theorists that one could, as it were, *achieve strategic victory by means of employment of one or another new weapon. There are no such weapons which pos-*

76

sess exceptional and all-powerful qualities. Historical experience teaches that with the appearance of new technology, new
more powerful and more destructive weapons, *the significance
of men on the battlefield not only does not decrease but increases all the more....*[33]

This tenet of Soviet military science is contrasted to alleged
Western over-reliance on particular weapons, especially nuclear
and thermonuclear ones. Bourgeois military thought is said to
"elevate to the absolute the destructive force of atomic and
hydrogen bombs."

In contradistinction to bourgeois military science, which over-
estimates the role of various types of military forces, Soviet
military science . . . considers that *all reliance upon any one
arm, or any one weapon, even on the most powerful, will inevitably lead to failure.* Any kind of new weapon represents
but one part of complex military technology, and hence is
incapable of solving all problems of contemporary combat. . . .
Victory in contemporary warfare is achieved by the combined
efforts of all arms.[34]

What, specifically, do the Soviets mean in criticizing and
denouncing "absolute" weapons and one-weapon strategies? As
the statement quoted above illustrates, criticisms are often directed against military thought in the United States, and against
specific Western theoreticians such as Douhet. Reliance predominantly upon strategic bombing, nuclear and thermonuclear weapons, and missiles are the generally designated objects
of the Soviet criticism. To cite but one reference, Lieutenant
General Krasil'nikov of the General Staff wrote (in 1956): "In
connection with the development of atomic, hydrogen and missile weapons, new unfounded and one-sided views on military
strategy have appeared in a number of imperialist countries."[35]
Of course this does not mean that the Soviets do not consider
these weapons to be both exceedingly powerful and necessary
to have in substantial quantities. But while necessary and even
of crucial importance, these weapons are *not* regarded as sufficient. The structure of the Soviet military establishment bears

77

eloquent witness to the seriousness of Soviet doctrinal anathema toward tendencies to rely on any absolute weapon.

The key point in the practical application of this doctrinal tenet has been the evaluation that nuclear and thermonuclear weapons, for all their destructive power, are not alone the decisive element in determining the outcome of war in the future. It has, in the West, frequently been assumed that Soviet derogation of the importance of atomic weapons in the period from 1945 to 1949 was a defensive measure to minimize the significance of the American monopoly. From 1949 to 1953, perhaps, it was a Stalinist "lag." But, as we have noted, this evaluation remains today when the Soviets boast (with, or more likely without, sound basis) of an alleged superiority in thermonuclear and missiles strength. Marshal Zhukov often remarked in 1955 and again in 1956 that: *"One must bear in mind that one cannot win a war with atomic bombs alone"* and *"Air power and nuclear weapons by themselves cannot determine the outcome of an armed conflict."*[36] Numerous statements (this author's survey located fifty-five in the years 1954 through 1957) argue, in the words of the official Soviet Army manual on atomic defense: "Atomic weapons significantly exceed conventional weapons in their destructive force, but there are simple and effective means of defense. Troops which are well prepared for actions under the conditions of the employment of atomic weapons can successfully accomplish their combat missions."[37] And, in fact, in 1955 Major General Pokrovsky (a prominent Soviet military expert on atomic weapons who is also a nuclear physicist and professor) declared: "Atomic and thermonuclear weapons at their present stage of development *only supplement the fire power of the old forms of armament.* Artillery, small arms, tanks, aviation, and other armaments were and remain the basic fire power of the army."[38] These statements, illustrative of the tone of serious Soviet military writing, reflect the continuing stress on theater or "tactical" combat. What of strategic bombing? The Soviet answer still returns the basic military *decision* to the battlefield.

Nuclear Concepts and Doctrines

As Major General Olisov put it several years ago: "Strategic atomic bombs, which are a source of great danger to cities and civilian populations, have little effect on the battlefield. It will not be strategic bombing which will decide the outcome of war, but the soldier on the battlefield."[39] Or, as Marshal of the Tank Troops Rotmistrov wrote in his celebrated article stressing the new importance of strategic surprise due to nuclear weapons: "It is entirely clear that atomic and hydrogen weapons alone, without the *decisive operations of the ground forces* with their contemporary materiel, cannot decide the outcome of war."[40] It is for this reason that the Soviets continue to maintain a very large modern ground army and tactical air power. Victory, to the Soviets, requires defeating the enemy's military forces in order to seize and occupy vast areas of land—and in the final analysis only a ground force can do this. In a nuclear war this requirement may even be *greater* than in a non-nuclear one. For one thing, industrial, economic, and labor resources of other countries would be harnessed to compensate in part for the extensive damage to the Soviet economic system in the bilateral strategic thermonuclear strikes. But there are also important military considerations. Lt. General Krasil'nikov of the Soviet General Staff noted one (in late 1956) when, in describing the requirements for nuclear warfare, he declared that it "calls not for the reduction of the numbers of combatants, but for their logical further increase, since the threat of wiping out of divisions grows, and for their replacement large reserves will be needed. The growth of the number of divisions is inevitable also as a consequence of the increasing extent of strategic fronts, since contemporary wars have the tendency to encompass not one, but several continents. . . ." Further, he adds, "The attempts of some bourgeois military theoreticians to show that new weapons—aviation, tanks, atomic and hydrogen bombs, guided missiles—relieve one of the necessity of having mass armed forces are bereft of any foundation. . . . Weapons of mass destruction not only require mass armed forces, but require their inevitable increase."[41]

The Soviet doctrinal tenet complementing their rejection of absolute weapon strategies is the principle of balanced forces and a combined arms team. Again, a long-held tenet of Soviet military doctrine has been retained, but modified, to accord with the needs and opportunities of atomic warfare. A survey of Soviet military writings located 95 sources from 1953 through 1957 reaffirming this principle (and, of course, *none* diverging from it). But more important than the frequency of expression (which does show this remains the *doctrine*) is the authoritative, practical application of this doctrine.

The conception of the combined arms team has undergone a significant evolution. It continues to be applied often to "combined operations on the battlefield," its prewar and wartime meaning. There is no doubt but that the Soviet experience, and ultimate success, in the recent Soviet-German war continues to influence Soviet military thinking even in the changed strategic arena and technological era of the present. Nonetheless, whether they have done so correctly or not, Soviet military thinkers believe that in their doctrinal review in recent years they have taken account of the new weapons developments in reasserting the continued reliance on the combined arms team. And the Soviets have now extended this concept to include coordinated operations not *only* on the battlefield, but in operations by long-range aviation, IRBM and ICBM missiles, and missile-launching submarines, all complementing the united actions of the still more closely combined land, air and sea "theater" forces. Major General of the Engineering Technical Services Pokrovsky, a rocket and nuclear weapons expert, recently stated the Soviet view:

> The only correct idea on the employment of various means of military technology in war is the idea of Soviet military science regarding the fact that all forms of armaments and technology must be employed in war in close and well-organized combined operation. Under such conditions strategic weapons must be regarded as part of the armament of the army and navy, entering into the general system as an important and

irreplaceable link, but not replacing and not supplanting any other means of combat. Soviet military science teaches that without well-organized combined operations of all arms and services—land armies, aviation, and the navy—one cannot successfully wage contemporary war.[42]

Thus the basic doctrinal concept governing the organization and role of the armed forces for the conduct of military operations continues to be the combined arms team, now more widely construed in terms of mission and forces, but still in furtherance of the strategic concept of destruction of the enemy's armed forces. Further, the combined team is seen as a balanced force. This is what the Soviets mean when they affirm this principle in contradistinction to one-weapon strategies to which they believe the United States has a proclivity. Marshal Zhukov authoritatively described the seriousness of this doctrine in stating (in 1957) : "In the postwar construction of the armed forces we are proceeding from the fact that victory in future war will be achieved *only* by the combined efforts of all arms of the armed forces and on the basis of their coordinated employment in war."[43] And after Marshal Zhukov's ouster the new Minister of Defense, Marshal Malinovsky, reaffirmed on November 25, 1957, in an address to the graduates of the Moscow military academies:

> Considering that victory in combat will be achieved by the combined efforts of all the arms and components of the armed forces, important significance is given in training to the organization of combined operations among the ground and airborne forces, aviation, the navy, rocket formations, and air defense forces, in the various forms of operations.

The organizational structure of the Soviet High Command reflects this principle. The unified Ministry of Defense directly controls the chief administrations for the various arms. There are first deputy Ministers who serve as commanders-in-chief of the Ground Forces, Naval Forces, Air Forces, and Air Defense Forces, and deputy ministers who head the Rear Services,

Long-Range Air Forces, Artillery, Tank Troops, and Airborne Troops. The Army is predominantly represented (the senior dozen military chiefs all are Army, including the head of the combined Air Defense Forces, with the Navy and Air Force chiefs currently ranking about thirteenth and fourteenth in standing), and the General Staff of the Armed Forces is the former Army General Staff upgraded.

"The Decisive Factors Which Decide the Outcome of Wars"

Soviet military doctrine has never been expressed in a summary of "principles of war," but there exists a partial equivalent in the "decisive" or "fundamental" factors which, it is said, "decide the course and outcome of wars." These factors are the basic morale, economic-military, command, and military qualitative and quantitative elements which *in the long run* the Soviets believe inevitably play the decisive role in war. From 1942 until 1956, these factors were formulated in a thesis originally expressed by Stalin, and were termed "the permanently operating factors which decide the course and outcome of wars." [44] These factors were contrasted with the transitory or temporary factors, such as surprise or advance mobilization. During the Stalinist postwar era virtually all Soviet discussions of military science and strategy invoked these factors. Since, unlike most other aspects of "Stalinist" military science, this formulation was in fact a contribution of Stalin's, it was moot whether the thesis on the permanently operating factors would survive the modifications of the post-Stalin era. But from 1953 through 1955, the concept continued to be reiterated, with no basic alteration in its meaning. At least fifty-seven reaffirmations were made in this period (including twenty-four in 1955 alone). The only change, in keeping with another earlier noted revision, was a recognition that the capitalist military theoreticians and commanders also could be

82

aware of the decisive importance of these factors, although it was held that they still could not utilize them as effectively.[45] The theoretical debate discussed earlier concluded that the thesis on the permanently operating factors was "often approached one-sidedly and in some cases even incorrectly," but that the thesis itself "retains its scientific value also in the present."[46]

During 1954 and 1955, especially after the publication of the aforementioned article by Marshal Rotmistrov in February 1955, the question of the role of surprise was raised and reviewed. We shall return to this shortly, but it is useful here to note that Rotmistrov and the others who called for—and obtained—a recognition of the greater importance of surprise in the nuclear era, explicitly reaffirmed the thesis that "the permanently operating factors, in the final analysis, have always decided and will always decide the course and outcome of wars."[47]

Since Khrushchev's denunciation of Stalin (in February 1956), reference to the thesis in the old formulation of the "permanently operating factors" has virtually ceased. The factors and their decisive significance are constantly reiterated and reaffirmed, but not under the old rubric. There are two reasons for the dropping of the old formulation: first, it was a codification made by Stalin and thus served to represent a claim to a perfect and unimprovable Stalinist military science; and secondly, uncritical parroting of the thesis for many years had served to freeze the doctrinal significance of the basic economic, political, morale and military factors into a stereotyped formula. In 1954 and 1955 experiments with reviving the real doctrinal essence of the factors through calls for a dynamic interpretation of the thesis were not fully satisfactory. Accordingly, in 1956 and 1957 the familiar stereotype has been discarded and succeeded by a concentration on the "fundamental" or "decisive" factors themselves. Finally, as has happened with so much of the Stalinist ideology and doctrine that the current Soviet leaders want to retain, the factors are now attributed to Lenin, in the new "cult of Lenin" which has replaced that of Stalin. Thus one key article in *Red Star* (in 1957) was entitled: "V. I. Lenin on the Fundamental Factors Which Decide the Course and Outcome of Wars." [48] What are the new "fundamental factors"? Precisely the old permanently operating factors paraphrased and reformulated. And this article, and others,[49] point quite clearly to the important purpose of the reformulation: the freeing of these vital and decisive factors from the old ossified formula in order to make more comprehensive use of their practical implications, and of certain other factors of increased importance such as surprise. Marshal Zhukov himself, while Minister, repeated the same factors, in paraphrase, as having "decisive influence on the character of war and the methods of its conduct." [50]

SURPRISE AND BLITZKRIEG

Perhaps the key point of innovation in Soviet military doctrine has been the belated recognition (in 1954 and especially in 1955) of the implications of nuclear weapons and modern delivery systems for strategic surprise. Surprise, previously somewhat downgraded as a transitory factor, had not been sufficiently appreciated. Since early 1955 surprise has been recognized as a possibly decisive condition for success in a war, and the premium attaching to successful surprise is now recognized to be highly important in a nuclear war. Yet, despite the greatly increased importance of surprise, the change in doctrine is far from revolutionary. Surprise has *always* been recognized as advantageous, but *never* regarded as decisive itself. This is one of the practical meanings of the reaffirmation of the decisive factors by the advocates of greater attention to surprise. For example, Marshal of the Tank Troops Rotmistrov carefully specified: *"Surprise cannot, however, yield a conclusive result, cannot bring victory, in a war with a serious and strong enemy."* [51]

84

We have seen earlier that *Military Thought* at first balked at publishing Rotmistrov's original article on the increased importance of surprise. The reason was probably not the doctrinal modification, but the practical policy step for Soviet strategy which Rotmistrov advocated: namely, that since a simple effort to *repulse* an attempted enemy surprise attack might be insufficient, a "preemptive" or "forestalling" strike was necessary. He specifically distinguished his idea of a preemptive strike from preventive war. A preemptive strike is the last-hour seizure of the initiative and surprise from the enemy whom the Soviets know (somehow) to be preparing an imminent surprise attack.[52] This was, evidently, a new operational consideration in Soviet war planning. Publication of Rotmistrov's article was accompanied by other signs that his view had gained official acceptance, including specific references to the concept in the limited-circulation *Military Thought*. Thus, in the May 1955 issue of *Military Thought* it was editorially stated that: "The task is to work out seriously all sides of this question [of surprise] and above all to elaborate ways and *means of warning of surprise attack by the enemy and of dealing to the enemy preemptive blows on all levels*—strategic, operational, and tactical."[53] Openly published articles described the new view of the increased importance of surprise, but none referred to the new preemptive strategy except very obliquely.[54] A high degree of vigilance and preparedness for the preemptive strike is expected to frustrate and substantially neutralize any advantage the enemy might gain through launching a surprise attack—and foil any enemy attempt at a quick victory by this means.

The Soviet evaluation of strategic surprise as extremely important, but not in itself decisive, is quite pertinent to an understanding of Soviet *offensive* strategy. Surprise is considered an unreliable foundation upon which victory can be anticipated, and hence not a sufficient basis to justify launching a war against a vigilant major opponent. It is recognized that under certain circumstances surprise may be a necessary condition for success, but never a sufficient basis for success in a war between prepared major powers.[55] Hence the Soviets will not be led to initiate a major war simply because they believe they can achieve surprise; but if on any other basis they decide to launch a war, they would doubtless seek the gains of surprise to bolster their presumed superiority in the ultimately decisive factors.

Surprise, then, is no recipe for blitzkrieg victory, even in the thermonuclear era. And the Soviets are most unambiguous in their rejection of the possibility of successful blitzkrieg between major powers. "Adventuristic, anti-scientific theories of 'atomic blitzkrieg'" are declared alien to Soviet military thought; "blitz-krieg can lead only to blitz collapse."[56] A powerful lightning blow may be non-adventuristic only if, when carefully calculated on the basis of the strength of the enemy, it yields not only a probability of success, but also involves no risk of disaster. Blitzkrieg in a general nuclear war, despite the much greater effectiveness of a surprise thermonuclear strike, necessarily involves unassumable risks. Soviet criticisms and rejections of blitzkrieg, often but not exclusively in the context of denying alleged American expectations of possible blitz victory, are related to the rejection of reliance on one-weapon strategies. Of the eighty references examined, many are explicitly directed against the idea of blitzkrieg. For the years 1953 through 1957, over forty specific critical rejections of blitzkrieg were found.

The doctrinal rejection of a blitzkrieg is probably also a reflection of calculations not made publicly. The Soviets, in considering a possible blitz thermonuclear strike on the United States (in particular on SAC bases in the U.S. and abroad, but also against other air bases, naval aircraft carriers, and other army and navy forces), must calculate on the possibility of a sufficiently strong force escaping the initial blow to retaliate against Soviet air bases and cities. Moreover, they would still not be in a position to occupy North America. A super-Pearl Harbor attack is reasonable only if there is expectation of defeating the United States by the initial attack itself. Every tenet of Soviet military doctrine is opposed to the conclusion that such a venture would lead to quick victory. Surprise, even if achieved, is not believed to be decisive, and attainment of blitzkrieg is not believed feasible in a major war between great powers.

Just as blitzkrieg is not adjudged a feasible strategy for the Soviet Union, neither is it considered a winning strategy for the West. Concretely, in considering the threat of an American biltzkrieg, they may estimate that even though powerful SAC forces might precede or evade their planned "preemptive" action and strike Soviet air bases (and cities), the Soviet Army would be able to operate effectively in driving the United States and allied military forces from the Eurasian continent and denying to the enemy any opportunity to occupy the U.S.S.R. Destruction would be great, but it would be mutual, with bilateral effects. Thus a long war or negotiated peace would still be the outcome of any attempted blitz action. Marshal of Aviation Vershinin has recently given us in part the Soviet reasoning for their conclusion that, in his words, "the possibility of a lightning annihilation of the Soviet Union by air strikes is excluded." For, he declares, "our country is not an island or a point on the globe; it has enormous territory over which our vital resources are dispersed."[57]

As we have previously seen, the Soviets are well aware of the importance of surprise in a thermonuclear attack. They intend to prepare in all possible ways to blunt any American-attempted surprise blow. They would certainly seek to utilize the advantage of surprise in any attack they would launch. But in the Soviet view surprise does not, even with hydrogen bombs and intercontinental missiles, provide the basis for a successful blitzkrieg.

THE LONG WAR

The obverse of the Soviet denial of attainability of blitzkrieg in war against a major power is thus the Soviet expectation

87

that a general war—nuclear as well as non-nuclear—would be a long and strenuous conflict, a "World War II radioactivated," as it were. Numerous Soviet military writings, in various contexts, reflect the views that "war inevitably develops a drawn-out character," and that "contemporary war is a long and severe contest." "Victory in war is achieved not by one, two, or several engagements, but by the achievement of a series of military campaigns and operations."[58] For, in the words of Lieutenant General Tsvetkov: "The ultimate result of the armed conflict —the complete defeat of the armed forces of the enemy—can be achieved only as the conclusion of frequently repeated blows, each of which is distinguished by objectives, scale, and character of forces used, by scope of time and space, and by results."[59]

The Soviet belief in a long war is evident in the important attention given to large, modern theater forces built around an atomically-prepared mass army. It is clear in Marshal Zhukov's statement that "large armies and a tremendous quantity of conventional arms inevitably will be drawn into military operations" in any future general war "along with atomic and hydrogen weapons, in spite of their tremendous destructive power."[60]

The economic, morale, and military factors are termed the "decisive" and "fundamental" factors because they clearly *are* decisive in a *long* war. This is the practical, operational significance of the Soviet stress on these factors and their efforts to attain a superiority in them. These factors, we are informed in the non-public General Staff organ *Military Thought*, "must be calculated in the working-out of strategic plans."[61] In fact, despite the expectation of extensive nuclear bombing in a total war, the Soviets continue to stress attention also on such matters as war production during hostilities[62] (though they also maintain very large stockpiles of finished war materiel and weapons to compensate for loss of productive facilities). Finally, the Soviet concept of large reserves of ground forces to maintain the "system of blows of mounting force" reflects their expectation of a long war. Thus, in the 1957 volume on *Marxism-*

Leninism on War and the Army, the military requirement for planning for a long war is stated as follows:

> In the strategic planning of war the correct employment of the troops must be estimated not only for its initial period but for its whole course. A genuinely scientific approach to the determination of the sizes of the first and succeeding strategic echelons, tempos of mobilization and strategic deployment, force levels of ready and reserve forces, reinforcement of combat field formations with fresh forces during the whole extent of the war is required. Hence Soviet military science attaches enormous significance to the working out of these problems. A correct decision on these problems determines the effectiveness of the employment of the quantity and quality of the armed forces in the interests of victory in war.[63]

Soviet military doctrine thus stresses the continued probability of a long war, waged by large armies and conducted by combined force operations, in which victory is won by the destruction of the enemy's armed forces and the seizure and occupation of his territory. The one major gap in Soviet capabilities is the apparent inability to occupy the United States even if the strategic thermonuclear exchange and initial ground campaigns were to give them an advantage. But save for this one very important deficiency, the Soviet armed forces are clearly prepared to attempt to implement their doctrine if general war should come.

Soviet Doctrinal Adjustment to the Nuclear Era

Soviet military doctrine appears to many of us to exhibit a certain lag in the appreciation of the growing potentialities for destruction and radioactive contamination on such a scale as to render almost meaningless the idea of fighting a total war. But is it a lag? The same Major General Pokrovsky who declared in 1955 that atomic and thermonuclear weapons "only supplement the fire power of the old forms of armament . . . which remain the basic fire power of the army,"[64] also declared in 1955 that "in contemporary major war atomic and thermo-nuclear weapons may be employed in quantities of hundreds, thousands, and even *tens of thousands.*" [65] One may dispute the realistic compatibility of the two statements, but in the context of Soviet military doctrine they are not at all contradictory. Soviet doctrine on mass armies in a long war may be unreal-istic, but is it a "lag" to say, as do the Soviets, that under con-ditions of reciprocal and mutual nuclear "saturation," "the decisive role of the old 'classical' light armaments . . . will be preserved?" [66] Is it a "lag" to point to the need for large reserves to replace units destroyed by hostile atomic strikes? Mutual thermonuclear destruction may be the last stage we care to con-template, but again is it a "lag" to face this and say that mutual nuclear strikes "may indeed result in equal losses to both com-batants. But from such equality it still does not follow that the war 'balances out' and ends without victory. . . . Operational bal-ance or equality achieved by reciprocal atomic blows will be broken to the advantage of one side or the other. . . ."? [67] A future war *might* be over in days, but if it weren't, would the side which had planned on a long war be guilty of a "lag"? A thermonuclear blitzkrieg *might* catch the enemy sufficiently off guard to win; but is it a "lag" to doubt the certainty of such a strategy? And surprise alone *is* no recipe for victory.

In visualizing the image of a future war, and calculating on its conduct beyond the first phase, the Soviets have the advan-tage of some relevant experience. The massive military loss undergone by the Soviet Union in 1941, in a relatively brief span of time, was more comparable to the loss from a nuclear assault than anything else experienced by a great power in modern times. The Soviets lost from their control 40 per cent of their population, 40 per cent of their grain production, ap-proximately 60 per cent of their coal, iron, steel and aluminum output, and 95 per cent or more of certain key military indus-tries such as ball-bearing production. They lost four million soldiers dead, wounded, or prisoners, and over two-thirds of their tanks and aircraft. Lend-lease would not, of course, be

90

available to them again, but in considering *mutual* losses of the scale noted, even multiplied, the Soviets may rightly or wrongly judge that they can better withstand the trial. Correctly or not, they apparently consider that such mutual losses would not necessarily mean that "the military decision" had been reached—hence the need for forces to fight on and win a long, arduous war leading to the destruction of hostile military forces and seizure of the enemy's territory.

The widely prevalent American view that the Soviets lag in understanding implications of modern high-yield weapons for their strategy is clearly as incomplete and incorrect a characterization as the opposite tendency to assume on a superficial basis that the Soviets "must have" come to hold the same views prevalent here. The Soviets *have* considered the implications of contemporary weapons and the geostrategic situation. They have amended, modified, and reinterpreted their military doctrine in several important respects—to the extent they presently believe justified. They also have reaffirmed and continued to demonstrate in their actions a continuing belief in the validity of the strategic concept which pursues the primary objective of destruction of the enemy's armed forces. Further changes in Soviet military doctrine must be expected. In such future modifications the traditions, experiences, and background of the Soviet Army and the senior Soviet military leaders will probably play a part. Also, the pressure of procurement of exceedingly expensive emerging weapons systems may compel further scrutiny of the allocation of the Soviet military budget, and manpower needs are under pressure from the short labor supply. But the main role will continue to be played by a calculation of risks and opportunities in terms of Soviet objectives and the Soviet strategic concept.

Notes to Chapter 4

1. Maj. Gen. N. V. Pukhovsky, *O sovetskoi voennoi nauke* (On Soviet Military Science), Voenizdat, Moscow, [November 16] 1953, pp. 84 and 85.

2. "On Some Questions of Military Science," editorial, *Voennaia mysl'*, No. 3, March, 1955, p. 6.

3. *Ibid.*

4. The present author's *Soviet Military Doctrine* (Free Press, Ill., 1953) by coincidence went to press in the very month of Stalin's death; it sums up Soviet military doctrine as it had developed until that time.

5. People's Commissariat of Defense Order No. 8, signed by Stalin, in *Krasnaia zvezda*, February 23, 1946.

6. Colonel I. S. Baz, *Istochniki voennogo moguchestva Sovetskogo Soiuza*, Voenizdat, Moscow, 1947, pp. 82-83.

7. Adm. of the Fleet N. Kuznetsov, *Pravda*, July 26, 1953.

8. Editorial, *Voennaia mysl'*, No. 11, November, 1953, p. 12

9. Maj. Gen. Eng. Tech. Service Prof. G. I Pokrovsky, *Nauka i tekhnika v sovremennykh voinakh* (Science and Technology in Contemporary Wars), Voenizdat, Moscow, [October 8] 1956, p. 88.

10. See Maj. Gen. Ye. Boltin, *Sovetskii flot*, June 6, 1957; Col. I. Baz, *Krasnaia zvezda*, March 6, 1957; Gen. of the Army A. I. Antonov, in *Slaviane*, No. 2, February, 1957, p. 4; Col. I. Korotkov, *Krasnaia zvezda*, August 29, 1956; and the editorial, *Voennyi vestnik*, No. 4, April 1956, p. 5.

11. "Conclusions on the Discussion of the Character of the Laws of Military Science," *Voennaia mysl'*, No. 4, April 1955, pp. 16-22. See also Maj. Gen. N. A. Talensky's original article, "On the Question of the Character of the Laws of Military Science," *Voennaia mysl'*, No. 9, September 1953, pp. 20-39; and a summary of the debate given in the unsigned article "On the Question of the Character of the Laws of Military Science," *Voennaia mysl'*, No. 11, November 1954, pp. 29-45.

12. *Ibid.*, p. 18. See also Major V. Zubarev, *Propagandist i agitator*, No. 13, July 4, 1955, p. 11.

13. *Ibid.*, p. 13.

14. Editorial, *Voennaia mysl'*, No. 3, March 1955, p. 3.

15. *Ibid.*, p. 4.

16. *Ibid.*, p. 4.

17. *Ibid.*, pp. 11 and 6.

18. See, in particular, the editorial "For Military-Scientific Work on the Level of Contemporary Requirements," *Krasnaia zvezda*, April 8, 1954; editorial, "Constantly Improve Military-Scientific Work," *Krasnaia zvezda*, January 26, 1955; Lt. Col. P. Derevianko, *Krasnaia zvezda*, March 26, 1955; editorial, *Voennaia mysl'*, No. 3, March 1955, pp. 12-14; Marshal of Tank Troops P. Rotmistrov, *Krasnaia zvezda*, March 24, 1955; editorial, *Krasnaia zvezda*, April 9, 1955; editorial, *Krasnaia zvezda*, June 10, 1955; Col. Gen. P. Kurochkin, *Voennaia mysl'*, No. 5, May 1955, pp. 32-33; Marshal K. Moskalenko, *Krasnaia zvezda*, February 23, 1957; Col. I. Baz, *Krasnaia zvezda*, March 6, 1957; Col. A. Goriachev, *Sovetskii flot*, May 24, 1955; Col. A. Strokov, *Krasnaia zvezda*, November 12, 1955; Maj. Gen. E. Boltin, *Krasnaia zvezda*, August 30, 1955; and

Nuclear Concepts and Doctrines

Marshal of Tank Troops P. Rotmistrov, *Voennyi vestnik* No. 11, November 1955, p. 94.

19. Editorial, *Voennaia mysl'*, No. 3, March 1955, pp. 7-8.

20. Col. Gen. P. Kurochkin, *Voennaia mysl'*, No. 5, May 1955, p. 16. See also esp. Lt. Gen. S. S. Shatilov, *Literaturnaia gazeta*, May 28, 1955; *Krasnaia zvezda*, May 6, 1955; and a whole series of articles which appeared in December 1956, and January 1957, commemorating the victory at Moscow fifteen years earlier.

21. Maj. Gen. Ye. Boltin, *Krasnaia zvezda*, August 30, 1955. See also Col. Gen. P. Kurochkin, *Voennaia mysl'*, No. 5, May 1955, p. 16; Marshal R. Malinovsky, *Voennye znaniia*, No. 2, February 12, 1957, p. 3; and Col. N. Sushko, *Sovetskii flot*, March 22, 1957.

22. *Voennaia mysl'*, No. 4, April 1955, pp. 21-22.

23. Lt. Gen. A. Tsvetkov, *Voennaia mysl'*, No. 3, March 1955, p. 52.

24. Maj. Gen. M. A. Mil'shtein and Col. A. K. Slobodenko, *Voennye ideologi kapitalisticheskikh stran o kharaktere i sposobakh vedeniia sovremennoi voiny* (Military Ideologists of the Capitalist Countries on the Character and Methods of Conducting Contemporary War), Znanie, Moscow, [April 22] 1957, pp. 46-47. In this passage, the authors describe a view which they state is in accord with "the objective requirements of contemporary war."

25. Col. P. Belov, *Voennaia mysl'*, No. 7, July 1949, p. 12.

26. *Bol'shaia Sovetskaia Entsiklopediia*, 2nd ed., Vol. 41, [April 21], 1956, p. 64.

27. E.g., see Maj. Gen. V. Khlopov, *Voennaia mysl'*, No. 1, January 1954, pp. 83 and 84; Col. A. Bagreev, *Voennaia mysl'*, No. 5, May 1955, p. 80; and Lt. Gen. of Aviation N. Zhuravlev, in *Sovetskaia aviatsiia*, January 10, 1957.

28. Col. N. Denisov, *Boevaia slava sovetskoi aviatsii* (The Combat Glory of Soviet Aviation) 2nd ed., Voenizdat, Moscow, [July 8] 1953, p. 67. See also Col. I. Maryganov, *Peredovoi kharakter sovetskoi voennoi nauki* (The Advanced Character of Soviet Military Science), Voenizdat, Moscow, [October 30] 1953, p. 32.

29. Lt. Gen. S. N. Krasil'nikov, in *Marksizm-leninizm o voine i armii* (Marxism-Leninism on War and the Army), Voenizdat, Moscow, [November 28] 1956, pp. 156-57. See also Marshal A. Vasilevsky, *Voennye znaniia*, No. 1, January 1957 p. 4; and Col. Yu. Pshenianik, *Sovetskaia aviatsiia*, March 17, 1957.

30. *Ibid.*, p. 154, and see p. 156.

31. Awareness of this consideration was published in several accounts; see Maj. Gen. G. Pokrovsky, *News*, April 1, 1955, p. 8; and Maj. Gen. F. Isaev *New Times*, March 26, 1955, p. 8.

32. Maj. Gen. M. A. Mil'shtein and Col. A. K. Slobodenko, *Voennye ideologi kapitalisticheskikh stran o kharaktere i sposobakh vedeniia sovremennoi voiny*, [April 22] 1957, p. 43. This statement is presented as a fact, not an attribution to foreign views.

33. Marshal (then Gen. of the Army) K. Moskalenko, *Krasnaia zvezda*, September 25, 1954. See also, in particular, for some recent restatements Marshal G. Zhukov, in *Krasnaia zvezda*, March 23, 1957; Col. Yu. Pshenianik, *Sovetskaia aviatsiia*, March 17, 1957; and Admiral V. Fokin, *Sovetskii flot*, February 23, 1957

34. Col. S. Mazhorov and Col. I. Tikhonov, *Krasnaia zvezda*, February 28, 1954.

35. Lt. Gen. S. Krasil'nikov, in *Bol'shaia Sovetskaia Entsiklopediia*, 2nd ed., Vol. 41, [April 21] 1956, p. 72.

36. Marshal G. Zhukov, *Pravda*, February 13, 1955, and August 7, 1956.

37. *Pamiatka soldatu i serzhantu po zashchite ot atomnogo oruzhiia*, Ministry of Defense, Voenizdat, Moscow, 1954, p. 1.

38. Maj. Gen. G. Pokrovsky, in *Marksizm-leninizm o voine i armii*, 1955, p. 168.

39. Maj. Gen. B. Olisov, *Krasnaia zvezda*, August 3, 1954.

40. Marshal of Tank Troops P. Rotmistrov, *Voennaia mysl'*, No. 2, February 1955, p. 25; italics in the original.

41. Lt. Gen. S. Krasil'nikov, in *Marksizm-leninizm o voine i armii*, 1956, pp. 148, 150 and 151.

42. Maj. Gen. G. I. Pokrovsky, *Nauka i tekhnika v sovremennykh voinakh*, [October 8] 1956, p. 48.

43. Marshal G. Zhukov, cited in *Krasnaia zvezda*, March 23, 1957. See also, for recent examples, Gen. of the Army A. Zhadov, *Krasnaia zvezda*, March 15, 1957; Lt. Col. V. Larionov, *Krasnaia zvezda*, March 19, 1957; Col. Yu. Pshenianik, *Sovetskaia aviatsiia*, March 17, 1957; Admiral V. Fokin, *Sovetskii flot*, February 23, 1957; Marshal R. Malinovsky, *Voennye znaniia*, No. 2, February 1957, p. 3; Marshal K. Meretskov, *Izvestiia*, February 23, 1957; Col. I. Baz, *Krasnaia zvezda*, March 6, 1957.

44. For the original statement, see J. V. Stalin, *O Velikoi Otechestvennoi voine Sovetskogo Soiuza* (On the Great Fatherland War of the Soviet Union), 5th ed., OGIZ, Gospolitizdat, Moscow, 1947, pp. 43-44; and see Garthoff, *Soviet Military Doctrine,* 1953, pp. 34-35.

45. For example, see Marshal of the Tank Troops P. Rotmistrov, *Krasnaia zvezda*, March 24, 1955; Col. A. Strokov, "Lenin's Elaboration of the Basic Issues of Soviet Military Science," *Krasnaia zvezda*, April 22, 1955; Maj. Gen. N. Pukhovsky, in *Marksizm-leninizm o voine*, 1955, pp. 99-100; and Col. G. Sapozhkov, cited in *Voennaia mysl'*, No. 11, November 1954, p. 37.

46. Editorial, *Voennaia mysl'*, No. 3, March 1955, pp. 4 and 5; and see the editorial, *Voennaia mysl'*, No. 4, April 1955, p. 20; Major V. Zubarev, *Propagandist i agitator*, No. 13, July 1955, p. 10; and the article on these factors by Maj. Gen. N. Talensky, *Bol'shaia Sovetskaia Entsiklopediia*, 2nd ed., Vol. 34, [June 20] 1955, p. 255.

47. Marshal of Tank Troops P. Rotmistrov, *Krasnaia zvezda*, March 24, 1955; and see Rotmistrov, *Voennaia mysl'*, No. 2, February, 1955, p. 21; Rotmistrov, *Voennyi vestnik*, No. 11, November 1955, p. 93; and Lt. Gen. S. S. Shatilov, *Literaturnaia gazeta*, May 28, 1955.

48. Col. I. Baz, *Krasnaia zvezda*, March 6, 1957. There was one precursor to this new line, in the theoretical journal of the Chief Political Administration, as early as mid-1955; see Major V. Zubarev, "V. I. Lenin and Military Science," *Propagandist i agitator*, No. 13, July 1955, pp. 10-12.

49. In addition to Col. Baz' article, see *Marksizm-leninizm o voine i armii*, [May 20] 1957, esp. pp. 209-81; Col. I. Nenakhov, "Military-Theoretical Ques-

tions in the Leninist Works," *Krasnaia zvezda,* September 14, 1957; Lt. Col. L. Korets, "V. I. Lenin on the Ways and Means of Armed Conflict," *Sovetskaia aviatsiia,* July 16, 1957; Cols. V. Gorynin, P. Derevianko, and V. Seregin, "Shortcomings of a Book on an Important Theme," *Krasnaia zvezda,* February 19, 1957; Col. G. Fedorov, "On the Content of Soviet Military Ideology," *Krasnaia zvezda,* March 22, 1957; Col. N. Sushko, "Soviet Military Ideology and Its Contrast to Bourgeois Military Ideology," *Sovetskii flot,* March 22, 1957; Col. I. Baz, *Krasnaia zvezda,* March 6, 1957; Marshal K. Meretskov, *Izvestiia,* February 23, 1957; D. Kondratkov, *Sovetskii flot,* January 6, 1957; and Col. N. T. Tsarev, *Ot Shliffena do Gindenburga,* [August 23] 1956, pp. 352 and 358.

50. Marshal G. Zhukov, *Krasnaia zvezda,* March 23, 1957, and March 20, 1957.

51. Marshal of Tank Troops P. Rotmistrov, *Krasnaia zvezda,* March 24, 1955; and see Rotmistrov, *Voennyi vestnik,* No. 11, November 1955, p. 94.

52. Marshal P. Rotmistrov, "On the Role of Surprise in Contemporary War," *Voennaia mysl',* No. 2, February 1955, pp. 20-21.

53. Editorial, *Voennaia mysl',* No. 5, May 1955, pp. 12-13; and see the editorials in No. 3, March 1955, p. 5; and No. 2, February 1955, p. 12; also Col. Gen. P. Kurochkin, *Voennaia mysl',* No. 5, May 1955, p. 18.

54. The most direct open statement was by Marshal V. Sokolovsky, *Izvestiia,* February 23, 1955; and see Lt. Gen. S. S. Shatilov, *Literaturnaia gazeta,* May 28, 1955; "The Great Strength of Leninist Ideas on Defense of the Socialist State," editorial *Vestnik vozdushnogo flota,* No. 4, April 1955, p. 8; and Lt. Gen. of Aviation P. Braiko, "Soviet Aviation in the Great Fatherland War," *Vestnik vozdushnogo flota,* No. 4, April 1955, p. 19.

55. The Soviets carefully define the possibilities for success based on surprise alone so as to *exclude* the U.S. and the U.S.S.R. See Rotmistrov, *Voennaia mysl',* No. 2, February 1955, p. 19.

56. The statement cited is by Lt. Gen. Gritchin, *Pravda,* January 7, 1955. See also, in particular, *Marksizm-leninizm o voine i armii,* [May 20] 1957, pp. 277-78; Maj. Gen. N. Talensky, *Mezhdunarodnaia zhizn',* No. 1, January 1957, p. 43; Col. N. Kramarenko, *Sovetskii flot,* December 26, 1956; and Marshal K. Moskalenko, *Slaviane,* No. 5, May 1955, p. 11.

57. Marshal of Aviation K. A. Vershinin, *Pravda,* September 8, 1957.

58. Col. A. Strokov, *Istoriia voennogo iskusstva,* Vol. 1, [October 17] 1955, p. xxix; and see Col. F. Dankovtsev, *Voennaia mysl',* No. 5, May 1955, p. 39; and Maj. Gen. N. Talensky, *Mezhdunarodnaia zhizn',* No. 1, January 1957, p. 43.

59. Lt. Gen. A. Tsvetkov, *Voennaia mysl',* No. 3, March 1955, p. 52.

60. Marshal G. Zhukov, *Pravda,* August 7, 1956.

61. Col. S. Kozlov, *Voennaia mysl',* No. 11, November 1954, p. 14 and see p. 28. See also Col. A. Strokov, *Istoriia voennogo iskusstva,* Vol. I, [October 17] 1955, p. xxviii, and the editorial, *Voennaia mysl',* No. 4, April 1955, pp. 18 and 22.

62. Col. I. N. Levanov, in *Marksizm-leninizm o voine i armii,* [May 20] 1957 p. 209; Col. G. Fedorov, in *Marksizm-leninizm o voine i armii,* 1955, p. 33; Col. F. Dankovtsev, *Voennaia mysl',* No. 5, May 1955, p. 35; Lt. Gen. S.

Krasil'nikov, *Krasnaia zvezda*, August 20, 1955; and Col. N. Tarasenko, *Sovetskii flot*, June 15, 1957.

63. Col. V. A. Zakharov, in *Marksizm-leninizm o voine i armii*, [May20] 1955, p. 262.

64. Maj. Gen. G. Pokrovsky, in *Marksizm-leninizm o voine i armii*, [February 3] 1955, p. 168.

65. Pokrovsky, *Voennaia mysl'*, No. 3, March 1955, p. 23.

66. V. Skopin, *Militarizm*, 1956, p. 424.

67. *Ibid.*, pp. 377-78.

CHAPTER 5

PERSPECTIVES ON LIMITED WAR

As the increasing Soviet nuclear power has made all-out thermonuclear war less and less attractive as even a reluctant undertaking, military thinkers in the West have been confronted with the problem of military (and political) substitutes for total war. Viewed in this perspective, it is not difficult to understand the long-standing *Soviet* preference for such substitutes in the face of American thermonuclear striking power. The mutual ability to destroy the opponent, regardless of who should strike first, is apparently in sight. While such a situation may lead to mutual deterrence from *all* war, it is only prudent to assume that it may only deter from *total* war, but not necessarily from other forms of armed conflict. Maintenance of a continuing thermonuclear capability for total war, is, of course, essential to the deterrence of total war and would always be available to implement a strategy of last resort.

The Soviets do not explicitly discuss possibilities of limitation in doctrinal terms. Their occasional discussions of Western views on possible limitation are usually couched in propagandistic terms. Nonetheless, it is possible and indeed most necessary to consider the probable calculations on limited war in Soviet policy-making.

Before discussing Soviet views of possible limitations (geographical or in the use of weapons) on war, it is perhaps useful to note that, in addition to such military substitutes for total war, there are a whole range of *political* substitutes for armed conflict. At the present, the Soviets favor the use of non-military substitutes such as political and economic pressures, inducements and blandishments, military demonstrations and threats, subversion, colonial rebellion and guerilla warfare, over direct military means, as a strategy to extend Soviet influence and control. Khrushchev, in his first major theoretical pronouncement (February 1956), stated that Marxism-Leninism in the contemporary era no longer considers that war is inevitable; socialism may be established throughout the entire world without war.[1] Thus, characteristically, the ideology is reinterpreted in terms of the practical situation: war is no longer a useful course of national policy, therefore it is no longer "inevitable." And, if military force is to be used, the Soviets well understand the value of "the use of *various means and forms* of armed conflict depending upon the circumstances."[2]

Non-Nuclear Major War

Soviet strategy is predicated upon the basic principle that war, as an instrument of policy, may assume various forms. It is not assumed either that nuclear weapons definitely will or will not be used; rather, it is recognized that under various circumstances they may or may not be employed. Consequently, the Soviets seek to build and maintain military forces necessary for conventional or non-nuclear warfare, and to prepare the forces necessary for nuclear war. Soviet recognition of the need to be prepared for general thermonuclear war is evident in many ways. Nonetheless, the available evidence suggests that the Soviets may believe it will be to their advantage to strive for the non-employment of nuclear weapons in a future war.

Soviet propaganda, ever since the war, has ostensibly sought the complete prohibition of nuclear weapons. There are obvious propaganda dividends from playing upon the fears of peoples everywhere. There is also obvious Soviet advantage in attempting to neutralize the nuclear deterrent strength of the United States. Less obvious, but more important, is the possibility that under certain conditions this objective might be achieved. The possibility of an effective international agreement to prohibit nuclear weapons must be recognized as very remote. But under circumstances of nuclear stalemate through mutual deterrence, the United States might forego use of nuclear retaliation if the Soviet provocation were clearly to involve less than a directly mortal threat.

In the Soviet political-military strategy, the wide belief in Europe and Asia of the existence of a general thermonuclear stalemate between the Soviet Union and the United States is regarded as an important advantage. Will other nations have confidence in the ability and resolve of the United States to invoke what is viewed as a virtually *suicidal thermonuclear strategy* to save Iran—or even West Germany? Or would such countries welcome even a "limited war" tactical nuclear strategy which is in any event virtually suicidal for them? The Soviet Union recognizes the value of exploiting this situation. The first objective presumably is the isolation of these countries from the United States. By offering blandishments and probably avoiding the appearance of the threat of war, the Soviets will seek to secure the abrogation of treaties of alliance with the U.S., as well as the abrogation of grants of base rights or atomic-weapons stations. At a later stage, the blandishments might even give way to more open pressures and threats and a further extension of Soviet influence and control. If the circumstances were deemed appropriate for resort to arms, in this context, it is quite possible that the Soviet Union in fact might favor non-use of nuclear weapons in a major war even in a situation of nuclear striking parity in which the U.S.S.R. holds the initiative.

Three important considerations might lead the Soviet to avoid initiation of the use of nuclear weapons. First, the Soviet bloc is stronger in non-nuclear military forces—increasingly so as the West comes to depend more and more upon nuclear military power. The *relative advantage* of the Soviet Union in seeking to avoid the employment of fission-fusion weapons, even at the risk of possible loss of initiative in the use of these weapons, is very great.

Second, the *absolute advantage* to both the Soviet Union and the Free World is a powerful force for mutual deterrence from their use in war. Soviet forfeiture of the opportunity for prior use of these weapons might lead to a Western decision on withholding their use. As the Soviet capability for delivering massive megaton attacks increases, the possibility of Western initiation of a mutual destruction duel in retaliation for a Soviet non-nuclear attack seriously diminishes. And of this the Soviets are doubtless aware. This possibility of Western failure to resort to massive retaliation for less than massive provocation would remain very great even if the West has failed to provide appropriate conventional or tactical nuclear capabilities, and is thus left no alternative but limited defeats (the American continents, at the very least, being unassailable by Soviet conventional weapons). Particularly is such deterrence likely since the Soviet Union, by initial non-use, would have shown an alternative —albeit unpleasant—to the vastly more unpalatable *certainty* of mutual destruction by reciprocal thermonuclear assaults.

Third, Soviet military thinkers do *not* regard nuclear and thermonuclear weapons as *all*-decisive; therefore, the risk of defaulting to American initiative in the use of the weapons *can be contemplated*, although to be sure not lightly. The gains of non-use may be so great, and the possibility of successful mutual deterrence from their use so large, as to make this strategy attractive.

It is, of course, a precondition of a strategy based upon non-use of nuclear weapons that the Soviet Union have a sufficiently powerful, and sufficiently invulnerable, intercontinental thermonuclear striking force to persuade and enforce mutual deterrence. Cognizant of this fact, the Soviet Union has been endeavoring, strenuously and successfully, to create such deterrent power. An air force suitable to this purpose is presently being acquired and perfected, and development of submarine-launched missiles and of an intercontinental ballistic missile provides weapons especially useful for such a mission of deterrence. Similarly, Soviet civil defense efforts may serve this purpose.

It is occasionally argued that that the Soviet Union would not create an expensive and large long-range bomber force and ICBM capability if it did not definitely intend to use them. The speciousness of this argument is evident by comparison to our own objective: we are building a powerful SAC as a deterrent which we hope never to have to use. And most important, *the Soviet strategic concept does not require the employment of an intercontinental striking force to gain a victory, while in the American concept and under current policy such use is assumed to be necessary.* In other words, the Soviets retain the flexibility of a strategy without use of the intercontinental thermonuclear striking force, and maintain the strong ground and tactical aviation forces to fight such wars.

In addition to the reasons noted, there are other doctrinal tenets which make views on possible non-use of nuclear weapons seem feasible to the Soviets. Particularly in view of the belief that such weapons are not decisive, even in an attempted surprise blitzkrieg campaign, there would be no gain in initiating a war with mortal risk and the certainty of enormous destruction. The Soviet objective is expansion of power and influence, but only by ways in which the Soviet Union itself is not risked as the stake in an "adventure." Finally, if nuclear weapons create a recognized stalemate, this stalemate would serve as a shield behind which the vastly superior Soviet conventional military power could, through threat and possibly in actual limited wars, be used to expand Soviet control at much reduced risk.

If the reasoning advanced above describes the Soviet position, favoring the non-use of nuclear military power through mutual deterrence both for defense and as a screen for possible future expansion, the Soviet Union may avoid initiation of the use of nuclear weapons. In a situation based upon necessary enemy "cooperation," enforced by the enemy's own advantage, there is of course always the risk of an irrational enemy use of his nuclear strength. Can the Soviet Union, or any country, take this risk? In view of the Soviet evaluation of the impossibility of attaining a decisive surprise nuclear blitzkrieg attack, it is reasonable to assume that this risk, while great, may be considered acceptable under some conditions. Moreover, *there is no alternative for expansion with less risk.* (Relative quiescence, which is not excluded from the reasoning, is of course less risky than limited moves of overt expansion.)

The Soviets themselves consider their preparations for nuclear war in terms reflecting implicitly the *contingent* alternative of nuclear war. For example, as Major General N. Pukhovsky put it in 1955, since the enemy "threatens to use atomic weapons" the Soviet must prepare "to win in contemporary combat *also* [sic] *under conditions of the employment of atomic weapons.*" [3] It is significant that Soviet descriptions of various tactical and protective measures in atomic warfare are typically stated in the terms "under conditions of the employment of atomic weapons." Clearly such specification indicates a belief that warfare *may* also be conducted under other conditions, under conditions of the non-employment of atomic weapons. The Soviets also sometimes state that the existence of nuclear weapons "in the hands of the imperialist states, and the *possibility* of their use in future war, seriously influences the character of contemporary combat. . . ." [4] The Soviet view that future wars, general and local, *may or may not* include the use of nuclear weapons was stated most authoritatively by Marshal Zhukov, in early 1957, when, in reply to questions on whether atomic and thermonuclear weapons would be used in future wars, he stated: "Neither I nor anyone else can answer completely all these questions now because all wars, major and small, arise, are waged, and end under specific political, geographical, and economic conditions."[5]

These various statements clearly imply *the contingent possibility* of nuclear war in Soviet thinking, in contrast to the presently dominant inclination in the United States (and projected into NATO) to assume that any major war *must* be nuclear, and accordingly to prepare only for that eventuality. For example, see the testimony in 1956 of General Nathan Twining, then Chief of Staff of the USAF, to the effect that the United States can not afford to prepare both for atomic and conventional war.[6]

Soviet interest in preparing for the contingency of all-out nuclear war is, of course, apparent, and anticipated on grounds of simple logic. The fact that it is advertised by such statements as those cited earlier, and others relating to nuclear weapons tests (in particular the thermonuclear tests of November 1955) is evidence of the Soviet attempt to maximize deterrence. Such deterrence purposes (and still less statements of alleged Soviet intent) by no means exclude the possibility that the Soviet Union may, under certain conditions, herself unleash a world thermonuclear war. But, as we have seen, there are cogent reasons for believing that the Soviet Union believes its greatest advantage would be served by avoiding a thermonuclear war and using her growing nuclear striking power to stalemate American deterrent power, and then to take advantage of this neutralization for purposes of gradual and probably indirect aggrandizement.

The Soviets are aware that the choice of limited or unlimited war may not be theirs. As one Soviet colonel has put it: "The selection of the means of armed conflict will depend not only on our wishes, on our means of armament and military technology, but also on the methods of combat action of the enemy and on many other factors which it is difficult to divine or to foresee."[7] Several senior Soviet military men have, in 1955 and 1956, cited a statement once made by Lenin that: "Anyone

103

would agree that an army which did not prepare to employ every kind of weapon and means of combat which the enemy has or might have would be foolish and even criminal."[8] And, as we have seen, the Soviets are building up powerful long-range air, naval, and missile forces capable of unlimited offensive thermonuclear war. But to be *prepared to employ* any weapon or to wage any kind of war does not mean it will be *necessary to employ* all kinds of weapons or wage all kinds of wars.

Several Soviet statements have hinted that general nuclear war will result only if the West initiates the use of nuclear weapons. Thus, in 1955, Major General Pukhovsky wrote: "If the enemy decided on such an adventure as the employment of atomic weapons, he will be destroyed by the same weapon."[9] It is quite significant that the specific threat to destroy the enemy with nuclear weapons is tied to American decision on the prior use of atomic weapons, rather than to American initiation of a war. The implication that the Soviet Union would not initiate the use of nuclear weapons is quite in accord with the reasons earlier advanced which make such a course both advantageous and plausible in terms of the Soviet strategic concept. Similarly, Marshal Zhukov in his speech to the Twentieth Party Congress in February 1956, said: "Future war, if *they* unleash it, will be characterized by atomic, thermonuclear, chemical and bacteriological weapons,"[10] a formulation carefully preserved in the frequent subsequent paraphrasings of this statement, and reflecting the Soviet belief in American intentions to use nuclear weapons. It is likely that since early 1955 the Soviet leaders have considered, in view of American and NATO planning and nuclear armament, that the West is increasingly bound to a nuclear strategy—if a general war is actually fought.

The other restriction on Soviet freedom of action in military development and strategic planning, then, is the possibility of enemy assumption of the initiative. This was the key impetus to an important Soviet re-evaluation in 1954 and 1955 of the

104

importance of surprise in the nuclear era, and the conclusion on the need to launch a preemptive initial nuclear attack if ever the United States should attempt to launch a surprise nuclear attack on the Soviet Union.

These qualifications indicate that, even if the Soviet Union should decide that total nuclear war should be avoided in favor of a major non-nuclear war, they might not be able to insure limitation of the war to a non-nuclear status. But the possibility of a major non-nuclear war in Europe remains strong enough—and may increase in likelihood—so that the question of preparation for waging such a war should concern all great powers. The Soviets realize this and plan accordingly.

A general war, limited by the non-usage of nuclear and thermonuclear (and probably bacteriological and chemical) weapons, might have no geographical limitations. What would be the characteristics of such a war? As Soviet nuclear striking power (weapons and delivery systems) has grown toward a balance with our own, this question has increasingly occupied Western political and military analysts.

A non-nuclear general war, in the fashion of World War II, seems indeed quite unlikely. Particularly in the past several years, the Soviets have shown signs of recognizing the decline of this possibility in view of American and NATO policy. But there is one case of a major, though not world, war under which the Soviets may attempt to place the West in a position where we will not use nuclear weapons: a major Soviet challenge which they deem insufficient to provoke us to all-out massive retaliation under prevailing circumstances of mutual strategic deterrence. Thus, at some time, the Soviets might launch a non-nuclear attack on West Germany, or on Western Europe in general, if they had been led to judge mutual deterrence to be so strong a restraint on American action that we would withhold our nuclear fire in response to such a major *conventional* attack in which neither major protagonist was directly threatened. This might at the least present us—and the people of the area involved—with a most difficult choice, and

105

conceivably lead us, in line with Soviet expectations, to forego our relative advantage in the use of nuclear weapons and to fight a major non-nuclear war.

In examining Soviet doctrine for a non-nuclear war the task is simplified by the relatively recent, and contingent, transition from a non-nuclear to a nuclear strategy and doctrine. The Soviet military doctrine of World War II, with postwar modifications, provides a general basis for the conduct of non-nuclear warfare. The ground forces have been mechanized and their firepower greatly increased, but their operations would be conducted on the basis of a modified form of traditional doctrine. The tactical air and naval forces similarly have improved weapons and a basically unchanged doctrine. In the case of all these arms, Soviet doctrine has provided precepts for training for tactical atomic warfare: but such provisions are explicitly conditional upon the circumstance of the use of such weapons. In the non-usage of such weapons, doctrine is also clear.

The major distinction of Soviet military strategy in a non-nuclear general war concerns intercontinental warfare. The world geostrategic arena of 1958 (and of the future), as noted earlier in this study, creates serious problems for the Soviet Union. In the event of the non-use of nuclear weapons, it is clear that the Soviet Union could not even seriously attempt to conquer the Americas and sub-Saharan Africa. The seizure of Western Europe, the Mediterranean, and parts of Asia would surely be attempted. But let us return to the central problem of intercontinental warfare.

It is unlikely, in view of the state of modern air detection and defense systems, that the United States would seek to defeat the Soviet Union by strategic bombing with high explosive bombs. The extent to which the United States did engage in intercontinental bombing in a non-nuclear war would probably determine the extent of Soviet efforts to attack SAC air bases in North America. It is also unlikely that the Soviet Long-Range Air Force would find it profitable to engage in strategic bombing of the economy of the United States. Soviet long-range raids might be made for reasons of home morale and foreign prestige, and also for a purpose which Marshal of Aviation Skripko specified as early as 1946: to tie down military capabilities for the defense of North America.[11] Naturally, as part of the mechanism of wartime deterrence, such air defense would in any case have to be maintained by the United States, but there might well be a greater drain on the American military effort from the main theater of the Eurasian rimland if Soviet bombers engaged in nuisance raids. Also, there would probably be prestige raids on such political centers and symbols as Washington and New York, to match such American raids as might be made on Moscow, Leningrad, Kiev, and other Soviet cities. American supply lines to Europe and Asia would be strongly attacked. But on the whole, *the intercontinental mission* would—at least for Soviet strategy—in a general non-nuclear war be relegated to secondary importance. The Soviets could not, in such a war, expect to defeat the United States itself. But they might well anticipate enormous gains in Europe and other areas on the Eurasian periphery. And, *so long as the mutual deterrence was maintained*, these gains could be made at assumable—indeed minimum—risks.

LIMITED NUCLEAR WAR

Soviet authorities, including Khrushchev and Bulganin, have on a number of occasions since 1955 declared that limitation of nuclear weapons to tactical employment is not possible. Moreover, the attempt to distinguish between strategic and tactical weapons or targets is declared "bourgeois propaganda" and "an attempt at criminal deceit of public opinion."[12] American statements about the "precision of tactical atomic weapons" and their use "exclusively against military targets" are said to be fraudulent. For, the Soviets aver, atomic weapons "do not cease to be weapons of mass destruction."[13] And intentions for

107

total war are not excluded; thus (in the official Soviet Ground Forces' journal *Military Herald,* in March, 1955):

> All the discussion of the "tactical use" of nuclear weapons is necessary to the propagandists of atomic war in order by consecutive steps to lead public opinion to a recognition of inevitability of the use first of tactical atomic weapons, and then of strategic ones. It is quite clear that the first attempt to use this "tactical" weapon would lead to the mass use of atomic and hydrogen bombs.[14]

Moreover, that tactical atomic weapons "would be used on a small scale is hardly likely because that would be inexpedient from the purely military and tactical standpoint. Small-scale tactical tasks can be achieved no less successfully with conventional weapons."[15] But there are said to be other reasons also for the inability to distinguish tactical from other nuclear weapons.

> . . the term "military target" applies to munitions plants, to naval bases, and to railway junctions, all of which are often situated within the limits of densely populated cities. So it is obvious that the use of tactical atomic weapons against such targets must inevitably result in immense loss of life among civilians.[16]

The employment of *tactical* atomic weapons would thus still lead to "the wholesale slaughter of civilians, devastation, gigantic fires, and contamination of numerous towns and villages by nuclear radiation and radioactive fall-out."[17] Most statements, such as the two immediately above, appear in popular press and radio media (although usually written by generals). But there is more than propaganda in the theme. The official ground forces' military journal stated in a serious discussion that "the radius of [explosive effects of] nuclear weapons and the nature of contemporary military objectives is such that it *completely excludes the possibility* of their employment *only* on a 'tactical' scale."[18] For propaganda to foreign audiences in particular, but probably reflecting a genuine military-political evaluaion, much is made of the fact that, as Major General Talensky put it (in 1955) :

> In modern war hostilities extend over huge areas. The zone of combat operations, and, consequently, of the use of armaments, includes a front line running for hundreds and thousands of miles and extending to a depth of at least 300 to 400 miles on both sides of the front, from the line of direct contact of the troops. The aggressive elements who are preparing atomic war do not intend to wage it in the deserts of Arabia, the pampas of Argentina, or even in our Siberian taiga. They are preparing to carry it on in Europe with its dense population, which in some areas reaches two hundred and even more people per square mile. Can it be imagined that in these conditions war and atomic attacks would be limited only to the zone of operations of the troops and would not affect the civilian population? In present conditions the density of the troops, at least in the case of defense, will frequently be much less than the density of the population in the same area adjacent to the field of battle, and the victims among the civilians would be incalculable just as the destruction would inevitably be immense. . . . *there is no difference in the tactical and strategic use of atomic weapons, nor could there be any.*
>
> And, what is more important, from the standpoint of the population subjected to atomic attack, there would hardly be any difference whether it is killed by a tactical or a strategic bomb. Both the strategic and the tactical means of atomic attack are equally barbarous weapons of mass destruction which would spell death to millions of people.[19]

Thus Soviet military commentators seek to refute the idea of precision employment of nuclear weapons, the sharp distinction of military targets from civilian populations, and the idea of limitation to a zone of combat operations which would spare civilian lives.

Soviet public rejection of the possibility of limitations on the use of nuclear weapons is based, at least in part, on the fact that to do so would seriously dilute the propaganda campaign for prohibition of *all* nuclear weapons. And it would wipe out any real Soviet hope of a major conventional war.

109

Moreover, the Soviets are well aware that a limitation would relatively favor the West, and the United States in particular. Marshal Zhukov reflected this view in his speech at the Twentieth Party Congress in February 1956, when he stated:

> Recently, political and military figures of the U.S.A. have more and more frequently expressed in their declarations the idea that American strategy must be founded on the employment of atomic weapons—as they express it "tactically;" that is, within the limits of operations on the battlefield and theaters of military operations.
> The American monopolists apparently understand the reality of retaliatory atomic blows . . . Already one cannot fight without suffering retaliatory blows. If one wishes to deal atomic blows on the enemy, then be ready to receive the same or perhaps more powerful blows from his side. War is an active process of two-sided combat.[20]

The prospect of a limited use of nuclear weapons would under certain circumstances assist the West to redress the balance of power for wars other than a total one. It is, moreover, possible that, in the Soviet view, this might encourage us to start limited nuclear wars against the Communist bloc.

Finally, it would create an alternative to any possible situation in which the United States might have to choose between massive but mutual retaliation or none at all, that is, between a strategy involving enormous destruction and one of either Western inaction or likely defeat. The Soviets evidently would not like us to know with certainty that the alternative of limited nuclear war was available.

Nevertheless, there are cogent reasons to support the conclusion that the Soviets might, in fact, agree to limitation to tactical use of nuclear weapons. So long as the Soviet Union gains greatly in propaganda by refusing to accept the idea of limitations, and so long as it does not anticipate an American attack, there is no reason for it to change its public disavowal of the possibility of limiting the use of nuclear and thermonuclear weapons. But the present Soviet rejection of the idea

110

of the distinction between tactical and strategic uses of nuclear weapons does not preclude its recognition of such a distinction in a war, were the United States to introduce it. The reasons are simple: so long as the Soviet Union gains most by *complete* abstention from the use of nuclear weapons, it will do nothing to encourage an alternative whereby the *limited* use of nuclear weapons relieves the enemy from facing a choice between a strategy of defeat and one of suicide. For the very same reason, and again in view of their belief that nuclear weapons are not in themselves decisive (especially when used against properly trained troops), it would be to the Soviets' advantage in wartime to "agree" in practice to limitations on use imposed by the enemy. The Soviets themselves might calculate upon Western recognition of the mutual advantages of limitation and themselves initiate a limited (especially local) nuclear war, but the reasons earlier noted for Soviet advantage in nonnuclear war would probably lead them in such particular circumstances to seek first of all limitation to conventional weapons.

The only two instances in which limitation would be impossible would be a sudden thermonuclear attack by the West (which would mean the Western idea of limitations was not serious anyway) or a similar attack by the Soviet Union (a situation in which the Soviets would have decided against limitations). But in all other cases—local wars, and general wars arising in any way other than a surprise strategic thermonuclear attack—the option on limitation would be available, and would probably be initiated or accepted by the Soviet Union.

The Soviets do not in general openly admit the possibility of limitations of nuclear weapons to tactical use or the distinction between "tactical" and "strategic" nuclear weapons. However, there has been at least one exception: Major General of the Engineering Technical Service G. I. Pokrovsky has on several occasions made the distinction. Thus in late 1956 he wrote: "Armaments may be divided into two categories: (1)

111

Tactical armament (weapons) having the function of direct employment against the troops of the enemy in the combat zone and on the route to this zone; (2) Strategic armaments (weapons) having as their function the aim of destroying the most militarily important centers of the enemy, as a rule located deep in the rear of the enemy." [21] Also, in some cases they have perhaps unwittingly slipped into using the term "tactical atomic weapons." The most significant to date was a statement by Marshal Zhukov in early 1957, in which he flatly declared that "tactical atomic weapons, if they are not banned, will in the next few years be introduced into the organic armament of the troops in place of conventional weapons." [22] Similarly, while not openly admitting the possibility of "tactical weapons," one Soviet military theoretician has implicitly revealed not only a form of acceptance of the idea but also has gone on to render an evaluation of the consequences of employment of tactical nuclear weapons. He wrote (in late 1956) that Western "hopes that tactical atomic weapons 'equalize the forces of large and small armies' . . . take the wish for reality." [23] Thus, at least according to that writer's view, use by both sides of tactical nuclear weapons is contemplated and with the effect of *not* equalizing differences in strength of conventional forces, with the result that these latter differences might decide the outcome of the conflict.

LOCAL WARS

The general view expressed by the Soviets is that, in the words of Major General Pokrovsky, "the era of local wars is over." [24] Khrushchev, in his letter to the British Labor Party in October 1957 declared: "It is to be recalled that both world wars started as limited military action, i.e., in their beginning both were local wars. In our time of rapid development of military technology it will be an even more difficult task to

112

put any limits on an armed conflict if this conflict starts in any single region." [25] Premier Bulganin, in his letter to President Eisenhower on December 11, 1957, declared:

> One of the arguments used by the military circles in the West in substantiation of their demands for the extension of military preparations is the so-called local wars theory. It should be stressed, most emphatically, that this theory not only is utterly inconsistent from the military point of view but is extremely dangerous politically.
> In the past, too, global wars are known to have started from local wars. Is it possible seriously to count on the possibility of localizing wars in our time when there exist in the world two opposed military groupings comprising scores of countries in various parts of the world and when the effect of modern types of weapons knows no geographical limits? [26]

Nonetheless, while suggesting that world wars are now more "typical," Lieutenant General Krasil'nikov has noted: "By their scale, contemporary wars can be local or worldwide." [27] Other Soviet sources have described local wars as the means used by imperialist powers to fight colonial wars, and against small powers. And an official Soviet declaration in early 1955 specifically indicated that if *Europe* becomes "an arena of war," *such* a war "would inevitably develop into another world war." [28]

There are good reasons for doubting that these statements represent the real Soviet expectation or foreshadow future Soviet behavior. The Soviets generally deny the possibility of future local wars (i.e., wars limited geographically to some particular theater of operations) because they want to deter the United States from initiating such wars and, perhaps, even from preparing defensively for them. But this present denial in no way limits future Soviet initiative or response.

The Soviet Union has, in the past, fought a number of local wars, such as the engagements with Japan at Lake Khasan and Khalkin-Gol' in 1938 and 1939, respectively. [29] In fact, this is the classic Soviet type of limited military action, for limited objectives, and at limited risk; the Korean war, most recently.

A history of local and peripheral wars is no indication of continuation of such wars in the future, under new conditions. But it does indicate that the Soviets are prepared, under circumstances of advantage to them, to localize conflicts involving Soviet troops and even Soviet soil. And future circumstances may make such behavior *increasingly* to Soviet advantage. Three circumstances greatly increase the possibility and danger of future local wars of Soviet aggression. One is American deterrence of the U.S.S.R. from general war as a means of attaining Soviet expansive aims. Second is the Soviet *counter-deterrence* of our retaliatory strength to prevent us from using this strength to deter or respond to *limited* Soviet aggression. Calculated risk by the Soviets of American non-use of SAC in retaliation for local aggression may increase as Soviet offensive striking power increases and the ICBM appears. Third, if increasing American reliance on nuclear weapons continues, it may be an inducement to the Soviets to engage in conventional local wars under the cover of mutual nuclear deterrence.

In fact, the Soviets occasionally even let slip hints of their interest in non-nuclear local wars. In a radio commentary in early 1957 it was said that so long as "further production and stockpiling of atomic weapons" continues, "any possible armed conflict will threaten to grow into an atomic war with all its terrible consequences. That is why adjustment of the question of banning atomic weapons is so very significant today."[30] Conventional local war is clearly considered possible if even under current nuclear preparations it only "will *threaten* to grow into an atomic war."

The Korean war offers an example of a local war waged by proxy—a favorable technique when it can be employed without serious risk of extension. But the possibilities for local wars by proxy are very limited, and the risks difficult to calculate, in view of the stated American policy of retaliation, particularly if this policy is clarified as selective local retaliation.

Local wars waged with Soviet forces would employ standard military capabilities and doctrine. The maintenance of large forces suitable for conventional warfare provides an appropriate basis for Soviet conduct of non-nuclear local wars.

Granting the possibility of local or peripheral wars, the question arises whether such conflicts can occur *with the use of nuclear weapons* and remain "local."

Available sources do not indicate Soviet views on this question. But the Soviet strategic concept does suggest an answer. In view of the Soviet conclusions on the disadvantages to the U.S.S.R. of a nuclear conflict, it seems improbable that the Soviet Union would *initiate* the use of nuclear weapons in a local war, regardless of the circumstances of the outbreak of the war. The most likely exception might be the extremely remote possibility of a non-nuclear local war launched by the enemy and involving Soviet territory.

There is another case of greater interest, because it is more likely (although also not probable). If a Soviet-sponsored non-atomic local war were converted by the United States into a local nuclear war, it is probable that the Soviet Union would not extend the theater of operations, but would use nuclear weapons locally in reply. Thus a local nuclear war would presumably result from American initiation of the use of atomic weapons in a Soviet-fomented local war. The particular circumstances of any local war would, of course, have to be taken into account, and the danger of a general war ensuing is never eliminated. But in general, the same reasons which make it disadvantageous for the Soviets to initiate a general nuclear war would probably lead them to avoid a nuclear local war, or if one developed to attempt to localize any peripheral nuclear war which might arise. The Soviet Union, as well as the West, would gain from not expanding the limits of a local war too widely.

Notes to Chapter 5

1. N. S. Khrushchev, *Pravda*, February 15, 1956; and see the discussion in Chapter 1 above.

2. Col. E. Chalik, *Voennaia mysl'*, No. 9, September 1954, p. 32.

3. Maj. Gen. N. Pukhovsky, in *Marksizm-leninizm o voine*, [February 3] 1955, p. 107. This statement did not appear in the original publication in *Voennyi vestnik*, January 1954, but was inserted in this reprinting of that article.

4. Col. F. S. Tiusin, *Bor'ba kommunisticheskoi partii za ukreplenie voennogo mogushchestva SSSR*, 1955, p. 99. See also *Uchebnoe posobie po MPVO*, 1956, p. 45.

5. Marshal G. Zhukov quoted in *Krasnaia zvezda*, March 23, 1957.

6. General Nathan F. Twining, quoted in "Twining Sees Lag in Nuclear Plan," New York *Times*, August 3, 1956. He further criticized the slowness of discarding conventional forces for "old-type warfare."

7. Col. A. Kapralov, cited in *Voennaia mysl'*, No. 11, November 1954, p. 45

8. See Marshal of the Tank Troops P. Rotmistrov, *Krasnaia zvezda*, March 26, 1955; Chief Marshal of Aviation P. Zhigarev, *Pravda*, March 21, 1955; Lt. Gen. S. Shatilov, *Literaturnaia gazeta*, May 28, 1955; and in a paraphrased reference, Col. N. Kuz'min, "Questions of Soviet Military Science in the Works of V. I. Lenin," *Sovetskii flot*, April 18, 1956.

9. Maj. Gen. N. Pukhovsky, in *Marksizm-leninizm o voine*, [February 3] 1955, p. 107. This passage was added to the text of his article as published in this work; it did not appear in the original version in *Voennyi vestnik*, No. 1 January 1954.

10. Marshal G. Zhukov, *Pravda*, February 20, 1956.

11. Marshal of Aviation N. Skripko, *Krasnaia zvezda*, August 11, 1946.

12. Col. Ye. Kosorukov and Lt. Col. V. Matsulenko, "The Atomic Problem and the U.S. Policy of 'Positions of Strength,'" *Voennyi vestnik*, No. 7, July 1955, p. 92. This was stated most authoritatively by N. A. Bulganin in his letter to President Eisenhower, *Tass*, December 11, 1957, and earlier by Marshal G. Zhukov, *Radio (East) Berlin*, April 20, 1957. See also Col. A. Kononenko, *Atomnoe oruzhie v voennnykh planakh SSha* (Atomic Weapons in U.S. Military Plans), Voenizdat, Moscow, [June 26] 1957, p. 22; Col. Vasil'ev, *Radio Moscow*, December 27, 1957; Col. V. Mochalov and Maj. V. Dashichev, *Krasnaia zvezda*, December 27, 1957; a Commentary by *Radio Moscow*, April 9, 1957; N. Khokhlov, "Philosophy of the Atomic Warriors," *Izvestiia*, March 22, 1957; V. Kamenev, "The Big Lie About 'Little' Atomic War," *Mezhdunarodnaia zhizn'*, No. 3, March 1957, pp. 94-97; Maj. Gen. Ye. Boltin, "Atomic Task Forces," *New Times*, No. 17, April 25, 1957, p. 8; and Maj. Gen. B. Olisov, *Krasnaia zvezda*, August 3, 1954.

13. Maj. Gen. F. Isayev, "The 'Small Atomic Weapons' Myth," *New Times* No. 13, March 26, 1955, p. 7.

14. Maj. N. Kopov, "The Employment of Atomic Artillery," *Voennyi vestnik*, No. 3, March 1955, p. 77.

15. Maj. Gen. F. Isaev, *New Times*, No. 13, March 26, 1955, p. 7.

16. K. Orlov, "Tactical Atomic Warfare Talk Abroad," *Radio Moscow*, April 13, 1955.

17. Maj. Gen. F. Isaev, *New Times,* No. 13, March 26, 1955, p. 8.

18. Col. Ye. Kosorukov and Lt. Col. V. Matsulenko, *Voennyi vesinik,* No. 7, July 1955, p. 92.

19. Maj. Gen. N. Talensky, *International Affairs,* No. 1, January 1955, pp. 27 and 28.

20. Marshal G. Zhukov, *Pravda,* February 20, 1956.

21. Maj. Gen. G. I. Pokrovsky, *Nauka i tekhnika v sovremennykh voinakh,* [October 8] 1956, p. 46; and see also his article in *Voennye znaniia,* No. 3, March, 1957, pp. 35-37.

22. Marshal G. Zhukov, *Krasnaia zvezda,* March 23, 1957.

23. V. Skopin, *Militarizm* [August 3] 1956, p. 423.

24. Maj. Gen. G. Pokrovsky, *News,* No. 7, April 1, 1955, p. 7.

25. Quoted in full in the New York *Times,* October 16, 1957.

26. N. Bulganin, in his letter to President Eisenhower, *Pravda,* December 12, 1957.

27. Lt. Gen. S. N. Krasil'nikov, in *Marksizm-leninizm o voine i armii,* [October 8] 1956, p. 145.

28. "Declaration of the Supreme Soviet of the U.S.S.R.," *Izvestiia,* February 10, 1955.

29. For a good review of the political problems and main incidents in these battles see C. S. Tinch, "Quasi-War Between Japan and the U.S.S.R., 1937-1939," *World Politics,* Vol. III, No. 2, January 1951, pp. 174-99; and see G. N. Sevost'-ianov, "The Military and Diplomatic Defeat of Japan in the Period of the Events at the Khalkin-Gol River,"*Voprosy istorii,* No. 8, August 1957, pp. 63-84.

30. "Soviet Plan for Atomic Weapons Ban is Workable," *Radio Moscow,* March 21, 1957.

CHAPTER 6

THE SOVIET IMAGE OF THE ENEMY

The Soviet image of American military views and strategy is an essential component of the over-all Soviet picture of future war. Evaluations of the enemy's military plans and capabilities necessarily affect one's own strategic thinking. In many respects the problem may appear to us not to be difficult for the Soviet leaders: views, doctrine, and even general strategic plans are widely propagated and debated in Congressional hearings and the press in this country. But the very proliferation of some-times conflicting statements by various American writers, official and unofficial, creates other difficulties for the Soviet analyst. In addition, Soviet ideological presuppositions influence their estimation of various points. Most important in Soviet calcula-tions are the hard results of American military policy—force allocations, budgetary allotments, deployment of forces, and the development and procurement of weapons. Because the conclusions drawn from this realistic approach are seen as con-sistent with their ideological expectations, certain Soviet con-clusions which otherwise might be dismissable as propaganda must be given credence. Also, the image of American strategy which is presented in organs of restricted circulation is very nearly the same as that which appears in the general military press. Finally, while views are distorted and motives are ma-ligned, the Soviet picture is nonetheless a recognizable reflec-tion of real American military thinking.

118

EVALUATION OF THE U.S. MILITARY STRUCTURE

Soviet military writers have concluded that the United States is building a military force structure with two main characteristics: (1) a major reliance on air-atomic striking power, but (2) maintenance of modern ground, sea, and air forces to complement the Strategic Air Command. In addition, military alliances with various countries around the world are understood to be, in part, a complement to these American military forces, to provide both bases and mass ground armies. A number of aspects of these general Soviet conclusions deserve attention.

Soviet analysis is faced with the problem of reconciling their own belief in the basic rationality of the "imperialist militarists," with other views they hold ascribing predilections for reliance on "miracle" weapons—currently air-missile-atomic power—predilections which are, in terms of Soviet beliefs, "irrational." However, the Communist dialectic explains such contradictions within the imperialist strategy by means we shall note below.

In an earlier chapter of this study, we have noted that the Soviets ascribe to the imperialists, and in particular to the United States, a proclivity to rely upon one-weapon strategies, particularly nuclear-thermonuclear air- and missile-delivered weapons, and to bank upon the advantages of surprise attack. To note but one statement, Major General Khlopov has envisaged an American war plan, in the General Staff organ *Military Thought,* as follows:

> Atomic bombs . . . will be employed by air forces in surprise attacks on important economic and political centers in the near and distant rear of the enemy with the aim of undermining his economic might and the morale of the population, and also against large concentrations of troops and military materiel in the rear.[1]

Many other statements, earlier and subsequently, have advanced this picture. Since early 1955 surprise has been particularly stressed: "At the basis of the 'preventive war' lies the expectation of the most complete exploitation of the results of a powerful surprise blow, especially by the air force employing means of mass destruction [i.e., nuclear weapons.]"[2] The most extensive discussion of alleged American and British intention to wage war by a surprise attack was contained in the key article by Marshal of the Tank Troops Rotmistrov in *Military Thought* in February 1955. In this article, he commented that "surprise attack is a favorite means of the aggressor for unleashing war and proceeds from the very nature of the imperialist states." And more precisely, he stated:

> The military figures of the United States and Britain openly declare that they intend to open war against us by means of surprise strategic blows with atomic and hydrogen weapons on the vitally important targets deep in the rear of the countries of the camp of peace and democracy, calculating in a few day to knock out the basic industrial targets, to paralyze transport, to demoralize the population. The American-British strategists suppose that, utilizing the enormous destructive power of atomic and hydrogen weapons, they can defeat the enemy as the result of an initial strike, and seize the initiative in the war.[3]

Rotmistrov considered that the imperialists "*correctly* value surprise as a strong element in the military art" but, reflecting the Soviet view, he regards the *degree* of reliance on surprise as fallacious and adventuristic. Thus, the Western imperialists today, "despite the crushing defeat of Fascist Germany" following the German use of surprise attack, "also place their stakes on a surprise attack, only under new conditions." The reason for the Western excessive stress on surprise is that "the imperialists are afraid of waging a long war because of political and economic considerations."[4]

This view of American strategy is noted here only as background to the question of Soviet evaluations of the American military force structure. As is clearly implied, the Soviets tend to attribute to the United States primary reliance on the capabilities of the Strategic Air Command.

Their Image of the Enemy

In the current military structure:

> The magnates of Wall Street, preparing a new world war, place their stakes on the employment of the atomic bomb. In this, *a special role is given to air power*. On it are placed great hopes as the weapon with which the American imperialists dream of accomplishing their delirious plans for world conquest. . . . *The relative weight assigned to their [the air force's] needs increases from year to year. . . .*[5]

Other writers also describe American reliance upon the development of the air forces, and state that the United States "places its stakes on aviation."[6]

Within the air forces, and in general within the military structure, according to the Soviets, "the major place in the plans of the aggressive circles of the U.S.A. is given to the air forces, *especially the strategic air force, which has become the dominating factor in the military strategy of the U.S.A.*"[7] This conclusion on the role of air power in American strategy is based not only on statements of American military leaders, but also on our budgetary allocations.[8] Both the increased expenditures for air power, exceeding those for the Army or Navy, and the increasing proportion of military personnel in the USAF are seen as indices of increasing reliance upon the air forces in the "New Look" budgets of the period since 1953. In the decade 1946 to 1956 the relative weight of the air forces in the armed forces structure is said to have doubled.[9]

The preeminent role of the air forces leads the Soviets to conclude that this is the army "for the select"—in the sense of political reliability.[10] And more specifically, the key role of SAC crews is recognized—although with an ideological twist alleging particular "dedication to the imperialists." The Soviets say that "considerable attention is devoted to the preparation of the crews of strategic bombers. Many important USAF leaders consider that the strategic aviation aircraft, and especially the atomic bomb carrier, must be flown by a crew consisting of the men most dedicated to the imperialists, capable of dealing treacherous surprise blows on vitally important enemy targets in the deep rear."[11]

Particular reference has been made to General Curtis LeMay, while he served as Commander of the Strategic Air Command. He is sometimes identified in terms claiming that he "feverishly prepares for war, and atomic war at that."[12] A speech by General LeMay was printed in the June 1955 issue of the official *Herald of the Air Fleet.* The brief introduction noted that strategic aviation, "the imperialists are convinced, is the decisive weapon in war," and further "LeMay obviously exaggerates the condition and combat potentialities of U.S. strategic air power."[13]

The Soviet evaluation of the United States Air Force as the main element of the American military forces is, as we have seen, based upon concrete data: expressions of doctrine and relative budgetary allotments. The Soviet expressed *explanation* of the presumed reasoning behind this American emphasis on air power is based upon three factors: (1) a fallacy in bourgeois military science, (2) an error in calculation of weapons potentialities, and, most important, (3) an awareness of a fundamental weakness in mass morale.

The alleged fallacy in bourgeois military science is the view that "chance" factors, rather than the fundamental "decisive" factors, can decide a war.[14] Moreover, "bourgeois military ideologists," it is said, "attempt to compensate for the weakness of the economic and morale potential of their countries by adventuristic military theories and strategic plans."[15] The error in weapons potentialities concerns both the general bourgeois vulnerability for the predilection to seek easy solutions through over-reliance on one-weapon strategies, and in particular an exaggeration of the role of nuclear and thermonuclear weapons.[16] But basic to these errors, and combined with them, is the last alleged factor: the necessity for reliance on substitutes for the true winning weapons system, a large modern combined arms force, because of a fundamental *morale* weakness inherent in the class nature of capitalist society.

Marshal of Aviation Vershinin voiced this explanation several years ago in the following passage:

> The underestimation of the infantry reflects *the fear of the imperialist bourgeoisie of their peoples, of mass armies* . . . . *Not having reliable reserves of manpower at their disposal. . . the warmongers boom and exaggerate the role of air power out of all proportion. . . . These ideas emanate from the completely distorted view that the outcome of war can be decided by some kind of weapon alone.* History has proved the reverse more than once.[17]

This particular statement was made in the Stalinist period, but it is typical of many others which continue in the post-Stalinist and thermonuclear weapons era.[18] One writer has declared that imperialist military theoreticians "have begun to propagate the idea of the withering away of existing arms (infantry, artillery) and to place their stakes on atomic, chemical, and bacteriological weapons."[19] And, with an explicitness which is rare, another Soviet military writer stated (in 1953) that, as a consequence of reliance upon nuclear air power, "the ground forces to this time continue to remain the weakest and most vulnerable point in the composition of the American armed forces."[20]

Nonetheless, as the Soviets recognize, there are countercurrents to the main stream of emphasis on air power in the United States. Thus, some Soviet military writers state:

> True, some bourgeois military theoreticians attempt to demonstrate that in contemporary war technology replaces man and that the size of the personnel of the army can therefore be significantly reduced. But the bankruptcy of such "theories" is obvious *even* to the imperialists themselves, who in practice conduct a policy of preparation of mass armies.[21]

Consequently, despite the *preference* of the imperialists for a military power based on advanced technology and weapons, "they are forced, more and more, to recognize that future war will be conducted by armies of millions and will have a long and drawn-out character."[22] Such statements have appeared

123

ever since 1950, and continue at present.[23] These Soviet affirmations that the imperialists are compelled to see the need for a mass ground army are based both upon statements of leading U.S. Army leaders (Generals Taylor, Bolte, Ridgway, Gruenther, Bradley, Collins, and Eisenhower in the period before his election to the Presidency),[24] and on the buildup in the strength of the U.S. Army from 1950 to 1953. The forced recognition of the need for large ground armies is explained particularly on the basis of two events: the American experience in the Korean War, and the Soviet acquisition of an atomic capability.

The war in Korea is held to have "demonstrated the adventurism" of such views "as the dominance of air forces in the military structure," and confirmed that mass ground armies are essential.[25]

Similarly, and roughly contemporaneously, Soviet procurement of atomic weapons is said to have "cooled in no small degree the interests of the military circles of the U.S.A." for the idea of an air-atomic strategy.[26] In fact, it is sometimes said to have led to a realization that "in the past the evaluation of the potentialities of the atomic bomb was grossly exaggerated."[27] And, of course, apprehension of the increased danger from a Soviet nuclear blow is believed to have had its effect. As one Soviet colonel, who has for years published articles on United States military affairs, stated in mid-1955:

> However, if one does not consider the self-confident youth of the strategic air force, dreaming with their commander General LeMay of a "lightning" war against the U.S.S.R., [one finds that] attitudes which are far from optimistic are prevalent among the other categories of American military men. Many have come to realize that in case of the unleashing of war a powerful retaliation blow will follow.[28]

Thus, under the pressure of circumstances and with the "lesson" of Korea, a substantial number of American military leaders are said to have been forced to the conclusion that

124

mass armies are needed. "However," in the words of Major General Pukhovsky, "from an awareness of the necessity for multi-million-man armies to their creation is a tremendous distance."[29] One way in which the imperialists are said to seek to overcome this obstacle is deception of the masses.

> Therefore bourgeois military science, although it understands the significance of the morale factor, is nonetheless in this connection forced to proceed on the basis of a false interpretation of the aim of war, and with false slogans of reactionary imperialist propaganda. In creating a mass army the imperialists try in every way to conceal and mask from the masses the true aim of these armies.[30]

In view of the difficulties in creating a mass army, despite a certain awareness of its need in modern war, the imperialists are thus forced to compromise with their preference for a war based on technology instead of man. And from this need was born the concept of "balanced forces."

Beginning in early 1954, and stressed particularly throughout 1955, Soviet writers paid considerable attention to this theory. Major General Khlopov, writing in *Military Thought* in January 1954, concluded: "The majority of influential political and military figures in the U.S.A. support the theory of balanced armed forces."[31] Another article, in April 1954, identified this concept as official:

> As is well known, the officially accepted theory in the U.S.A. in recent years is the so-called theory of "balanced armed forces," which considers that in contemporary war the army, aviation, and the navy have equal significance. . . . In accordance with this theory, the three basic forms of armed forces are relatively equally divided and allocated.[32]

Subsequent statements in 1955, and even in 1956 and 1957, have repeatedly stressed the theory of balanced forces.[33] Major General Boltin in August 1955 declared that imperialist theories of atomic blitzkrieg and push-button war were not held as "the official doctrines of contemporary armies of the powerful capitalist countries."[34] According to General Boltin, "attention is being devoted in the major capitalist countries to the development of all branches of the armed forces, all arms and means of combat." But the continued trend in American military thinking toward reliance on air-atomic deterrent power has led to a Soviet reassessment of American views on "balanced forces." Thus Colonel Kononenko, writing in September 1956, concluded that the three-year "new look" plan for 1954-1957 "marks the funeral of the former official conception of 'balanced forces,' according to which the army, navy, and air force were considered as relatively equally important elements of military power" and with approximately equal budgetary allocations.[35]

Even when Soviet commentators have indicated the prevalence of the *concept* of balanced forces, they also have noted that in accordance with the recognition of air power as the dominant army *"in practice,* the American military have given *preference to the air forces."*[36] In fact, it has even been stated that: "The military leaders of the U.S.A. *in practice* devote predominant attention to military air power and the navy, *as if* they could in largest measure determine the fate of the entire war. Her ground forces are in fact considered as auxiliary forces, a strategic reserve. . . ."[37]

The existence of a variety of military views in the United States is explained by Soviet writers on the grounds of selfish service conflicts, of failures by bourgeois military science, and especially by underlying conflicts among competing bourgeois business interests. Thus an article in *Red Star* (in 1955) declared:

> . . . the existence of a great number of these theories is evidence that American military circles have met with difficulties in working out the plan of a new aggressive war. It is impossible not to take into consideration that while some military theories are designed for the disorientation and deception of the masses, others express the struggle of various monopolistic groups for receiving high profits from military orders.[38]

The ideological foundation for the belief that American policy is made by the interplay of pressures of monopoly capitalists

126

and financiers is, in the Soviet view, substantiated by the fact that in recent years a number of prominent civilians directing the military departments, and retired military men, have been associated with business and financial enterprises engaged in military production and construction. The significance of this Soviet belief is attested to not only by its frequent reiteration, but by the fact that the conflict of competing monopolies is even said to be more important than doctrinal differences and service rivalries in determining the American military budgetary allocations and military force levels.[39] It is on this basis, according to General Khlopov (in 1954), that:

> Some monopolistic groups in the U.S.A. and their advocates in the Pentagon attack the main theses of the theory of balanced armed forces. The wrangling among the representatives of the land, air, and sea forces of the U.S.A. for priority of one or another form of the armed forces in a future war has not ceased to this time. For the various monopolistic circles this is no simply technical [military] question. Recognition of the leading role in the system of the armed forces, for example, of the air forces, leads to their increase, investment in their development of more significant budget appropriations, an increase of government orders to aviation firms, and in the final analysis solid profits to the latter. . . .
> The widespread theory in the United States of a decisive, dominating role of the air forces in future war also represents the narrow aims of American monopolists who receive enormous profits from filling government orders for the production of aircraft.[40]

Other military writers also state that in the preeminence given in practice to the air forces "no small role is played by the struggle of the most powerful monopolist firms for receiving profitable military orders at high prices."[41]

The current Soviet view is well summarized by Major General Mil'shtein and Colonel Slobodenko in their booklet, *Military Ideologists of the Capitalist Countries on the Character and Means of Conducting Contemporary War*, which appeared in 1957. They review the theories of "air war," "sea power," "balanced forces," and the "new look." Their conclusion is

127

extremely interesting not merely because it reiterates the long-expressed views noted above, but because it reveals so clearly *Soviet* military thinking: Air power in the atomic age "has enormous significance for the achievement of victory in contemporary war. . . . *However,* the views of American military ideologists, tying their hopes in future war only to aviation and underevaluating the role of other branches of the armed forces, borders on adventurism."[42] Similarly, while "of course it would be a crude mistake to underestimate the role of naval forces in combat operations in war. . . . *nonetheless* the contentions of the military theoreticians of American imperialism on an 'exceptional' role for the navy in war must be considered erroneous, not meeting the objective requirements of the armed conflict."[43] The "new look" is recognized as "a compromise between two theories of conducting war. On the one hand, it recognizes the necessity [sic] of the equal development of all forms of the armed forces . . . but on the other hand, it still gives a preference to the development of the air forces. . . . ."[44] What does this leave? The theory of balanced forces recognizes that "the aim of military operations must be the defeat of the armed forces [of the enemy], and not strategic bombing of targets in the rear."[45] This, of course, is the *Soviet* strategic concept. And thus in contrast to its evaluation of the theories of air war, sea power, and "new look" as respectively adventurist, erroneous, and falling between two strategies, the theory of balanced forces is seen as the correct one. "Many bourgeois military theoreticians have been compelled to consider *the objective requirements of contemporary war, victory in which can only be achieved by closely combined operation* of all three services of the armed forces."[46]

Thus we see that the Soviet image of the United States military force structure is characterized by the following conclusions:

1. American military policy has at least until recently set as its goal the creation of "balanced forces"—land, air and sea

—but with a powerful bias toward reliance upon strategic nuclear air power. While the Soviets now sometimes recognize that the "new look" has dropped the idea of balanced forces, they cannot imagine that the United States fails to recognize the great importance which they themselves attribute to maintenance of continued powerful ground forces.[47] Nonetheless, they must and do recognize the increased reliance on air power, though at the same time they exaggerate the degree of continued attention to the ground forces.

2. One cause of the reliance upon air power is said to be a fear and distrust of mass armies, who cannot be expected to maintain, in capitalist military forces, the necessary morale resilience required by modern war (nuclear or non-nuclear). Nonetheless, the need for mass ground armies cannot be escaped; hence the compromise idea of balanced forces, and more recently attempts to maintain a modern if smaller army.

3. Another cause of the bias toward air power is an exaggeration of the properties of advanced military technology and new weapons, especially nuclear weapons.

4. A third cause of bias toward air power is the influence of powerful monopolies whose profits derive from aircraft production, although other monopolies compete for military expenditures and support the balanced-forces concept.

EVALUATION OF U.S. MILITARY STRATEGIES

The dominant Soviet image of American military strategy is a massive, surprise air blow with weapons of mass destruction (nuclear, thermonuclear, and bacteriological) delivered primarily against Soviet urban-industrial centers. In General Khlopov's words in the General Staff journal:

> American and allied air forces, armed with the newest contemporary means of destruction and annihilation, will attack military-political and economic centers of the countries of Eastern and Central Europe, in order to undermine the eco-

nomic and morale might of the U.S.S.R. and peoples' democ
racies [Satellites] . . .[48]

Such an attack, however, is not conceived by the Soviets as
representing the full picture of American strategy.

American military strategy is usually described in terms of
two or three phases. "The main element of the first phase," as
General Mil'shtein and Colonel Slobodenko put it, "will be
not only gaining dominion in the air and on the sea. . . .
[but] also the mass and determined operations of the air forces
and navy and long-range guided missiles with the employment
of means of mass destruction [nuclear and thermonuclear war-
heads] against the main population centers of the enemy, the
most important economic-political targets, industrial regions,
rail centers, oil-processing factories and reserves of fuel, stockpiles, air and naval bases, etc. It is presumed that by these
operations the economic and morale condition of the enemy
will be undermined, breaking the resistance of the democratic
[Communist] camp. . . ."[49]

The second phase (for those who picture the strategy in
three phases) is the exploitation stage, with extended land
campaigns conducted primarily by the American allies. Then,
"the American army, according to the plans of these strategists,
will enter the war only in its concluding stage (the second or
third stage) to complete the defeat of the weakened enemy
and to affirm rule over the world."[50]

The theory of the two- or three-phase strategy is widely
stated in both public and limited-circulation publications. It
is, of course, criticized as "false" and "adventuristic."[51]

Two aspects of this strategy deserve further attention. One
is the role assigned to air power, the other is the role of allied
armies in the first stage or stages of the war. The first of these
is discussed directly below, the second in the following section.

Colonel Rodin expresses the Soviet view as follows: "According to this theory, in the most difficult initial period of the
war the United States will participate only by means of 'strategic
bombing.' It is not difficult to see these theories are built on

130

sand. . . ."[52] There is one additional role which some Soviet writers have ascribed to American air power: the use of airborne troops to occupy strategic rear areas.[53] In fact, Colonel Kononenko has even declared: "The majority of representatives of American military circles consider that the key to success is air mobility of the troops," and he cites Lieutenant General Gavin to this effect.[54]

The American strategy of employing only strategic air power in the first phase is considered as the basis for American establishment of a network of overseas air bases. American military (especially air) bases "located on the territory of others . . . are a component of the adventuristic strategy" of the United States.[55] In fact, "the creation of a net of air and naval bases is one of the fundamental conceptions of the American 'global' strategy."[56] The United States was said in April 1957 to have over 950 military bases on foreign soil.[57] The very existence of overseas American air bases is said to be evidence of American aggressive intent, although this may be but propaganda. Marshal Zhukov could hardly have been serious, in claiming the existence of bases as *proof* of aggressive intent, when he stated in May 1955:

> Soon after the end of the war the American government . .
> began to create aggressive military blocs and a whole system
> of military bases on foreign territories. For the purpose of de-
> ceiving peoples all this was masked under allegations of "de-
> fense," although any thinking person understands that the
> military bases of the U.S.A., created around the U.S.S.R.,
> China and the countries of the peoples' democracy, are absurd
> from the standpoint of a defensive strategy for the United
> States, since they are so far from the objectives which must
> be defended that at any moment they can be annihilated one
> by one. It is another matter to use these bases in the aims of
> aggressive strategy, for dealing blows by an atomic air force.
> And it is precisely for that purpose that they are being
> built.[58]

Nonetheless, he may have been expressing genuine apprehension over the danger of American air attacks from these bases.

131

Marshal Bagramian, on the same occasion, also stated that the existence of a net of American bases "indubitably means" that American deployment is not defensive.[59]

Marshal Zhukov's statement also implies a high degree of vulnerability to the advanced American air bases (although hardly by their being attacked "one by one"). As early as 1953 it was said that "the closer their [U.S.] military bases are to the objective of attack, the more vulnerable these bases become."[60] The Commander-in-Chief of the Soviet Air Forces, Marshal of Aviation Vershinin, declared more recently (1957) that "one can only wonder at the shortsightedness of those who do not consider that if these [NATO and U.S.] bases are close *to* us, then they are also not far *from* us."[61]

It is interesting, and perhaps significant, that Soviet discussions of American military strategies do not reflect awareness of the Western objective of *deterrence*. To be sure, the Soviets would not publicly admit any justifiable American *need* to deter them, since they deny aggressive aims. But just as American claims of various defensive measures are raised and defensive purpose denied by the Soviets, it would be feasible for them to note but deny in their propaganda the need for deterrence. But the very idea of deterrence has not, as of this writing, been raised in serious Soviet discussions of American military thought.

In summary, in the Soviet evaluation, the main aspects of American strategic plans are:

1. The theory of a two or three phase war, in which the first phase (s) are marked by active American strategic bombing of the Soviet bloc, and limited land and sea holding actions to maintain the necessary overseas air bases and bridgeheads.

2. The first and/or intermediate phase is also marked by dependence upon allied ground forces to hold the enemy generally in check while strategic bombing destroys his economic and morale resources, and while the American Army is mobilized and readied.

132

3. The final phase is marked by commitment of U.S. ground forces to destroy the greatly weakened enemy, after the outcome of the war has been decided.

4. In the Soviet view, this theory is not well founded, and, in published discussions at least, they aver that it would not be successful. The reasoning behind this conclusion will be reviewed later in discussion of Soviet views on the enemy's strengths and weaknesses.

ARMED ALLIANCES OF THE FREE WORLD

The United States is seen as the main enemy and the driving force behind "a new coalition of capitalist states" in the postwar period. Moreover, it is conceded that "the ruling circles of the U.S.A. do not lack forces and means for the welding of North Atlantic, Mediterranean, Pacific, and other military-political aggressive blocs."[62] Nonetheless, "the anti-Soviet blocs include states divided by contradictions," and are therefore not stable or reliable.[63] The system of military alliances, like the manning of overseas air bases, is declared to be "a concrete manifestation of the aggressive policy and ideology of the imperialists."[64] Marshal Zhukov declared (again in 1956) that the alliances are a demonstration of aggressive intent:

> The officials of the United States attempt to describe their bases [overseas, in alliances] as of defensive significance. However, anyone literate in military affairs understands that military bases deployed thousands of kilometers from the territory of one's country cannot serve defensive aims.[65]

This argument is obviously specious in logic, but may be in part seriously accepted by Soviet leaders on the basis of their general suspicions of Western "imperialist" motives.[66] *Military Thought* has, in an analysis of the causes of wars, declared that "contemporary wars *begin* with preliminary welding of aggressive military blocs."[67]

The most interesting aspect of the Soviet view of armed

133

alliances in the Free World is their interpretation of the role of these alliances in American strategy. On the whole, the less powerful states of the West are considered more as object than subject in the creation and operation of alliances. In addition to the United States, only the United Kingdom is sometimes specified as an active power—and then usually as but one of a number "in support" of United States policy.[68]

The American theory of "balanced forces," and still more the recent increasingly unbalanced American forces, are said to be predicated upon the use of allied ground forces.

> For conducting the war in land theaters, especially in its initial phase, the American militarists, in accord with the strategy of global war, count upon utilizing above all the armies of countries dependent upon the U.S.A. Such "balances" of the armed forces at the expense of the armies of the allies and satellites of the U.S.A., is nothing more than a continuation of the traditional American imperialism of fighting "with the hands of others." [69]

Thus, while the United States builds its favored strategic air atomic power:

> Military circles of the U.S.A. want to place the main burden of war on the peoples of Europe and Asia who, according to the calculations of the Pentagon, must establish the major portion of the ground forces, and the U.S.A. only strategic air power and the navy.[70]

As a consequence of this division of military force contributions, "in the first stage or phase of the war, the brunt of the fighting will be borne by the land armies of the European NATO members, the Near and Middle East countries and Japan." [71]

Thus, the primary role of the armed alliances in American strategy is "to wage the war on foreign territory and with foreign armies. . . ." [72] This view of "using the armies of American allies as cannon fodder" in the first phases of a war has long been a standard Soviet view.[73]

An additional role of the alliances is relevant to an understanding of the Soviet picture of American strategy. The alliances also are recognized as providing advanced bomber and missile bases for the atomic air offensive of the initial phase of the war.

Finally, to note one other alleged purpose of the alliance systems, Soviet writers assert that by means of bases and troops established in other lands the United States seeks also "to hold in compulsory service those countries on whose territories these bases are located, and also other nearby states," to perform, in short, "tasks of a gendarme character." [74]

EVALUATION OF ENEMY STRENGTHS AND WEAKNESSES

Soviet strategy is considered to possess a scientific form of decision-making, a "calculation of the relation of forces" between the Soviet power and the enemy.[75] In calculating the relation of forces in national military strategy, the key element is a balancing of relative strength and potential in the permanently operating factors. In general terms, as Lieutenant General Krasil'nikov of the General Staff has put it: "The ability of a country to conduct a war depends not only on military potential, but also on economic and political [morale] potentialities." [76] It is useful to elucidate the Soviet evaluation of the strengths and weaknesses of the enemy in terms of Soviet conceptions of the enemy's strategy.

As we have seen, Soviet military thinking continues to reject reliance on any "atomic," strategic air, surprise, or blitzkrieg strategy. Consequently, tendencies in the enemy's strategic planning toward reliance upon these factors are believed faulty. Nonetheless, the enormous destruction—even though not necessarily defeat—which enemy nuclear and thermonuclear attack and strategic bombing would bring causes serious apprehension. In particular, it is feared that Western failure to recognize the true requirements for winning a war may lead "gambling" Western strategists into "adventures." Since the Soviets profess to have a superiority in the decisive factors, an appreciation of true strategic requirements by the enemy is more to be desired than a false enemy assurance which leads to a losing, but terribly destructive, strategy.

The military strengths of the enemy are appreciated, particularly American strategic nuclear air power. Nonetheless, not only is the American military strategy judged faulty on doctrinal bases, but it also is seen as presupposing a weaker opponent than the Soviets believe themselves to be. As Major General Khlopov stated it in the non-public General Staff journal *Military Thought* as early as 1950 (but reflecting a continuing Soviet view):

> The bankruptcy of the [American] plans for future war . . . consists in the fact that they almost all proceed from extremely favorable conditions, in which the enemy [the U.S.S.R.] will be so weak in the air that it will be possible in the first phase of the war to complete, with impunity, flights to targets selected by the Americans. The enemy will be so weak on the ground that the coalition army which will face him in the initial period of the war (an army composed of allies and, in part, of Americans themselves) can successfully hold the enemy troops and gain time for the transfer of forces and materiel from across the ocean. If one discards these favorable circumstances and takes real conditions—i.e., when the enemy [the Soviet bloc] places in the air active opposition and makes mighty air raids with the use of the newest means of armament to disrupt and destroy the transfer and concentration of troops, and when the enemy will have ground forces which are in a condition (American transfers from across the ocean not being anticipated) to deploy powerful offensive operations on a large scale with a high tempo of advance—then the bridgehead on which the American militarists count to concentrate and deploy their forces for land engagements will be liquidated and the plans for the war will be buried with it. The war will in this case assume an entirely different character from that which is planned by the representatives of the military-political circles of the U.S.A.[77]

This passage is also quite revealing in its statements on the "enemy" (Soviet) strategy, making explicit a unique confirmation of the Soviet objective, in a major war, of completely seizing the European continent. Thus both the bases and bridge-heads on the European (and Asian) continents will be lost to the United States.

An additional flaw seen in the American strategy is its neglect to recognize that the United States itself would be subjected to retaliatory nuclear attack, with its morale weakened, and its economic and military mobilization and military deployment seriously disrupted. We have earlier noted that the American overseas bases are said to be highly vulnerable.

Finally, the Soviets claim that there is also a political factor which will work to undermine the holding mission of the ground forces in the first phase of the war. The political foundation for the reliance upon the masses who must be called upon to form the necessary large ground armies is believed to be weak. This is especially, but not exclusively, said to be true of the non-American allied armies: "The calculations of the American aggressors to fight with the hands of others is doomed in advance to failure. The masses do not want to fight for the interests, hostile to them, of Wall Street," [78] And in referring to professional soldiers: "The armies of the imperialist countries preserve their martial spirit, their combat esprit, only so long as they experience successes in combat, while they plunder. But once they meet with a serious enemy, once they begin to experience failures and defeats in battle, little will remain of their martial spirit, of their morale." [79]

Western sources are cited to show that in the West the basis of morale is incorrectly sought in physical comforts, in the psychology of the individual rather than in social and class role (Liddell Hart is cited), and in religion (General Ridgway), but as a consequence of this false approach, despite extensive "propaganda" indoctrination, morale is so low that most infantrymen don't even fire their weapons (Brigadier General S. L. A. Marshall's report on Korea) .[80]

Morale is crucial in other ways as well. "Morale of the army" is considered a decisive factor; so is morale-political "stability of the rear." And in a total nuclear war:

137

The rear of the aggressors, subjected to a retaliatory atomic blow from the defending side, will be faced with a very great trial. *The use of atomic weapons against the unstable rear of the aggressor will lead to incomparably greater consequences than in the use of these weapons against a strong monolithic rear,* inseparably connected with the armed forces fighting for the achievement of the just aims of the war. The attitude of the people toward the war, its readiness to undergo very great sacrifices in the name of victory, assumes still greater significance under new conditions.[81]

The "aggressor" is, of course, the West; and the strong monolithic rear is that of the Soviet Union.[82]

The other major element of strength is the whole complex of economic, industrial, and transportation resources, and in particular the base for armaments production. Consequently, in evaluating the enemy's strength, the Soviet military leaders are told to study the enemy's economic strength. In particular, "The tempo of increasing military production changes the relation of forces of the sides in the course of the war, influences the course of the war and, in the final analysis, the outcome of the war as a whole."[83]

In estimating American industrial potential for war-making, the Soviets cannot escape the substantial superiority of American production facilities. Nonetheless, the potential alone is held to be insufficient:

A high economic potential is only the potentiality for victory, though it is a necessary condition. In order to convert the potentiality for victory into actuality, it is necessary to utilize the resources on hand and to convert them into real military factors which directly determine the outcome of war.

Wars of the [current] machine period have shown that it is insufficient to have a developed economy. It is necessary to be able swiftly to convert one's economy to a military basis, and to create in wartime an integrated and continually growing military economy. . . . Only a swift and basic reorganization of the economy on a military base makes possible the conversion of potential resources of the country into real military factors.[84]

138

And, the realization of economic potentialities, it is said, "depends directly upon the social and state structure of the country." The industrial production ability of the United States is specifically said to be *not* equatable with economic-military potential.[85] Even to the extent that the United States places its economy "on a military basis already in peacetime, capitalists all the more disorganize their rear, weaken their economic and morale potentialities."[86] And, in general, the Soviet system, the Soviet "social and state structure," is declared to be superior to that of the United States in economic mobilization and utilization of economic potential for military ends.[87] Despite the high productivity of the American economy and despite alleged preparations for war, American war plans are still considered to be adventuristic.

In summary, the Soviet evaluation of the enemy's strengths and weaknesses is that in all major aspects—military, morale, and economic—the enemy is fundamentally inferior. Nonetheless, his very substantial strength in the military and industrial sectors is recognized. In particular, even with a losing strategy, the enemy could in his defeat unleash a rain of thermonuclear destruction on the U.S.S.R. Consequently, Soviet strategy must seek by all measures short of provoking this disaster to neutralize the danger.

This Soviet evaluation of the strengths and weaknesses of the United States and of its strategy may not represent a complete and candid picture of the actual high-level military and political estimate. In particular, they may be less sanguine about the weaknesses of the American "rear," and less certain about the strength of their own. Such considerations would not appear in military and other publications for obvious reasons. But the general evaluation given by military officers, as described and discussed in this chapter, probably reflects *on the whole* the view held by the Soviet leadership.

Notes to Chapter 6

1. Maj. Gen. V. Khlopov, *Voennaia mysl'*, No. 1, January 1954, p. 82.

2. Lt. Col. P. Derevianko, *Krasnaia zvezda*, March 26, 1955. See also V. P. Skopin, *Militarizm*, 1956, p. 430.

3. Marshal of Tank Troops P. Rotmistrov, *Voennaia mysl'*, No. 2, February 1955, p. 19.

4. *Ibid.*, pp. 19 and 20.

5. 134. Col. A. Bozhenko, "The U.S. Air Force—A Tool of Aggression and Piracy," *Vestnik vozdushnogo flota*, No. 6, June 1955, p. 86.

6. See B. Borisov, "The Air Forces of the USA," *Kryl'ia rodiny*, No. 10, October 1956, p. 22; Eng. Maj. S. Lidin, *Vestnik vozdushnogo flota*, No. 3, March 1955, p. 88; Col. A. Kononenko, "Conceptions of Military Circles in the USA," *Mezhdunarodnaia zhizn'*, No. 9, September 1956, p. 67; Eng. Lt. Col. B. Surikov, "The Development of Air Defense," *Krasnaia zvezda*, March 23, 1957; V. Linetsky, *Sovetskii flot*, February 14, 1957; Lt. Gen. of Aviation P. Braiko, "Soviet Aviation in the Second World War," *Vestnik vozdushnogo flota*, No. 4, April 1955, p. 19; Col. N. Kramarenko, "In Search of the 'Decisive Forces' for Aggression," *Sovetskii flot*, December 26, 1956; Col. S. Kozlov, "Man and Technology in Contemporary War," *Sovetskii flot*, January 25, 1957; and Chief Marshal of Aviation P. Zhigarev, "The Air Fleet of the Soviet Power," *Pravda*, July 3, 1955.

7. Eng. Lt. Col. P. Safonov, *Vestnik vozdushnogo flota*, No. 9, September 1954, p. 79; and see esp. Col. A. Bozhenko, *Vestnik vozdushnogo flota*, No. 6, June 1955, pp. 87 and 90.

8. See Lt. Gen. of Aviation N. Zhuravlev, *Sovetskaia aviatsiia*, April 25, 1957; Maj. Gen. V. Khlopov, *Voennaia mysl'*, No. 1, January 1954, p. 81; M. Krementsev, *Krasnaia zvezda*, April 10, 1954; Lt. Gen. A. Sukhomlin, *News*, No. 12, June 1954, p. 10; Col. N. Rodin, *Vestnik vozdushnogo flota*, No. 11, November 1954, p. 71; Col. A. Bozhenko, *Vestnik vozdushnogo flota*, No. 6, June 1955, p. 86; Lt. Col. P. Derevianko, *Krasnaia zvezda*, March 26, 1955; Col. M. Mil'shtein, *Krasnaia zvezda*, February 25, 1955; Lt. Gen. of Aviation P. Braiko, *Vestnik vozdushnogo flota*, No. 4, April 1955, p. 19; N. Glagolev, *Krasnaia zvezda*, January 20, 1956; and Col. A. Kononenko, *Mezhdunarodnaia zhizn'*, No. 9, September 1956, p. 67.

9. Col. B. Karpovich, *Voennyi vestnik*, No. 6, June 1955, p. 78.

10. Col. A. Bozhenko and Col. V. Osipov, "Who Commands the American Air Forces?" *Vestnik vozdushnogo flota*, No. 11, November 1951, p. 90.

11. Eng. Lt. Col. P. Safonov and Eng. Lt. Col. T. Andreev, "Preparation of the Crew of a Strategic Bomber (According to the Foreign Press)", *Vestnik vozdushnogo flota*, No. 7, July 1955, p. 91.

12. Col. A. Bozhenko, *Vestnik vozdushnogo flota*, No. 6, June 1955, p. 88.

13. "On the U.S. Strategic Air Command," *Vestnik vozdushnogo flota*, No. 6, June 1955, pp. 91-94; introductory statement on p. 91.

14. See the earlier discussion in Chapter 4; and see Garthoff, *Soviet Military Doctrine*, pp. 253-57. For a later statement, see Col. S. Kozlov, *Vooruzhenie armii*, 1954, pp. 3-4.

15. Col. E. Chalik, *Voennaia mysl'*, No. 9, September 1954, p. 28. See also Col. V. Petrov, "What Is Military Potential?" *Sovetskii flot*, September 20, 1956.

16. See the discussion in Chapter 4.

17. Marshal of Aviation K. Vershinin, *Pravda*, July 19, 1949.

18. See especially D. Kondratkov, "The Morale Factor in the Evaluation of Bourgeois Military Science," *Sovetskii flot*, January 6, 1957; and also Maj. Gen. M. Mil'shtein and Col. A. Slobodenko, *Voennye ideologi kapitalisticheskikh stran o kharaktere i sposobakh vedeniia sovremennoi voiny*, Znanie, Moscow, [April 22] 1957, p. 46 (hereafter cited as *Voennye ideologi*); a Retired General, *Izvestiia*, January 19, 1954; Maj. Gen. V. Khlopov, *Voennaia mysl'*, No. 1, January 1954, p. 83; Col. S. Kozlov, *Krasnaia zvezda*, August 18, 1954; Col. I. Sokolov, in *Marksizm-leninizm o voine*, [February 3] 1955, p. 150; and Col. N. Kramarenko, *Sovetskii flot*, December 26, 1956.

19. Col. I. Sokolov, in *Marksizm-leninizm o voine*, 1955, p. 154.

20. Col. I. Maryganov, *Peredovoi kharakter*, [October 30] 1953, p. 124.

21. Col. G. Petrov, in *Marksizm-leninizm o voine*, 1955, p. 144. See also Col. P. Kashirin, *Voennaia mysl'*, No. 10, October 1952, p. 16.

22. Maj. Gen. M. Smirnov, in *O sovetskoi voennoi nauke*, 1954, p. 168.

23. Maj. Gen. N. Petrov, "The Military Ideology of the American Imperialists," *Krasnaia zvezda*, October 6, 1950; Col. B. Karpovich, *Krasnaia zvezda*, July 9, 1952; Maj. Gen. V. Khlopov, *Voennaia mysl'*, No. 1, January 1954, p. 80; Col. I. Sokolov, in *Marksizm leninizm o voine*, 1955, p. 150; Col. A. Kononenko, *Mezhdunarodnaia zhizn'*, No. 9, September 1956, pp. 66-67; Col. Yu. Pshenianik, *Sovetskaia aviatsiia*, March 17, 1957; and esp. see Maj. Gen. M. Mil'shtein and Col. A. Slobodenko, *Voennye ideologi*, 1957, p. 50.

24. For example, Eisenhower and Bradley are mentioned by Maj. Gen. N. Petrov, *Krasnaia zvezda*, October 6, 1950; Col. B. Karpovich, *Krasnaia zvezda*, July 9, 1952; and Maj. Gen. V. Khlopov, *Voennaia mysl'*, No. 1, January 1954, p. 80; and Bradley also by V. Skopin, *Militarizm*, [August 3] 1956, p. 407. Ridgway is cited, *inter alia*, by Maj. V. Garin, *Voennyi vestnik*, No. 11, November 1954, p. 77; Lt. Col. Derevianko, *Krasnaia zvezda*, March 26, 1955; Maj. Gen. N. Tsigichko, *Voennaia mysl'*, No. 4, April 1955, p. 80; Maj. Gen. Ye. Boltin, *Krasnaia zvezda*, August 30, 1955; and Col. A. Kononenko, *Mezhdunarodnaia zhizn'*, No. 9, September 1956, p. 66. Gruenther is mentioned by N. Kondratkov, *Sovetskii flot*, January 6, 1957. Generals Taylor and Bolte, Ridgway and Bradley are singled out by Maj. Gen. M. Mil'shtein and Col. A. Slobodenko, in *Voennye ideologi*, 1957, p. 46.

25. Maj. Gen. N. Pukhovsky, *Voennyi vestnik*, No. 1, January 1954, pp. 20-21, and in *Marksizm-leninizm o voine*, February 1955, pp. 103-104; and Col. N. Kramarenko, *Sovetskii flot*, December 26, 1956.

26. Lt. Col. P. Derevianko, *Krasnaia zvezda*, March 26, 1955. For an earlier statement, see Maj. Gen. N. Petrov, *Krasnaia zvezda*, October 6, 1950.

27. Maj. V. Garin, *Voennyi vestnik,* No. 11, November 1954, p. 77.

28. Col. B. Karpovich, *Voennyi vestnik,* No. 6, June 1955, p. 81. See also Col. A. Kononenko, *Mezhdunarodnaia zhizn',* No. 9, September 1956, p. 67.

29. Maj. Gen. N. Pukhovsky, *Voennyi vestnik,* No. 1, January 1954, p. 21.

30. Maj. Gen. Ye. Boltin, *Krasnaia zvezda,* August 30, 1955; and Major A. Sapronov, *Voennyi vestnik,* No. 12, December 1956, pp. 74-78.

31. Maj. Gen. V. Khlopov, *Voennaia mysl',* No. 1, January 1954, pp. 79-80.

32. M. Krementsev, *Krasnaia zvezda,* April 10, 1954.

33. See esp. Maj. Gen. M. Mil'shtein and Col. A. Slobodenko, *Voennye ideologi,* 1957, pp. 46-50; Col. Yu. Pshenianik, *Sovetskaia aviatsiia,* March 17, 1957; Col. S. Kozlov, *Sovetskii flot,* January 25, 1957; Col. N. Kramarenko, *Sovetskii flot,* December 26, 1956; Maj. Gen. N. Pukhovsky, in *Marksizm-leninizm o voine,* [February 3] 1955, p. 103; Col. M. Mil'shtein, "The Structure and Organization of the American Armed Forces," *Krasnaia zvezda,* February 25, 1955; Lt. Col. P. Derevianko, *Krasnaia zvezda,* March 26, 1955; Maj. Gen. N. Tsigichko, *Voennaia mysl',* No. 4, April 1955, pp. 80-81; and Col. A. Bagreev, *Voennaia mysl',* No. 5, May 1955, p. 87.

34. Maj. Gen. Ye. Boltin, *Krasnaia zvezda,* August 30, 1955.

35. Col. A. Kononenko, *Mezhdunarodnaia zhizn',* No. 9, September 1956, p. 68. See also Col. A Kononenko, *Atomnoe oruzhie v voennykh planakh SShA,* 1957, p. 49.

36. Lt. Col. P. Derevianko, *Krasnaia zvezda,* March 26, 1955. See also Maj. Gen. M. Mil'shtein and Col. A. Slobodenko, *Voennye ideologi,* 1957, pp. 52 and 63; Admiral V. Platonov, *Krasnaia zvezda,* December 14, 1956; Col. M. Mil'shtein, *Krasnaia zvezda,* February 25, 1955; Col. V. Vasilenko, *Marksizm-leninizm o voine,* 1955, p. 103; M. Krementsev, *Krasnaia zvezda,* April 10, 1954; and Maj. Gen. V. Khlopov, *Voennaia mysl',* No. 1, January 1954, p. 84. The only exception was Maj. Gen. Ye. Boltin, *Krasnaia zvezda,* August 30, 1955.

37. Col. V. Vasilenko, *Marksizm-leninizm o voine,* 1955, p. 216.

38. Lt. Col. P. Derevianko, *Krasnaia zvezda,* March 26, 1955.

39. See esp. Col. A. Kononenko, *Mezhdunarodnaia zhizn',* No. 9, September 1956, p. 71; Col. A. Bozhenko and V. Osipov, *Vestnik vozdushnogo flota,* No. 11, November 1951, p. 85; and S. M. Vishnev, *Sovremmennyi militarizm i monopolii* (Contemporary Militarism and Monopolies), Academy of Sciences, Institute of Economics, Moscow, [November 29] 1952, *passim.*

40. Maj. Gen. V. Khlopov, *Voennaia mysl',* No. 1, January 1954, pp. 80 and 84.

41. Lt. Col. P. Derevianko, *Krasnaia zvezda,* March 26, 1955; and see Col. N. Kramarenko, *Sovetskii flot,* December 26, 1956.

42. Maj. Gen. M. Mil'shtein and Col. A. Slobodenko, *Voennye ideologi,* 1957, p. 45.

43. *Ibid.,* p. 51.

44. *Ibid.,* p. 52.

45. *Ibid.,* pp. 46-47.

46. *Ibid.,* p. 50.

47. *Ibid.*, pp. 36-38.

48. Maj. Gen. V. Khlopov, *Voennaia mysl'*, No. 1, January 1954, p. 77; see also p. 82.

49. Maj. Gen. M. Mil'shtein and Col. A. Slobodenko, *Voennye ideologi,* 1957, p. 55.

50. Col. N. Rodin, *Vestnik vozdushnogo flota,* No. 11, November 1954, p. 70. See also Maj. Gen. M. Mil'shtein and Col. A. Slobodenko, *Voennye ideologi,* 1957, p. 56.

51. Col. N. Kramarenko, *Sovetskii flot,* December 26, 1956; Col. V. A. Zakharov, in *Marksizm-leninizm o voine i armii,* 1957, p. 278; Lt. Gen. A. Sukhomlin, *News,* No. 12, June 1954, p. 10; Lt. Col. P. Derevianko, *Krasnaia zvezda,* March 26, 1955; Col. V. Vasilenko, in *Marksizm-leninizm o voine,* [February 3] 1955, p. 216; Col. A. Mikhailov, *Voennaia mysl',* No. 9, September 1955, p. 73; Col. N. Rodin, *Vestnik vozdushnogo flota,* No. 11, November 1954, p. 70; Maj. Gen. V. Khlopov, *Voennaia mysl',* No. 1, January 1954, p. 83; V. Khlopov, *Voennaia mysl',* No. 6, June 1950, p. 73; Col. M. Milantsev, *Voennaia mysl',* No. 4, April 1949, p. 81.

52. Col. N. Rodin, *Vestnik vozdushnogo flota,* No. 11, November 1954, p. 70.

53. Lt. Gen. S. Krasil'nikov, "Military Strategy," *Bol'shaia Sovetskaia Entsiklopediia,* 2nd ed., Vol. 41, [April 21] 1956, p. 73; and Col. M. Milantsev, *Voennaia mysl',* No. 4, April 1949, p. 82.

54. Col. A. Kononenko, *Mezhdunarodnaia zhizn',* No. 9, September 1956, p. 71.

55. Col. Ye. Kosorukov and Lt. Col. V. Matsulenko, *Voennyi vestnik,* No. 7, July 1955, p. 92; and see Col. B. Karpovich, *Krasnaia zvezda,* December 10, 1955.

56. M. Krementsev, *Krasnaia zvezda,* April 10, 1954.

57. M. Kazantsev, "U.S. Military Bases—A Threat to the Peace and Security of Peoples," *Sovetskii patriot,* April 10, 1957; Col. M. P. Tolchenov, *Amerikanskie voennye bazy na chuzhikh territoriiakh—ugroza miru i bezopasnosti narodov* (American Military Bases on Foreign Territories—A Threat to Peace and the Security of Nations), Znanie, Moscow, [January 20] 1955, p. 6. See also Lt. Gen. A. Sukhomlin, *News,* No. 12, June 1954, p. 10; Col. N. Chistov, "American Air Bases," *Vestnik vozdushnogo flota,* No. 10, October 1951, pp. 81 ff; and T. Belashchenko, "The Real Purpose of American Military Bases [Overseas]," *Krasnaia zvezda,* October 11, 1956.

58. Marshal G. Zhukov, "The Tenth Anniversary of a Great Victory," *Pravda,* May 8, 1955.

59. Marshal I. Bagramian, "The Historic Victory of the Soviet People," *Oktiabr',* No. 5, May 1955, p. 112.

60. Col. M. Tolchenov, *Radio Moscow,* Home Service, October 14, 1953.

61. Marshal of Aviation K. Vershinin, *Pravda,* September 8, 1957.

62. Maj. Gen. V. Khlopov, *Voennaia mysl',* No. 1, January 1954, p. 78.

63. *Ibid.*

64. Col. B. Karpovich, *Krasnaia zvezda,* December 10, 1955.

65. Marshal G. Zhukov, *Pravda*, February 20, 1956; and see Zhukov, *Pravda*, May 8, 1955.

66. See also Marshal V. Sokolovsky, *Pravda*, February 23, 1956; and the editorial, *Voennyi vestnik*, No. 4, April 1956, p. 4.

67. Editorial, *Voennaia mysl'*, No. 5, May 1955, p. 11.

68. Lt. Col. P. Derevianko, *Krasnaia zvezda*, March 26, 1955.

69. *Ibid.*

70. Col. M. Mil'shtein, *Krasnaia zvezda*, February 25, 1955. And see Col. A. Kononenko, *Mezhdunarodnaia zhizn'*, No. 9, September 1956, p. 67.

71. Lt. Gen. A. Sukhomlin, *News*, No. 12, June 1954, p. 10. See also Col. A. Kononenko, *International Affairs*, No. 2, February 1957, pp. 63-64.

72. *Ibid.*, p. 11.

73. Maj. Gen. M. Mil'shtein and Col. A. Slobodenko, *Voennye ideologi*, 1957, pp. 54 and 63; Marshal G. Zhukov, *Pravda*, February 20, 1956; Col. A. Kononen-ko, *Mezhdunarodnaia zhizn'*, No. 9, September 1956, p. 67; Col. M. P. Tolchenov, *Voennye bloki imperialisticheskikh gosudarstv—ugroza miru i bezopasposti parodov* (Military Blocs of the Imperialist States—A Threat to Peace and the Security of Peoples), Znanie, Moscow, [May 16] 1956, p. 7; Col. B. Karpovich, *Krasnaia zvezda*, December 10, 1955; Lt. Col. P. Derevianko, *Krasnaia zvezda*, March 26, 1955; Col. M. Mil'shtein, *Krasnaia zvezda*, February 25, 1955; Col. N. Rodin, *Vestnik vozdushnogo flota*, No. 11, November 1954, p. 70; Lt. Gen. A. Sukhomlin, *News*, No. 12, June 1954, pp. 10-11; M. Krementsev, *Krasnaia zvezda*, April 10, 1954; Maj. Gen. V. Khlopov, *Voennaia mysl'*, No. 1, January 1954, pp. 76-77 and 81-82; Karpovich, *Krasnaia zvezda*, July 9, 1952; Khlopov, *Voennaia mysl'*, No. 1, January 1950, pp. 73 and 76; and Col. M. Milantsev, *Voennaia mysl'*, No. 4, April 1949, p. 81.

74. N. Krementsev, *Krasnaia zvezda*, April 10, 1954; Col. A. Kononenko, *Mezhdunarodnaia zhizn'*, No. 9, September 1956, p. 67; and A. Leont'ev, on *Radio Moscow*, Home Service, March 7, 1957.

75. See Garthoff, *Soviet Military Doctrine*, pp. 16-19, and Garthoff, "The Concept of the Balance of Power in Soviet Policy-Making," *World Politics*, Vol. 4, No. 1, October 1951, pp. 85-111.

76. Lt. Gen. S. Krasil'nikov, *Krasnaia zvezda*, August 30, 1955.

77. Maj. Gen. V. Khlopov, *Voennaia mysl'*, No. 6, June 1950, pp. 75-76.

78. Col. B. Karpovich, *Krasnaia zvezda*, July 9, 1952. See also Lt. Gen. S. Krasil'nikov, "Military Strategy," *Bol'shaia Sovetskaia Entsiklopediia*, 2nd ed., Vol. 41, [April 21] 1956, p. 66.

79. Col. P. Kashirin, *Krasnaia zvezda*, May 28, 1955; and see Kashirin, *Voennye znaniia*, No. 8, August 1956, p. 13.

80. Col. V. B. Belyi, in *Marksizm-leninizm o voine i armii*, 1957, pp. 230-33; and see D. Kondratkov, "The Morale Factor in the Evaluation of Bourgeois Military Science," *Sovetskii flot*, January 6, 1957; and Major A. Sapronov, "American Views of the Role of the Morale Factor in War," *Voennyi vestnik*, No. 12, December 1956, pp. 74-78.

81. Maj. Gen. G. Pokrovsky, in *Marksizm-leninizm o voine,* [February 3] 1955, p. 169.

82. Cf. for example, Col. P. Sidorov, "Morale Propaganda and Its Significance in Modern War," *Krasnaia zvezda,* August 3, 1955.

83. Col. P. Belov, *Voennaia mysl',* No. 5, May 1951, p. 18. See also Lt. Gen. S. Krasil'nikov, *Krasnaia zvezda,* August 20, 1955.

84. *Ibid.,* pp. 23-24. See also Maj. Gen. V. Khlopov, *Voennaia mysl',* No. 6 June 1950, p. 69.

85. Col. A. Strokov and Col. I. Maryganov, in *O sovetskoi voennoi nauke* 1954, p. 56.

86. Col. V. Petrov, in *Marksizm-leninizm o voine,* 1955, p. 111.

87. For example, see Col. A. Lagovsky, "Economic Potential and Its Role in Contemporary War," *Krasnaia zvezda,* July 1, 1955; and Col. N. Sushko, *Sovetskii flot,* March 22, 1957.

145

CHAPTER 7

LAND POWER IN SOVIET STRATEGY

The Soviet Army continues to play a major role in Soviet strategy for nuclear war. The very fact of the maintenance of 175 divisions makes this clear, and Soviet military writings are replete with statements that reflect and affirm the Soviet belief in the importance of large ground armies in the nuclear era.

Marshal Zhukov described the continuing view on the role of of large ground forces even in general nuclear war as follows: "*Air power and nuclear weapons by themselves cannot decide the outcome of armed conflict.* Along with atomic and hydrogen weapons, in spite of their tremendous destructive power, *large armies and a tremendous quantity of conventional arms inevitably will be drawn into military operations.*"[1] Another Soviet general put it: "Mass armies are needed for victory in atomic war, too. ..."[2]

THE NEED FOR LARGE ARMIES

"Mass armies," in the current Soviet doctrine must not be confused with the mere masses of soldiers which formed the Red armies of the Second World War. A continuous postwar modernization program has converted the Soviet Army into a potent modern force. The fifteen-million-man Red Army of

149

1945 was a massive but motley conglomeration of over 600 "divisions," the vast majority of which were infantry formations of brigade strength with horse-drawn transport. During the postwar period a drastic reorganization was undertaken. The demobilization in this period was selective and part of the program of modernization. In 1945 there were ten infantry divisions to each armored (tank or mechanized) division; by 1947 the ratio was two to one, and it may now be approaching parity. By the end of 1947 the Soviet armed forces had reached the level of the initial postwar standing force: approximately 4,000,000 men in the three services (plus 400,000 security troops), of whom 2,500,000 were in the ground forces, organized in 175 line divisions. During the Korean war the force grew.

In 1955 and 1956, the Soviet government announced, with much fanfare, reductions in military manpower totaling 1,840,000 men.[3] While it remains uncertain, indeed doubtful, if reductions of this size were in fact made, there was a sizable gradual demobilization to the 1947 levels.

The main cause of the cut was economic and demographic: the men were badly needed in industrial and especially agricultural work, more so than they were as soldiers. It was a calculated reallocation of manpower resources from a sector of state power overstrong in comparison to the West to the relatively understrong economic sector.[4]

Reports of Western military specialists indicate that, as a result of the reductions to 1958, there was no decrease in the number of divisions.[5] In general the reductions appear to have been made by shifting a number of divisions from new full-strength combat-ready status to "cadre-strength," preserving the officer and non-commissioned officer complement and a reduced enlisted force. Also, there was some decrease in support elements. An estimated 30,000 junior *political* officers were dropped as the post of full-time political assistant at company level was abolished in 1955.

Another cause of the reductions in standing ground forces is the fact that it is becoming too expensive for the Soviet

150

Union to maintain the traditional level of massive (and economically parasitic) ground forces, and simultaneously to compete with the United States in acquiring the exceedingly costly modern strategic offensive and defensive weapons systems. Faced with a problem of choice between pulling abreast of the United States in modern weapons or maintaining the enormous existing standing army, *and in view of the tremendous Soviet preponderance in ground strength,* the Soviet leadership of course has reduced the Army. Even *after* the announced Soviet (and Satellite) reductions in force, the Soviet bloc *retains* a superiority of nearly three to one over Free World combat forces both in Europe and in Asia.[6] In this perspective it is significant that, impressive as the numbers may seem at first glance, the reduction has been as *limited* as it has (to say nothing of the fact that it apparently falls short of the announced goals).

The Soviet reduction of the ground forces is often cited as an illustration of a presumed nuclear "new look" paralleling that made in the United States and Great Britain in recent years. In a sense this is true, but it is necessary to note the other influences which led to this decision: the severe ethnographic-economic pressure, and the continued weakness (in fact, decline) in numbers of United States and NATO ground forces. The real "new look" of the Soviet ground forces has been their systematic modernization over the past decade.[7]

The reduction of the standing force does *not* mean that the Soviets consider a large army to be unnecessary for nuclear war. The continued maintenance of between 140 and 175 divisions and other ground units, plus the continued training of a multi-million-strong reserve force, provides the basis for rapid mobilization of the modernized mass armies which the Soviets expect to employ in a major war, nuclear or non-nuclear. The *Great Soviet Encyclopedia* (in 1956) continued to declare that: "The ground troops are *the main element* of the armed forces. . . ."[8]

The Soviet concept of modern mass armies must be considered in terms of its relation to the doctrine of combined arms operations, centered upon support of the ground forces by tactical aviation and coastal sea forces, but now broadened to include actions of the long-range air, sea, and missile components. Marshal Zhukov declared, in a speech in 1957 to a military audience in Moscow: "In the postwar construction of the armed forces we are proceeding from the fact that *victory in future war will be achieved only by the combined efforts of all arms of the armed forces* and on the basis of their coordinated employment in war." [9] There is no sign of change since Zhukov's dismissal.

The Soviet ground forces are being maintained on the substantial scale considered sufficient to permit both immediate commitment in a war, and simultaneous use of the remainder as the cadre in mobilizing the large reserve strength. The Soviet ground forces are preparing for tactical nuclear warfare, but, as we shall see, this by no means implies a reduction in strength, particularly since divisions in the Soviet Army have in the past been smaller and less encumbered with support and service troops than have Western divisions.

The Soviets maintain large ground armies for a number of purposes. The extremely long land frontiers require Soviet military planners to calculate on the possibility of simultaneous military operations on several fronts. The maintenance of order and guard duty over numerous installations spread over vast areas, together with frontier patrol and guard duty, is a function shared by the Army with the Internal Troops of the KGB and Frontier Guards of the MVD. Maintenance of internal order in the Soviet empire, especially in the satellites, requires large-scale ground forces. The quelling of the revolution in Hungary in November 1956 required commitment of a reported seven to twelve divisions. But in addition to all these considerations, the basic reason for Soviet maintenance of over one hundred combat-ready ground divisions, plus many other divisions in cadre forms, is the belief that the winning of any major future war, despite the employment of nuclear and thermonuclear weapons, will require defeating enemy forces and the seizure and occupation of vast areas of land. In a nuclear war this requirement might even be more essential than in a non-nuclear one because industrial, economic, and labor resources of other countries would be harnessed to compensate in part for the extensive damage which the Soviet economic system would suffer in the mutual strategic exchange.

The requirements of a military establishment with a large land army as a central component can be met only with the resources of a large and mobilized economic-military potential. And since employment of mass armies can only be contemplated in the present geostrategic arena in a long war, it is clear that the Soviet conception of a long war and of an irreplaceable role for massive land armies are interdependent.

In viewing the course of a general nuclear war the Soviets evidently do not subscribe to the view that mutual devastation spells mutual defeat. The destruction of a number of Soviet and American cities would have an effect difficult to predict, but one which would affect both sides. The Soviet mobilization and dispatch of ground forces would probably be much less critically disrupted than would ours, due to their larger force in being and to its deployment. The mutual destruction of strategic air bases, and probably cities and industry, would presumably consume the major part of the long-range air forces, and the Soviets apparently calculate that the continued efforts of these forces would in a sense cancel each other out. If the Soviets consider the level of destruction both at home and in the combat theater to be roughly symmetrical, as they apparently do, no matter how great this level the remaining Soviet land armies would still be able to defeat the proportionately weakened enemy forces on the ground. But the Soviets believe that in the face of enemy nuclear strength the overcoming of all enemy resistance on the Eurasian periphery may require major campaigns and large armies, and they intend to be prepared. The Soviets visualize the role of the combined ground and supporting aviation forces not as a subsequent "mopping up" stage, but as a contemporaneous significant element in determining the outcome of the war. As Marshal of the Tank Troops Rotmistrov put it, in the General Staff journal *Military Thought,* in 1955: "It is entirely clear that atomic and hydrogen weapons alone, without *the decisive operations of the ground forces* with their contemporary materiel, cannot decide the outcome of a war." [10]

We have noted that the Soviets continue to believe in the maintenance of a mass army. More specifically, they have concluded that nuclear warfare will require *larger* armies than were needed before. Thus, to cite at length but one authoritative source, Lieutenant General Krasil'nikov of the General Staff has observed (in late 1956):

> The employment in war of means of mass destruction [i.e., nuclear weapons] calls not for the reduction of the numbers of various divisions of the combatants, but their logical further increase, since the threat of wiping out a division grows, and for their replacement large reserves will be needed. The growth of the number of divisions is inevitable also as a consequence of the increasing extent of strategic fronts, since contemporary wars have the tendency to encompass not one, but several continents. . . . The attempts of some bourgeois military theoreticians to show that new weapons—aviation, tanks, atomic and hydrogen bombs, guided missiles—relieve one of the necessity of having mass armed forces are bereft of any foundation. . . . The atomic or hydrogen weapons, and in general any single weapon, can not decide the fate of a war. All forms of armament are necessary, and together with them massed armed forces capable of waging a strenuous struggle on land, sea, and in the air. . . . Weapons of mass destruction not only require mass armed forces, but require their inevitable increase. [11]

Before turning to a more detailed comprehensive review of Soviet views on nuclear warfare, it is useful to focus on one peculiar Soviet problem. What would be the morale of these large armies in a war waged in Europe and the Middle East? Would the Soviet soldier fight as courageously and well in a war on foreign soil as in defense of Russia? The question is not susceptible of definite answer, but it is possibly very important. For the first time, *Military Thought* in May 1955 broached this subject indirectly:

> In the further working out of the questions of the morale factor in war it is necessary to attain an ability to calculate and to utilize realistically all its potentialities in the interests of the military art and the achievement of victory over the foe. . . . [political instruction] *in the spirit of conducting active offensive operations directed toward the complete crushing and annihilation of the enemy,* assumes particularly important significance.[12]

Very soon after the appearance of this article, a Soviet military "specialist" on the role of morale, Colonel Kashirin, raised the issue in *Red Star* as follows:

> The Soviet state is a peaceful state. . . . But that does not mean that the Soviet armed forces cannot conduct military operations on the territory of the enemy if the imperialists unleash a war and attack the Soviet Union. . . . Unfortunately, some of us often confuse two entirely different conceptions. This is explained by the fact that there exist among us military comrades of the opinion that in the case of an attack on us of imperialist aggressors our mission will be to defend, to repulse their attack, not to permit them to enter deep in our country—and only that.

This view, he explains, is faulty and dangerous.

> And if it is necessary to advance on the territory of other states, not in order to seize their territories, to suppress some people, but in order to destroy barbarous imperialist robbers, *to defend to the end the state interests of the U.S.S.R.* . . . this requires of the entire personnel of the Soviet armed forces high morale qualities.[13]

It is a remarkable disclosure, indeed, that some "military comrades" were so bold as to hold the view that in case of war the Soviet armed forces should not attempt to advance into other countries. And the defense of the official view on advance sees that it is necessary to deny the aim of suppression and to argue for advances not only to destroy an "aggressor," but "to defend *the state interests* of the U.S.S.R." This is as far as the Soviets can go, even in discussions intended for their own officers, toward admitting their interest in *offensive* wars.

In discussing the Soviet armed intervention and suppression of Hungary in November 1956, the Soviets still claim (in the words of Colonel I. N. Levanov, a professor at the important Lenin Military Political Academy) that "fulfilling their alliance obligations and international duty, Soviet troops helped the Hungarian people to crush the forces of internal and international reaction."[14] But this is not believed by the vast majority of Soviet citizens—and soldiers. The author knows from hundreds of personal conversations in Moscow and other Soviet cities that the Soviet intervention in Hungary has had a profound impact. It is one issue on which most Russians are sufficiently informed to know that their regime used force to conquer another people. And they are not proud of this fact. The absence of post-Hungary references in Soviet military literature to the need for indoctrination on fighting abroad reflects sensitivity on "the Hungarian events."

PREPARATIONS FOR NUCLEAR WARFARE

The Soviet Army was tardy in facing the challenge of preparation for nuclear warfare. Under the influence of "Stalinist stagnation" in military doctrine, incredible though it seems, there was literally *no preparation for atomic warfare* prior to the autumn of 1953. At that time the first small-scale experimental maneuvers hastily tested the initial defense plans against tactical atomic attack.[15] Also, as we have noted, not until 1954 and 1955 did the first series of articles on nuclear weapons appear in *Red Star,* the service journals, and other military

156

publications. During most of the first year these discussions were limited to elementary explanations of the nuclear physics of an atomic explosion, structure of a "basic" atomic bomb, and effects of a nuclear explosion (using, almost entirely, published American data based on a nominal 20 KT explosion). Later, in 1954 and 1955, protective measures against atomic attack were discussed. In 1954 a series of Army manuals on atomic warfare appeared, including one for enlisted men and sergeants. During these two years, 1954 and 1955, substantial strides were made in training for atomic warfare. A large mortar-howitzer reportedly capable of firing nuclear shells was paraded publicly. The atomic age had come, if belatedly, with a real impact on the Soviet Army. In the period since 1955 training and preparation for nuclear warfare has been standard.

Thus, when Marshal Zhukov addressed the Twentieth Congress of the Communist Party in early 1956, he could state with assurance: "In recent years considerable work on the training of troops in the art of conducting combat operations under conditions of the use of atomic weapons and other new weapons in the ground forces, aviation, and the navy has been conducted."[16]

Defensive measures against atomic attack have been extensively discussed in Soviet writings. Discussions of personal and unit measures for protection from blast and radiation effects of nuclear weapons are frequent. Passive defensive measures emphasized are the importance of cover, protective clothing, use of protective features of the terrain, and thorough decontamination of personnel, equipment and weapons.[17] But while Soviet soldiers are taught protective measures against atomic weapons, they are also taught that, in the words of their official manual on atomic defense: "The fulfillment of the combat mission is the first and basic duty of the soldier." Thus: "At the signal of the atomic alert the fulfillment of combat tasks does not cease. . . . In the offensive the best means of action at the warning is determined closing with the enemy. . . . In the defense, in deployment, and in the concentration for the offensive departure, continue to fulfill your mission. . . . On the march, at the signal of atomic alert, movement does not cease"[18]

Engineering preparation of the terrain, as well as individual "digging in," is stressed also: "The significance of engineering work increases considerably under the threat of the enemy's using atomic weapons."[19] Development of special high-speed mechanized engineering equipment has been urged. The construction of revêtments and bunkers for command posts, artillery emplacements, tanks, and aircraft is advocated. But, of course, such provisions are not permitted to encourage a tendency to sacrifice maneuver for static protection. In the first place, maneuver is generally *better* protection, and in addition the Soviets do not want to lessen offensive spirit by stressing emplaced protective shielding. The general de-emphasis on fixed positions and lines in nuclear warfare is parallel to our own.

The Soviets well recognize the tactical implication of atomic weapons: "Above all, the concentration of a large quantity of troops and materiel will be significantly more difficult. The enemy will attempt to drop atomic bombs on concentrations of personnel and materiel and on strong defense points."[20] Defense against enemy air attack, in particular, assumes greater importance.[21] Hence, the recognition of the need for dispersion.

Dispersal, as we know, is an easily recognized *requirement* for tactical nuclear warfare, but a most difficult one to satisfy without sacrificing the requirements of defensive, and especially of offensive, deployment. The doctrinal "solution," as stated by Major General of the Tank Troops Losik (in early 1957), was: "Under conditions of the employment of atomic weapons, troops will in general operate dispersed in order to save men and materiel, collecting into a striking concentration only at the time of the attack."[22] The means of dispersing, and of gaining concentration when necessary, have been indicated in some of the Soviet writings and training. In general, of

course, they all involve solutions to the second main requirement of atomic warfare: mobility.

"*Mobility* of the troops is considered the *key to victory* in
all forms of combat operations under conditions of the employment of means of mass destruction," we are told by Colonel
Mochalov (in 1956).[23] We shall return in a moment to note
the Soviet measures planned to effect this mobility.

A third major problem, and heightened need, seen by the
Soviets in tactical atomic warfare is increased effectiveness of
reconnaissance. Detection both of enemy attacks and of targets
for their own attacks requires (in Colonel Mochalov's words)
"a more precise organization of reconnaissance than in usual
[i.e., non-atomic] circumstances."[24] The fleeting nature of attractive targets is recognized, as is the fact that "combat targets
will be more mobile and more dispersed."[25] And, as Major
General Pokrovsky stated in an authoritative non-public source
in 1955, "the role of timely detection and destruction of the
enemy's atomic weapons, in particular, increases."[26]

In addition to mobility, dispersal, and improved reconnaissance, another measure of achieving defensive security emphasized by the Soviets is the "hugging" technique. As Colonel
Yakovkin has put it: "The *best defense* against an atomic strike
is precipitate closing with the enemy,"[27] so that he cannot use
atomic weapons without endangering his own front lines. Thus
the Soviets are led to implement the old principle that "the
best defense is offense."

The Soviets are, of course, studying both the defensive and
offensive effectiveness and characteristics of tactical nuclear
warfare. On balance, the Soviets conclude (in the words of
Major General Tsigichko, in the semi-classified General Staff
organ *Military Thought*) that "atomic weapons *significantly
increase the offensive potentialities* of the ground troops."[28] In
particular, as another recent authoritative Soviet source put it,
they can be employed in the offensive to achieve "a swift break-
through of defensive lines and destruction of the tactical and
close operational reserves of the enemy."[29]

Traditional Soviet military doctrine on the forms of offensive maneuver is considered to be upheld and enhanced in atomic warfare.[30] Use of nuclear weapons "dealing powerful surprise blows on the enemy" may permit tactical achievement of "decisive results in a shorter period of time."[31] Moreover, we read in *Military Thought* that: "Employing atomic weapons, the attacker has the potentiality of breaking through the enemy's defensive in high tempo, quickly converting the struggle into the operational depth, and creating favorable conditions for dealing blows on the flanks and rear of his defending groupings with the aim of their encirclement and annihilation."[32] And, after an encirclement has been effected, "the use of atomic weapons in annihilating encircled troops will significantly speed the period of their liquidation."[33] Key targets for tactical atomic attacks in a large encirclement are: (1) "the most important points of command," (2) "the most solid points of resistance," and (3) troops preparing for a breakout.

The heightened requirement for mobility and maneuverability leads to increased emphasis on armored forces. Marshal of the Tank Troops Rotmistrov, Colonel General of the Tank Troops Poluboiarov, and others, have in recent years expressed the authoritative Soviet view on the larger role of the armored forces.[34] Defensively, it is pointed out that "tanks, in comparison with other weapons, are less vulnerable to atomic weapons."[35] But armored forces are essentially an offensive arm. In nuclear warfare their role is primarily to penetrate enemy defenses and then to maintain the tempo of advance. As Major General of the Tank Troops Pinchuk has put it (in 1956): "The mobility, maneuverability, great fire-power and shock-power of the armored forces permits tankists to participate in the initial echelons in the break-through of strongly fortified defensive positions, and to develop a high tempo of offensive in the course of battle."[36] In particular, as Marshal of the Tank Troops Rotmistrov has indicated, tank forces are considered as the most suiltable for effecting a break-through by assault, exploitation of a break-through or of an atomic strike, and encirclement of large enemy groupings.[37] More generally, Soviet infantry also is relied upon to keep up with the necessary pace of movement by means of wide-scale use of tracked, armored infantry-carrier vehicles and infantry-carrying tanks. Artillery support is, in significant degree, to be provided by the wide variety and large numbers of armored self-propelled guns that are organic to all Soviet divisions and by short- and long-range rockets.

In addition to the increased importance of armored forces, airborne landings also assume a greater role in achieving mobility in nuclear warfare. Airborne troops can serve in nuclear warfare to exploit advantage in the offensive, particularly after disruption caused by nuclear strikes, and to block enemy advances when the defense has been punctured by enemy nuclear blows. They also serve as a major reserve in tactical nuclear combat. Finally, as we read in the semi-classified *Military Thought:* "Airborne troops can conduct independent operations in seizing the most important targets and regions in the territory of the enemy. In addition they participate in combined operations . . ."[38] in particular, in the combined forces offensive: "For the swifter isolation of encircled groupings and the achievement of success of operations of the troops in encircling and destroying the enemy, airborne landings will find wide use."[39]

Helicopters are accorded a large-scale role in achieving tactical mobility. Major General Pokrovsky, writing in *Military Thought* in 1955, declared that the wide use of helicopters "will lead in the near future to significant changes in the character of military transport and the tactics of troops operating in the enemy's rear and in mountainous and difficult terrain."[40] Soviet air shows, notably the one in June 1956, have demonstrated this technique, and disclosed the active Soviet research and development of a variety of suitable vertical-lift carriers such as the Yak-24 and Mi-6.

The Soviets are not only providing helicopter transport to troop units, but also are intent upon securing adequate air transport for *all* troops, not only for the airborne forces (which command has its own transport aircraft). Again, Major General Pokrovsky has noted that in nuclear warfare "the perfection of transport aviation will enable the development of the airborne troops and significantly increase the maneuver potentiality of [all] troops, permitting the conduct of operations in great depth, swift creation of superiority in forces in the main sectors, and also the reinforcement of troops on those sectors where an unfavorable situation has developed." [41] Again, too, the Soviets have demonstrated their active research effort to meet this recognized requirement. The most significant step has been the design of a new large turboprop assault transport, publicly unveiled in June 1956. Also, the expansion of the Soviet civil air fleet, now headed by Chief Marshal of Aviation Zhigarev, clearly has the purpose of providing an adequate reserve transport fleet for war as well as expanding civil air service. The Soviet air transports, such as the Tu-114, the Tu-104A, the *Ukraina* (an enlarged version of Antonov's assault transport described above), and the IL-18 *Moskva*, are directly based on military types. But more important than this design economy, they are also readily convertible to wartime military personnel and freight uses.

Mobility is the keynote for forces in the field. Other considerations must be met for strategic dispersal of permanent stations. Most supplies can be prestocked, but the provision of power supply for isolated military installations and forces is a problem. For this purpose, according to Major General Pokrovsky, "the possibility of atomic electric stations at naval bases and fortified areas, etc., deserves serious attention." [42] Engineering preparation, the increased importance of which we have noted earlier, is of course also especially applicable to efforts at "atomic-bomb proofing" submarine pens, airfields, etc.

There has been some inconsistency in Soviet-published estimates of the vulnerability of airfields. One Soviet air officer, writing in late 1954, stated that it was difficult to knock out airfields with atomic bombs, while another Air Force writer stated in 1955 that "at the present time there is no more vulnerable military target than a present-day airfield with armaments and aircraft disposed in a limited area." [43] From these and other discussions, it is clear that the Soviets recognize that airfields are vulnerable, but that certain "hardening" measures can be taken which reduce the vulnerability considerably. But even in 1957 discussions continued to refer to the problem primarily in terms of the danger from a nominal 20KT atomic bomb. [44]

Tactical air delivery of atomic weapons is described primarily, but not exclusively, in terms of the missions of interdiction of supply and operations against enemy air forces. Targets mentioned in Soviet discussions include: airfields, "large concentrations of troops and materiel," bridges, and command and communication centers. [45]

It is useful to recall that the major part of the Soviet air forces remain assigned to support of the surface forces. In all, about two-thirds of Soviet military aircraft are assigned to support (including the airborne forces' transports and naval aviation), and a little over one-half are assigned to the Frontal Aviation, direct equivalent to our TAC (with USAFE and PAF). The Soviet Long-Range Air Force and the fighter component of the joint Air Defense Forces (headed by a ground-forces marshal), have significantly increased in importance. But this increased importance of strategic air offense and defense has not been developed at the expense of the large modern tactical air force with its jet fighter, attack, and light bomber aircraft.

Soviet discussions have not been very informative on the tactical employment of atomic artillery and missiles. Missiles, including even "long-range [ballistic] rocket weapons . . . of operational and strategic types," are said to "constitute *a form of artillery*," in addition to "atomic [gun] artillery" and conventional artillery, and to mark "a new qualitative leap in the development of artillery." [46] Some of their tactical rockets and missiles were shown in the parade on November 7, 1957. Also, in the Soviet view, conventional artillery pieces "still have many combat missions on the contemporary battlefield which cannot be accomplished by atomic weapons, and implementation of which by atomic weapons would not be expedient." [47]

The traditional Soviet emphasis on reserves, operational and strategic, has been heightened by the Soviet evaluation of the requirements for nuclear warfare. We have noted the Soviet belief in the continued need for a *large* ground army. The Soviet belief is directly tied to the need for reserves as replacement for the anticipated heavy losses from enemy nuclear attacks on a wide scale. The most revealing statement of this view is one made in late 1956 by Lieutenant General Krasil'nikov of the General Staff. He declares that nuclear warfare "calls *not* for the reduction in the numbers of various divisions of the combatants, but for their logical further increase, since the threat of wiping out of divisions grows, and for their replacement large reserves will be needed." [48]

In the discussions above, we have surveyed Soviet indications of operational planning and training for tactical nuclear warfare. As one Soviet general noted, as early as 1955, "all the combat preparations of the troops is now permeated with the task of creating an army for the conduct of atomic warfare." [49] The modification of Soviet military doctrine concerning the field employment of the combined armed forces has to date perhaps not been drastic, but it has certainly been significant. The increased attention to mobility and dispersal adds impetus to the Soviet efforts to be more selective in the employment of the principle of mass. The much increased fire-power of present Soviet weapons and units—even aside from atomic weapons— makes this feasible. One additional aspect of the change is the need for greater initiative at all levels of command. The smaller role of political officers at the lower levels in recent years is, in part, intended to instill greater responsibility and initiative in company and field-grade commanders. Marshal of the Tank Troops Rotmistrov has been most explicit in noting the need for greater initiative in modern battle. In his words (in *Military Thought*, in 1955) : "In future war, in which the situation will doubtless be distinguished by its dynamic and sharp changes, it is very important that military commanders at all levels and ranks be able to take audacious and bold decisions. . . . Great independence in the operation of troops will be required, without looking back on neighboring units, without the presently usual elbowing of neighbor units." [50] This requirement is one that presents particular difficulties for the Soviet Army. They have not yet overcome some of the various influences that have distinguished their past record in this respect as a poor one. Nonetheless, the combination of senior commanders who did display initiative in the Second World War, and of new junior officer cadres who have been given a somewhat greater opportunity to exercise initiative than were their predecessors of the 1930's and 1940's, may reduce the problem to acceptable proportions. It would be unwise to *rely* upon past Soviet weaknesses in initiative, though the Soviets probably do not at present meet the standards of the professional American officer in this respect.

The Soviets conclude that "troops that are well trained in anti-atomic and anti-chemical defense can successfully execute any combat mission." [51] Soviet preparation for tactical nuclear warfare extends to training of the troops, development of corresponding doctrine, and of course procurement of the various forms of mobile weapons, transport and communications. Tactical aircraft, mortars, artillery and rockets capable of delivering atomic weapons have been disclosed as forming part of the continuing re-equipment and modernization of the Soviet ground, air and sea forces.

Preparation for tactical nuclear warfare in no way reflects irrevocable decisions on the use of nuclear weapons. It is, however, true that in *any* future war the constant danger of *possible* use of atomic weapons will require the maintenance of "nuclear-ready" forces in the battlefield even if a mutual restraint on the employment of such weapons is exercised. The Soviets intend to be prepared.

The Army remains the major component of the Soviet

armed forces, though without its former predominance, in the thermonuclear era. The basic reason is that the Soviet strategic concept continues to hold that the primary objective of military operations is the destruction of the enemy's military forces and the seizure of his territory. While the Soviets have not yet succeeded in solving the problem of ultimately overcoming the United States itself, the Soviet Army is being groomed for the mission of overrunning the Eurasian continent, overcoming all resistance in the face of tactical nuclear opposition.

Notes to Chapter 7

1. Marshal G. Zhukov, in *Pravda*, August 7, 1956. See also a similar statement by Zhukov on February 4, 1957, cited in *Krasnaia zvezda*, March 23, 1957; and another by Marshal Bulganin, *Pravda*, September 25, 1955.

2. Maj. Gen. Prof. G. Pokrovsky, "Atomic Deadlock?" *News*, March 6, 1956, p. 13. See also Col. N. Sushko, *Sovetskii flot*, March 22, 1957; Yu. Arbatov, *International Affairs*, No. 9, September 1955, p. 60; Col. N. Tsarev, *Ot Shliffena do Gindenburga*, [August 23] 1956, p. 360; Col. A. Strokov, *Istoriia voennogo iskusstva*, [October 17] 1955, p. xxix; Col. V. Vasilenko, in *O sovetskoi voennoi nauke* [June 30] 1954, p. 76; a Retired General, *Izvestiia*, January 19, 1954; Col. I. Sokolov, in *Marksizm-leninizm o voine i armii*, [February 3] 1955, p. 148; Maj. Gen. N. Pukhovsky, *Voennyi vestnik*, No. 1, January 1954, p. 20; Lt. Gen. S. Krasil'nikov, "Military Strategy," in *Bol'shaia Sovetskaia Entsiklopediia*, 2nd. ed., Vol. 41, [April 21] 1956, p. 66; Maj. Gen. M. Smirnov, in *O sovetskoi voennoi nauke*, [June 30] 1954, p. 168; statements by other writers in *O sovetskoi voennoi nauke*, 1954, pp. 54, 104, and 115; Lt. Col Y. Sidel'nikov, *Krasnaia zvezda*, January 24, 1956; Cols. S. Mazhorov and I. Tikhonov, *Krasnaia zvezda*, February 28, 1954; Rear Adm. V. Andreev, *Krasnaia zvezda*, April 25, 1957; and the editorial *Voennaia mysl'*, No. 2, February 1955, p. 12.

3. *Pravda*, August 13, 1955; and May 15, 1956.

4. See R. L. Garthoff "What's Behind Soviet Disarmament?" *Army* [*Combat Forces Journal*], October 1955, pp. 22-24; and Marshal G. Zhukov, *Pravda*, August 7, 1956.

5. *The Economist*, London, December 10, 1955, p. 947, reports a statement to this effect by General Sir John Whitely, Chairman of the NATO Standing Group. Gen. A. Gruenther repeated the figure of 175 Soviet divisions in mid-1956, cited in *U.S. News and World Report*, June 8, 1956, p. 102; so did Hanson W. Baldwin in the New York *Times*, February 3, 1958, in an account based on official interviews.

6. Garthoff, *Army [Combat Forces Journal]*, October 1955, pp. 24-27.

7. For a good review, see Lt. Col. Irving Heymount (USA), "A New Look at the Soviet Ground Forces," *Military Review*, Vol. 36, No. 10, January 1957, pp. 54-62.

8. "Tactics (Military)," *Bol'shaia Sovetskaia Entsiklopediia*, 2nd ed., Vol. 41, [April 21] 1956, p. 334.

9. Marshal G. Zhukov, in *Krasnaia zvezda*, March 23, 1957.

10. Marshal of Tank Troops P. Rotmistrov, *Voennaia mysl'*, No. 2, February 1955, p. 25. Italics in the original.

11. Lt. Gen S. Krasil'nikov, *Marksizm-leninizm o voine i armii*, [November 28] 1956, pp. 148, 150 and 151.

12. Editorial, *Voennaia mysl'*, No. 5, May 1955, p. 14.

13. Col. P. Kashirin, *Krasnaia zvezda*, May 28, 1955.

14. Col. I. N. Levanov, in *Marksizm-leninizm o voine i armii*, [May 20] 1957, p. 227.

15. This feature of the autumn 1953 maneuvers was broadly hinted at in Marshal Bulganin's speech on the anniversary of the Revolution (*Pravda*, November 8, 1953) and a number of subsequent statements.

16. Marshal G. Zhukov, *Pravda*, February 20, 1956; see also Marshal I. Bagramian, *Trud*, February 23, 1956.

17. See, for example, the numerous articles in *Krasnaia zvezda*, particularly August 3, 4, 6, 25, 26, and 28, October 23 and 31, November 13, December 7 and 24, 1954; January 29 and 30, February 1 and 17, May 25, June 29, October 18 and 25, and December 2, 1955; April 18, May 8, 20, and 25, July 21, and September 6, 1956; *Voennye znaniia*, Nos. 8, 9, 10, 11 and 12 (August through December), 1954, and Nos. 2, 3, 6, 7, 9, 11 and 12, 1955, and Nos. 1, 4, 6, 7, and 8, 1956; *Sovetskii flot*, November 13, 18, 23 and 28, and December 7, 1954; January 5, 1955; January 10 and March 30, 1956; *Radio Volga*, February 15 and 17, March 4, April 18, and June 17, 1955; May 21, June 12 and 18, and August 14, 1956, and February 8, and 21, 1957; and various articles in the military journals.

18. *Pamiatka soldatu i serzhantu po zashchite ot atomnogo oruzhiia*, 1954, pp. 34-36.

19. "Engineering Work on the Terrain," *Radio Volga*, June 18, 1956. See Eng. Col. N. Georgievsky, "On the Mechanization of Engineering Work in the Conduct of Operations under Contemporary Circumstances," *Voennaia mysl'*, No. 10, October 1955, pp. 15-25; and see Maj. Gen. of Eng. Tech. Service G. Pokrovsky, in *Marksizm-leninizm o voine i armii*, 1955, p. 169 (reprinted from *Voennaia mysl'*, No. 9, September 1954, p. 24).

20. G. Starko, in *Atomnoe oruzhie (Atomic Weapons)*, 2nd ed., Voenizdat, Moscow, [October 31] 1955, p. 203 (reprinted from an article appearing in *Vestnik vozdushnogo flota*, No. 6, June 1954).

21. Lt. Gen. A. Tsvetkov, *Voennaia mysl'*, No. 3, March 1955, p. 51.

22. Maj. Gen. of Tank Troops O. Losik, *Krasnaia zvezda*, March 30, 1957. See also Lt. Col. V. Larionov, *Krasnaia zvezda*, January 10, 1957.

167

23. Col. V. Mochalov, "Mobile Defense," *Krasnaia zvezda,* March 30, 1956. See also Maj. Gen. Tsigichko, "Some Questions of the Tactics of American Troops under Conditions of the Employment of Atomic Weapons," *Voennaia mysl',* No. 4, April 1955, p. 82; Lt. Col. V. Larionov, "Maneuver in Defense," *Krasnaia zvezda,* January 10, 1957; Larionov, "Command of Troops in Contemporary Combat," *Krasnaia zvezda,* March 19, 1957; and Maj. Gen. of Tank Troops O. Losik, "An Important Condition for the High Mobility of Troops," *Krasnaia zvezda,* March 30, 1957.

24. Col. V. Mochalov, "Peculiarities of Offensive Operations of a Field Army in Contemporary Circumstances," *Voennaia mysl',* No. 7, July 1954, p. 82.

25. Maj. Gen. G. Pokrovsky, *Voennaia mysl',* No. 9, September 1954, p. 23 (reprinted in the collection *Marksizm-leninizm o voine i armii,* 1955, p. 168).

26. *Ibid.,* p. 23 (p. 169).

27. Col. V. Yakovkin, "Atomic Weapons and Anti-Atomic Defense of the Troops: Special Features of the Actions of Tank Troops," *Krasnaia zvezda,* June 29, 1955. See also the manual *Pamiatka soldatu i serzhantu po zashchite ot atomnogo oruzhiia,* 1954, p. 36.

28. Maj. Gen. N. Tsigichko, *Voennaia mysl',* No. 4, April 1955, p. 81. And see Col. N. Kupenko, "Employment of Atomic Weapons in the Offensive," *Krasnaia zvezda,* September 21, 1957.

29. "Tactics (Military)," *Bol'shaia Sovetskaia Entsiklopediia,* 2nd ed., Vol. 41, [April 21] 1956, p. 541.

30. For the pre-atomic (pre-1953) development of Soviet doctrine, see Garthoff, *Soviet Military Doctrine,* 1953, pp. 97-120.

31. Lt. Col. V. Parno and Lt. Col. A. Ekimovsky, "On the Question of Encirclement and Annihilation of the Enemy," *Voennaia mysl',* No. 9, September 1955, p. 16.

32. *Ibid.*

33. *Ibid.,* p. 26.

34. Marshal of the Tank Troops P. Rotmistrov, *Voennaia mysl',* No. 2, February 1955, p. 25; Rotmistrov, *Voennye znaniia,* No. 9, September 1955, p. 5; Col. N. Garvysh, "The Development of the Armored Troops and Their Influence on the Military Art," *Voennaia mysl',* No. 9, September 1955, p. 11; Col. V. Yakovkin, *Krasnaia zvezda,* June 29, 1955; Col. V. Mironov and Engineer Col. A. Rokhmachev, "Armored Troops of the Soviet Army," *Voennye znaniia,* No. 7, July 1956, p. 5; Col. Gen. of Tank Troops P. Poluboiarov, "On Guard Over the Peaceful, Creative Labor of the Soviet People," *Pravda,* September 9, 1956; and Maj. Gen. of Tank Troops P. Pinchuk, "The Armored Forces of the Soviet Army," *Krasnaia zvezda,* September 9, 1956.

35. Cols. V. Mironov and A. Rokhmachev, *Voennye znaniia,* No. 7, July 1956, p. 5. See also Marshal of the Tank Troops P. Rotmistrov, *Voennaia mysl',* No. 2, February, 1955, p. 25.

36. Maj. Gen. of Tank Troops P. Pinchuk, *Krasnaia zvezda,* September 9, 1956.

37. Marshal of Tank Troops P. Rotmistrov, *Voennaia mysl',* No. 2, February

1955, p. 25; Col. Gen. of Tank Troops P. Poluboiarov, *Pravda*, September 9, 1956; Col. N. Garvysh, *Voennaia mysl'*, No. 9, September 1955, p. 11.

38. Capt. 2d Rank N. V'iunenko, *Voennaia mysl'*, No. 2, February 1955, p. 27. See also Lt. Gen. V. Margelov, "A Young Developing Service," *Krasnaia zvezda*, December 28, 1957.

39. Lt. Cols. V. Parno and A. Ekimovsky, *Voennaia mysl'*, No. 9, September 1955, p. 18.

40. Maj. Gen. G. Pokrovsky, *Voennaia mysl'*, No. 3, March 1955, p. 27. See also M. L. Mil', *Vertolety* (Helicopters), Znanie, Moscow, 1957, pp. 29-30.

41. The quoted statement is by Maj. Gen. G. Pokrovsky, in *Marksizm-leninizm o voine*, 1955, p. 169 (reprinted from *Voennaia mysl'*, No. 9, September 1954, p. 23). See also Col. Yu. Pshenianik, *Sovetskaia aviatsiia*, March 17, 1957.

42. Maj. Gen. G. Pokrovsky, in *Marksizm-leninizm o voine*, 1955, p. 170 (reprinted from *Voennaia mysl'*, No. 9, September 1954, p. 25); and Engineer Lt. Col. M. Gvozdev, "Some Means of the Employment of Atomic Energy for [the Generation of] Power for Military Purposes," *Voennaia mysl'*, No. 9, September 1955, p. 34.

43. Maj. R. Batalov, "The Operation of Tactical Aviation Employing the Atomic Bomb," *Vestnik vozdushnogo flota*, No. 12, December 1954, p. 68; and Eng. Maj. S. Lidin, "The Atomic Weapon and Anti-Atomic Defense of Airfields," *Vestnik vozdushnogo flota*, No. 3, March 1955, p. 88. Also, see V. Skopin, *Militarizm*, [August 3] 1956, p. 433, for the latter view.

44. Eng. Lt. Col. P. Mikhailov, "The Effects of an Atomic Weapon on an Airfield," *Sovetskaia aviatsiia*, January 16, 1957. See also I. Goviazin and G. Zapol'sky, "Anti-Atomic Defense of Airbases," *Kryl'ia rodiny*, No. 7, July 1956, p. 20.

45. Eng. Lt. Col. P. Safonov, "Aircraft, Carriers of Atomic Bombs, and Their Employment," *Vestnik vozdushnogo flota*, No. 9, September 1954, p. 79; and Col. V. Emelin, "On Aircraft, Carriers of Atomic Bombs," *Krasnaia zvezda*, January 25, 1955.

46. Col. Gen. of Artillery N. S. Fomin, "Soviet Artillery Day," *Sovetskaia rossiia*, November 18, 1956; Col. Gen. of Artillery F. A. Samsonov, "On the Eve of Artillery Day," *Radio Moscow*, November 17, 1956; and Marshal of Artillery M. N. Chistiakov, "Artillery of the Soviet Army," *Krasnaia zvezda*, November 18, 1956.

47. Col. Gen. of Artillery F. A. Samsonov, *Radio Moscow*, November 17, 1956.

48. Lt. Gen. S. Krasil'nikov, *Marksizm-leninizm o voine i armii*, [November 28] 1956, p. 148.

49. Maj. Gen. N. Tsigichko, *Voennaia mysl'*, No. 4, April 1955, p. 81.

50. Marshal of the Tank Troops P. Rotmistrov, *Voennaia mysl',* No. 2, February 1955, p. 26. See also Lt. Col. V. Larionov, "Command of Troops in Contemporary Combat," *Krasnaia zvezda*, March 17, 1957.

51. Maj. Gen. N. Tsigichko, *Voennaia mysl'*, No. 4, April 1955, p. 82.

CHAPTER 8

AIR POWER IN SOVIET STRATEGY

The Second World War everywhere provided an impetus to the re-evaluation of the role and potentialities of air power. Paradoxically, in the Soviet Union the war also served indirectly to retard development of air doctrine by the virtual canonization of the "Stalinist" military doctrine of 1945. Intemperate and uncritical praise of Soviet wartime operations—which featured almost exclusively air support of ground forces—inhibited constructive criticism and innovation. The period from the end of the war until 1953 was consequently dominated by the dogmatization of World War II doctrine limiting air power to the role of supporting the ground forces. Belatedness in recognition of the significance of new weapons and the new world geostrategic picture was born of the "freeze" on doctrine during Stalin's lifetime and of the retardation caused by excessive devotion to the doctrine that had suceeded for the Soviets in World War II. A natural impetus for re-evaluation of the role of air power, for seeking new perspectives in doctrine, and for speculation on atomic and other new weapons existed in 1946, but was silenced and curbed from mid-1947 until mid-1953. For this reason it is useful to begin by looking back briefly at the few premature expressions of a "new look" in air doctrine which appeared in 1946, and then at the Stalinist postwar period, as background to the developments since 1953.[1]

170

Air Power

The main focus here will be on the development of Soviet views of strategic air power, because the missions of support to the surface forces and of air defense have in general been less affected both by the Stalinist freeze and subsequent thaw. But it is quite important to realize that the Soviet development of a strategic air doctrine and capability has *not* been at the expense of a steadily modernized and large air establishment to provide support capability for the ground forces, airborne troops, and the Navy, and an increasingly important and strong air defense force. Soviet strategy continues to regard these air-power missions as crucial, as well as now recognizing a greater role for long-range air forces.

POSTWAR AIR DOCTRINE UNDER STALIN

Major General of Aviation Tatarchenko, former Imperial Army flyer and prewar neo-Douhetist, was the author of a thought-provoking article which appeared in the Air Force journal *Herald of the Air Fleet* in mid-1946. In this unusual article he surveyed (albeit superficially) recent developments in atomic energy, radar, jet propulsion, aerodynamics, and missiles, and sought to raise the problem of revision of doctrine on air power in the light of these developments. In his survey Tatarchenko assumed that a greater role would be given to strategic bombing:

> . . . it has now become an indisputable fact that along with operational-tactical aviation, the main task of which consists of direct support to the operations of ground troops, *there must also exist strategic aviation.*
> It would appear that contemporary air forces are capable of deciding not only tactical, but also operational and *strategic tasks, which no arm other than aviation can fulfill.*
> Concerning the form of future war the following thoughts suggest themselves: *in future engagements the place of application of the main force will be not so much the front as the rear of the enemy. . . .*[2]

171

General Tatarchenko, although unique and unsuccessful in his ambitious attempt to suggest that the meaning of new techlogical developments for Soviet air doctrine was a reorientation of strategic concept, was not alone in recognizing an increased role for strategic air power. A General Staff officer, Major General Korkodinov, in a contemporary article, wrote that while usually air (and sea) operations were "component parts" of strategic operations by the ground forces, in some cases air or sea operations might have "strategic significance, that is be [independent] strategic operations."[3] As an example he cited the Allied strategic bombing of Germany in 1944-45. Another author, in 1946, in surveying Allied air operations, also recognized the increased role of air power: "In the course of the Second World War it [aviation] proved able to solve a series of operational *and even strategic missions* both in combined operations with other arms and the fleet *and independently*, and its combat operations assumed an unprecedented scale."[4] Nonetheless he also repeated the doctrinal dogma upholding the primacy of the combined-arms team: "Of course, its increased relative standing does not at all provide grounds for considering aviation an exceptional or the only means of combat and victory. Of this the experience of the Second World War eloquently bears witness, showing that victory can be achieved only as the result of the combined forces of all arms of ground troops, aviation, and the navy."[5] Marshal of Aviation Skripko, then Deputy Commander of the Long-Range Air Force, also declared: "One of the means of active operations against the military potential of the enemy is strategic aviation. The threat of its massed operations alone compels the enemy to hold large forces in his air-defense system, diverting them from the front. . . ."[6]

It would not be correct to conclude that these few statements from the early postwar period marked a prevailing trend toward full recognition of the increased importance of strategic air power. The statements above, moderate as they are, none-

172

theless are exceptional. More typical was the comment in the authoritative journal *Military Thought* by the Soviet Air Force reviewer of General Spaatz's article in *Foreign Affairs* in 1946. He attributed a "hyperbolic exaggeration of the role and significance of strategic aviation" to General Spaatz.[7]

In tracing the integration of strategic bombing into Soviet air doctrine in the postwar era, it is necessary to bear in mind the persistence of conservatism. We have seen the continuity to the present of the doctrinal rejection of reliance on any one arm and reaffirmation of the concept of the combined-arms team. Moreover, strategic bombing has often been expressly held to a supplementary role. An Air Force officer, Colonel Volkov, writing in the General Staff publication *Military Thought* in 1949, flatly stated that *"no* independent sections of aviation can play such a role as operations conducted in the interests of the ground troops."[8] But this judgment did not mean a lack of interest in long-range bombing.

A comprehensive statement of the Soviet doctrine in the postwar period appeared in an article by Colonel General of Aviation Nikitin in 1949 in the authoritative *Military Thought*:

> Soviet military science holds alien any form of the one-sided theory, widely prevalent in the capitalist countries, which considers aviation as the most important factor of contemporary war, capable practically independently of deciding the outcome of war. Our military science recognizes that victory in modern war is achieved by the combined efforts of all forms and arms of the armed forces, that no one arm can replace another, and that each of them must participate on the basis of able employment of all their characteristics and combat capabilities. On the basis of this deeply scientific principle, *Soviet military science considers that the outcome of war under contemporary conditions is decided on the field of battle by means of the annihilation of the armed forces of the enemy,* and that one of the most important tasks of aviation is active assistance to the ground and naval forces in all forms of their combat activity. *This definition of the fundamental mission of aviation is not contradicted by the need to*

employ part of its forces to strike the deep rear of the enemy, on his military-industrial targets, but our military science does not consider such blows an end in themselves, but only a helpful means of creating favorable conditions for the success of the combat operations of the ground and naval forces. The structure of our military air forces is established on the basis of the scientific definition of the role and significance of aviation in contemporary war.[9]

Thus we see that in the postwar Stalinist era strategic bombing came to be accepted as a supplement to, or perhaps a new member of, the essentially ground-oriented combined-arms team.

Before we examine the post-Stalinist period, it is useful to note two other signs of the rising role of strategic air power in the Stalinist period. One is the way in which Soviet military men described their own long-range bombing in World War II; the other is the actual construction of a fleet of long-range bombers.

The great emphasis placed on the study of the experience of the Soviet-German war, as we have noted, affected doctrinal development relating to air power. However, there was recognition of the need to give a greater, even if only complementary, role to strategic aviation. Consequently, an interesting characteristic of the postwar attempt to integrate the strategic aviation mission into the established doctrine has been the retroactive ascription of strategic bombing to Soviet operations in the Second World War.

The tendency to "make history" the easy way, by sleight-of-writing-hand, had begun during the war. Lieutenant General (later Chief Marshal) of Aviation Golovanov, wartime chief of the Long-Range Air Force, wrote in *Red Star*, in November 1942, of his force: "Its aircraft, from the first day of the war, made mass raids on the deep rear of the enemy, making attacks from the air on political and economic centers of Fascist Germany and its satellites."[10] This statement was quite false. After a number of attempts which ended in complete failure, Berlin had finally been bombed by a regiment of bombers of the Baltic Fleet air arm under Naval Colonel (now Colonel General of Aviation) Preobrazhensky on August 7, 1941.[11] There were no further long-range raids on the enemy's political and industrial centers until 1943.

In the early postwar period, however, Marshal of Aviation Vershinin, Marshal of Aviation Skripko, Colonel General (now Marshal) of Aviation Sudets, and others had quite correctly stated (in Sudet's words) that "long-range aviation in the course of the war worked predominantly in the interests of the [ground] front operations."[12] Marshal of Aviation Skripko, in addition to noting that "our heavy bombers operated predominantly in the interests of the front operations," also provided the interesting information that "approximately one-third of the sorties of long-range aviation were conducted in attacks on the enemy's *troops* and his tactical deployment."[13] The remainder were almost all interdiction missions, with the exception of some for supply of partisans in the enemy's rear.

In the period since 1949 there have been a number of statements exaggerating the wartime role of strategic bombing in Soviet operations. For example, in 1950, Colonel General (now Marshal) of Aviation Rudenko declared: "Long-range bomber flights against strategic targets in the deep rear of the enemy occupied a significant place in the operations of Soviet aviation. These flights were begun in the very first months of the war."[14] But the limited aspect of this doctrinal revision is also apparent in the tenor of Rudenko's article. He was quite critical of what he termed "the pseudo-scientific theory that a war can be won by air bombing alone," which he attributed to the United States in World War II and which he said had "proved itself worthless." All of these statements discuss long-range and strategic bombing as a supplement or complement to the basic and decisive combined-arms operations on the battlefield.

The true nature of the Soviet wartime bombing strategy, allegedly "completely confirmed" by the war, was described in the *Herald of the Air Fleet*, official Air Force organ, by an Air Force colonel:

The 1941-45 war completely confirmed the *correctness of the views of Soviet military science on the place and role of bomber aviation* in contemporary war. In the Great Fatherland War our bombers, together with fighters and attack planes, were widely employed *to secure the operations of the ground troops,* operating in close combined action with them.[15]

Nonetheless it is clear that by 1949 strategic air power was being allotted a higher role than previously. In the years since, the retroactive attribution of a strategic or long-range bombing history to the Soviet air forces of World War II has continued.[16] One of the recent accounts is also of interest for the emphasis on the economic and morale disruption missions. Colonel General Kurochkin wrote in *Military Thought* in mid-1955:

> The Soviet command, even in circumstances of an unfavorable relation of forces in the air, was able to organize and to conduct a number of air attacks on targets in the strategic rear of the enemy, including his economic centers such as sources of oil. These blows weakened the military-economic potential of the enemy, undermined the morale of his people and troops, and made possible raising the morale of our army and people.[17]

Thus the Soviet military leadership has, throughout the postwar period, sought to integrate long-range aviation into its air-power establishment within the basic framework of the continuing strategic concept. Bombing of the enemy economy in a general nuclear war would complement the actions of the Soviet long-range air force and all other military forces against the enemy military forces, ranging in their deployment from "front lines" to SAC bases in the United States.

As Soviet military thinking evolved toward these views on the role of long-range air power, a strenuous effort was under way to provide the long-range capability to correspond to this emerging doctrinal requirement.

The wartime decision by Stalin in the spring of 1942, to

establish an independent long-range air force, shows that he realized such an arm had potentialities. It is quite likely that Marshal Golovanov impressed upon him the need for better bombers with which to equip this force. The obsolete TB-3 heavy bomber of the mid-1930's, which the Soviets still had in 1941 when war broke out, was ineffective. The TB-7 and Pe-8 which replaced it were, while an improvement, not adequate to the needs of the time, and no match for the German fighters of the day. Consequently the backbone of the Soviet "long-range" air force was the American twin-engine B-25 bomber, provided in substantial numbers under lend-lease aid. The Soviets insistently requested B-24 and B-17 heavy bombers, but only a single B-24 and no B-17's were provided. In 1943, at Teheran, according to General Arnold, Stalin asked "innumerable and very intelligent questions . . . about our long-range *bombers*," although "he was just beginning to learn something about strategic bombing." [18] It is probable that this attitude—placing the weapon ahead of the doctrine—has characterized much of subsequent Soviet development. By chance four American B-29A aircraft crash-landed in Siberia in 1944, giving to the Soviets an unexpected major gain in their efforts to construct a heavy bomber. The Soviets publicly unveiled the Tu-4, Lieutenant General A. Tupolev's copy of the B-29, in August 1947, precisely three years after acquiring the American bombers.

But again, history is not permitted to stand in the service of truth when it can be distorted to Soviet advantage. And so we read, as early as 1949, in the *Great Soviet Encyclopedia*: "In the period of the Great Fatherland War, Tupolev created a bomber superior in its tactical flight characteristics to aircraft of a similar class in Germany, England, and the U.S.A." [19]*

Subsequently while producing the Tu-4 in quantity and training a resuscitated and enlarged long-range air force in its

---

* In 1946 Marshal of Aviation Skripko had admitted that the American B-29 was "the most powerful long-range bomber participating in the recent war." (*Red Star*, August 11, 1946.)

use,* the Soviet aviation research and development organization worked toward the attainment of modern jet bomber aircraft suitable for long-range operations. The talent of German scientists and engineers was exploited to prepare parallel aircraft designs and even prototypes. But German scientists were not permitted to work on the actual jet bombers in the Soviet design bureaus headed by Lieutenant General A. Tupolev, Lieutenant General S. Iliushin, and Major General V. Miasishchev, all of the Aviation Engineering Service. In May 1954 the twin-turbojet medium *Badger*† and the four-turbojet heavy *Bison* bombers were publicly flown in Moscow. A year later the *Badger* and *Bison* were flown in operational-unit numbers, and a new multi-turboprop long-range bomber, the *Bear*, was disclosed. The Soviet Air Force is closing the gap in aircraft types available for long-range employment although for the next few years the United States will continue to have a substantial lead over the Soviet Union in numbers of modern jet bombers.

So we see that beginning in the Stalinist period efforts which have since borne fruit were under way to develop modern long-range bombers. A former Soviet Air Force officer who defected to the West reports that Stalin gave increased attention to strategic bombing after he had been in Potsdam in 1945 and personally observed the destruction in Berlin caused by the strategic aviation of the Western Allies.[20] Lieutenant Colonel Tokaev, a former Soviet Air Force technical officer, has reported that the long-range bomber force was being given special attention by the Politburo at the time of his defection in 1948.[21] In any event, it is evident that Stalin gave his approval to the development of this new arm (the West's primacy

---

* The wartime Long-Range Air Force (ADD) was converted into the Eighteenth Air Army of the Air Force of the Soviet Army in December 1944. In early 1946 it was re-established as an autonomous Long-Range Air Force (now termed DA).

† *Badger, Bison, Bear* are Western designations to identify these aircraft. The Tu-4 is called *Bull*. In Soviet parlance, the heavy four-jet *Bison* is called the *Sledgehammer* (*Molot*).

in which, as with the atomic bomb, he may have envied for reasons of prestige as well as for its undeniable military utility). But it is equally clear that Stalin did not permit Soviet military doctrine to be basically altered by interest in strategic bombing. He was providing a useful arm for this purpose to supplement the decisive action of the combined forces on and over the battlefield.

This policy was Stalin's because at the least he gave it his approval. But it was not Stalin's alone. The post-Stalin Soviet military leadership has continued to adhere to the essential doctrine of combined-arms action in implementation of the strategic concept of destruction of the enemy's military forces.

In discussing Soviet views on the role of strategic air power in the postwar Stalinist period we have noted no reference to an obviously crucial aspect: the influence and effect of nuclear weapons. Similarly there was no sign of attention to the geostrategic problems posed by the intercontinental combat ranges. It is quite likely that technical and operational aspects of these issues were considered by the Soviet General Staff and air and naval staffs, although no indication of this is known.

Soviet Air Doctrine since Stalin

Now let us turn to the post-Stalinist period. It has been characterized by explicit awareness of the influence of nuclear capabilities on the significance of strategic bombing. This is evidenced in an article in *Red Star* (in 1955):

> The creation of atomic bombs has significantly increased the striking power of bombers. The utilization of turbojet propulsion led to a growth in speed and practicable ceiling of flight. As a consequence, the significance of heavy bomber aviation with a large operational radius, as a means of air attack for the destruction of important strategic targets in the deep rear, has been raised.
>
> With the development of air science and technology, strategic

179

bombers have become all the more powerful and effective a weapon for air attack. However, the means of air defense have been perfected simultaneously.[22]

And, less explicitly, an article in *Military Thought* in early 1955 marked as "an important task" of Soviet military science "the further working out of new forms and means of crushing blows against the enemy."[23]

Thus the Soviets have been developing a greater understanding of the implications of nuclear weapons. Nonetheless, as Marshal Zhukov asserted, both in 1955 and 1956: "One must bear in mind that one cannot win a war with atomic bombs alone" and that "air power and nuclear weapons by themselves cannot determine the outcome of an armed conflict."[24] And again in 1957 he re-emphasized that *"in the postwar construction of the armed forces we are proceeding from the fact that victory in future war will be achieved only by the combined efforts of all arms of the armed forces and on the basis of their coordinated employment in war."*[25]

And an air force officer, Colonel Pshenianik, wrote in *Soviet Aviation* in March 1957: "No one arm or component of the armed forces can replace another, and cannot decide the outcome of an operation, much less of war as a whole. . . ."[26]

Several Soviet accounts for general popular reading have described the role of "long-range bomber aviation" (presumably the enemy's, but also possibly their own) in terms including economic and city bombing. For example, a civil defense manual (in 1953) stated:

> Long-range bomber aviation is intended for attacks on targets deep in the rear of the enemy with the objectives of undermining his military-economic power, affecting the morale of his armies and population, disorganizing communications, and gaining air supremacy. Long-range aviation is the main threat to the rear.[27]

Nonetheless long-range striking capabilities continue usually to be discussed in terms of attacks on enemy military forces

180

deep in the rear, in indirect combined action with the main combined operations forces in the theater. Lieutenant General Tsvetkov declared in the authoritative *Military Thought* in 1955:

> The great operational radius of contemporary aviation creates the conditions for the conduct of independent air operations seeking the destruction of important targets or groupings of the enemy deep in the rear. Such an activity as air operations to destroy strategic military targets of the enemy, and also the disruption of naval and airborne operations, may not be connected directly with operations of the ground forces or navy. Positive results of such air operations can show significant influence on the general course of the armed conflict and thus predestine the subsequent success of the operations of the land and sea forces, and especially if they are properly harmonized with one another.[28]

"Strategic bombing" is variously construed in the West, sometimes as all the operations of the Strategic Air Command, sometimes as a strategy of massive destruction of the enemy's economic and political-morale base by bombing in order to win a military decision. The importance of strategic bombing in the first, general, sense has greatly increased in the Soviet Union. At the same time, Soviet military thinkers continue to reject reliance on a strategy of destroying the enemy's economy. They assign to economic-population bombing an important role complementary to the main military effort by combined military forces seeking a decision by destruction of the enemy's military forces in being. In a general nuclear war, this "combined action" to destroy the enemy's military forces includes of course a major and indeed crucial role for the long-range air forces: destruction of the enemy's strategic striking power—SAC, the British Bomber Command, and probably U.S. and U.K. fleet carrier forces. And in a general nuclear war we can expect additional direct bombing of selected economic targets, in view of the Soviet recognition of the value of "simultaneous action against the army and the economy of the enemy."[29]

181

Colonel Denisov, an Air Force writer, stated in 1953: "Our air doctrine considers necessary the action of air power against military-industrial centers and communications of the enemy, evaluating this action as a means *complementing but by no means replacing* operations conducted by the combined efforts of all the armed forces."[30] Thus, within an over-all strategy of military action directed primarily against the enemy's military forces in being, the Soviets recognize the value and even necessity of bombing military industry, and even the economy in general "with the aim of undermining the economic potential of the country."[31] Thus the Soviets have come to recognize the importance of strategic bombing along with operations against the enemy's armed forces. Lt. General Krasil'nikov (in 1956) spelled this out very clearly:

> Powerful blows against the armed forces—land, air and sea— will clearly be combined with intensive and determined operations against the rear of the enemy country, against its economy, since only such a combination of attacks can speed victory. . . . Thus intensive and determined operations of the ground forces with the aim of defeating the armed forces of the enemy, and operations of the air forces to gain air supremacy, must have combined with them powerful systematic strategic air attacks on the basic military-economic centers and communications centers of the hostile countries, constant intensive submarine surface and air combat against his sea communications, and other forms of combat aimed at undermining the economic might of the enemy and weakening his will for resistance.[32]

But while now giving conscious and explicit recognition to the increased importance of bombing the enemy rear with high-yield modern weapons, the Soviets, as we have seen, have continued to reject a strategy based on this action at the expense of the primary "counter-force" missions against all enemy military capabilities. Major General Khlopov, writing in *Military Thought* in 1954, described as "defective in its foundation" the American reliance on "the theory of strategic air war, exaggerating the potentialities of this one form of the

182

armed forces" and *erroneously* assuming that "powerful flights of strategic bombers can so effectively and quickly undermine the military-economic might and morale of the enemy that his will and ability to resist will be broken."[33]

How then is a major war to be won today? In the nuclear era as before, according to the General Staff organ *Military Thought* in 1955, "the defeat of the enemy will be achieved above all by means of the annihilation of his armed forces."[34]

It may be significant that the Soviet long-range heavy and medium bomber force is titled the "Long-Range Air Force" rather than the "Strategic Air Force." The former designation reflects simply the capability which distinguishes the weapon system—range of striking power. The latter may imply by inference the target system of strategic capabilities for war. Marshal Zhukov, in his speech to the Twentieth Party Congress, mentioned various categories of aviation including both "strategic" and "long range," suggesting that part of the Long-Range Air Force may secretly be designated as the "Strategic Aviation" and be assigned missions of strategic bombing of the enemy's economy and cities.[35]

At present we can only speculate on the influence that Western views on strategic air power may have in the future on Soviet doctrine. The new tendency to study bourgeois military science more seriously should acquaint Soviet airmen with views previously not expressed in the Soviet Union. One illustration was the translation and publication in the official *Herald of the Air Fleet,* in June 1955, of an address by General Curtis LeMay on the mission of the Strategic Air Command. There were no comments or "corrections," and there was no refutation, except for one statement introducing the translation, which claimed: "LeMay obviously exaggerates the condition and combat potentialities of U.S. strategic air power."[36] Earlier at least one volume of the *United States Strategic Bombing Survey* (The War in the Pacific) had been published in translation, in 1949, reissued in 1956. It is perhaps of interest that this translation was made and published by the

Soviet Navy, rather than by the Air Force of the Soviet Army. The introduction to the translation contained a *caveat* that the data was not entirely trustworthy and alleged that the purpose of the USSBS was to prove superiority of the Air Force, by fair means or foul, as a bargaining tool of the USAF in interservice budgetary competition.[37] Nonetheless the translation of the volume (and perhaps others) was hardly undertaken to "demonstrate" this propaganda point.

Belated recognition of the strategic implications of the greatly enhanced striking capabilities of long-range air power came from Marshal of Aviation Rudenko (First Deputy Commander-in-Chief of the Air Forces) in 1955:

> Under conditions of contemporary war, when atomic and hydrogen weapons are in the armament of armies, and jet aircraft are capable of covering great distances, the role of the air forces has still further risen. They must be prepared not only to annihilate any hostile aircraft which appears in the Soviet sky, but also to deal crushing blows to an aggressor.[38]

In his speech at the Twentieth Party Congress in February 1956, Marshal Zhukov stressed the increased importance of air power:

> In the composition of our armed forces the relative weight of the air forces and air defense forces have significantly grown. . . .
> The Central Committee of the Party and the Government devotes particular attention to the development of the air forces, as a most important means of maintaining the security of our Motherland. At the present time we have first class jet aviation capable of meeting any tasks which are placed before it in case of attack by an aggressor.[39]

And a few months after Marshal Zhukov's statement, Chief Marshal of Aviation Zhigarev commented more specifically:

> The relative weight of aviation in the composition of the armed forces has significantly grown in the postwar period.

> And this is entirely understandable since weapons of enormous destructive power are now part of the armament of contemporary armies, and in order to guarantee the security of our country it is necessary to have strong and perfected means of air defense, and also our own powerful aviation ready at the call of the Party and Government to fulfill any mission in the interests of our state and our people.[40]

Though these are but statements of an obvious truth, they are unprecedented and unsurpassed as "air force self-assertion" in the U.S.S.R.

Perhaps the most significant signs of awareness of the potentialities of a long-range nuclear and thermonuclear striking capability have been displayed by the post-Stalin *political* leadership. Their evaluation of the importance and necessity of such a capability is implicitly in terms of its effectiveness for *deterrence,* and possibly also for aggressive political purposes of threat or blackmail. It is important to realize that such a view is quite consonant with the strategic concept for winning a war without *reliance* upon strategic bombing. That is to say: While long-range air and missile attacks on the enemy's long-range striking power would be crucially important in a general nuclear war, if any limitation on use of nuclear weapons were found advantageous and possible, the Soviet deterrence employment of this capability could be extended into war to enforce restrictions to a non-nuclear or limited nuclear campaign. Since the Soviet strategy and force structure are not based upon a necessary reliance on strategic air power, the Soviets thus retain the choice on non-use of this weapon system, Soviet superiority in other forms of military power being assumed to ensure a high probability of success in achieving the objectives of a non-nuclear or even limited (tactical) nuclear war.

In the Soviet view, even in a general nuclear war the role of strategic air power, while absolutely necessary and crucial, is not "decisive" in the sense of fully determining the outcome of the war. Great as the importance of long-range striking

Soviet Strategy in the Nuclear Age

power would be in such a war, the use of massive ground forces to seize and hold territory after destroying the balance of the enemy's military forces is considered ultimately decisive.

The earliest Soviet allusions to intercontinental weapon systems appeared in late 1953 and early 1954. The first appeared in a Soviet government statement commenting on President Eisenhower's "atoms for peace" address to the United Nations in December 1953.[41] Similar statements have been repeated by Khrushchev and Bulganin since 1955. These statements have referred primarily to the "state of the art" of weapons development rather than to specific achieved Soviet capabilities. On the other hand, ever since the early 1950's the Soviets have declared themselves "ready to deal a crushing rebuff to any aggressor." These statements have continued to appear frequently in the post-Stalinist period and have been characteristic of both the Malenkov and Khrushchev administrations. During the past several years the Soviets have on a number of occasions alluded publicly to their growing intercontinental aviation and missile capability.

In military writings, in political statements, and in their weapons procurement program, the Soviets display their increasing interest in developing a long-range striking force. The objectives of this weapon system are: first, to serve as a deterrent (and perhaps as a threat) in peacetime or limited war, and possibly extending into a major war; and second, in a general nuclear war, to form one important weapon in the total effort to destroy the enemy's military strength. To destroy the key enemy weapons launched from another continent, it is necessary to have and to use an intercontinental capability. Under the Soviet strategic concept, long-range bombing forces would be employed primarily against distant enemy military capabilities, especially bases of the Strategic Air Command located in the United States and advanced areas overseas, and probably also against key military-industrial targets.

Since it is generally accepted that the priority target of long-range bombing forces of each side is the enemy's long-

186

range bombing force, one may question the practical significance of the distinction between the strategic concept of destruction of the economy and population and the concept of destruction of the military forces of the enemy, especially with the
employment of multi-megaton weapons of extremely large
destructive radius. But the distinction remains very great. In
the American concept, use of SAC to neutralize the Soviet
Long-Range Air Force is essentially a necessary prior *diversion*
of effort from strategic bombing. The way to *win* a war is still
seen as the subsequent destruction of the Soviet economic-
population structure; or, at the least, the threat to do so
followed if necessary by its fulfillment. In the Soviet concept,
the use of the Long-Range Air Force to neutralize SAC is not
a diversion but the primary mission of that force. The way to
win a war is still considered to be the subsequent destruction
of the rest of the enemy's military forces, of all arms, wherever
they may be, and the physical seizure and control of territory
and its resources.

There are many important implications of this difference.
One is that the *employment* of nuclear and thermonuclear
weapons is *necessary* in the United States concept, but *not* in
the Soviet one. The Soviets thus retain greater freedom of
choice. If a genuine stalemate in intercontinental capabilities
is achieved in a pre-hostilities period, the United States might
be endangered by the neutralization of its entire strategy, and
hence of its ability to act, whereas the Soviet strategy would
be served by this development.

Strategic bombing of the economy and population thus has
not been adopted as the foundation of Soviet strategy in the
nuclear era. In a general nuclear war the role of the Soviet
Long-Range Air Force and missiles in neutralizing the enemy
(American and British) strategic air power by powerful strikes
would be of crucial importance. But in the Soviet view, while
crucially important, long-range air power remains one of several
broadly complementary key elements in total military power,
all of which are essential. And in a non-nuclear or limited

war, the role and significance of strategic aviation would clearly be less, although it could perform important missions complementing the combined operations of land, air, and possibly sea forces within a theater. The current Soviet military and political leadership do have a clear awareness of the need for powerful long-range bombing (and, later, missile and possibly other intercontinental) capabilities to attempt to neutralize SAC, either by stalemate or by its destruction.

The mission of conducting the struggle for air superiority or supremacy has other aspects, too, in an atomic war. The highest priority in time would, as we have implied, be given to attacking the enemy's air-atomic delivery forces. Colonel Safonov (in 1954) made a rare specific mention of this obviously key target, *"airfields on which atomic-carrying aircraft are based."*[42] Soviet air doctrine on the gaining of air superiority and supremacy has, however, since the prewar period emphasized that a combination of measures is required: attacks on the enemy's airfields, bombing of the aviation industry, and especially air battle by fighter-interceptor aviation.[43] Even as recently as 1956 the *Handbook for Civil Defense* stated: "Fighter aviation is the most powerful means of combat with the enemy's air force."[44] Until 1955 Soviet Air Force writers explicitly denied that attacks on enemy airfields or aviation industry could be the major means of gaining air superiority or supremacy. But in 1957 the Soviet Air Force newspaper declared that "under contemporary circumstances ever more significance is due to the annihilation of the enemy's air force on its air bases."[45] Moreover, some of the most recent statements emphasize attacks on enemy airfields as well as fighter interception, reflecting awareness of the increased importance of this mission. Lieutenant General Tsvetkov stated in 1955 in *Military Thought:*

> In the course of the recent war it became quite clear that the ground and sea forces can successfully operate only with domination in the air by their aircraft. In winning this superiority the main role is played by air forces destroying

the enemy's aviation on its airfields and in air battles. Domination in the air is achieved by a series of air engagements and blows on basing points of the enemy's aviation, which taken together are an independent operation of the air forces.[46]

Thus in the Soviet view air supremacy in contemporary war is achieved by a combination of air interception and attacks on the enemy's air bases. According to the *Great Soviet Encyclopedia* (in 1956) attacks may also be made on aviation industry, petroleum stocks and facilities, and even aviation training centers.[47] In 1957 a Soviet Air Force colonel summed it up in *Soviet Aviation*:

> Aerial superiority has enormous significance for success of an operation and the conduct of war as a whole. It is achieved by aviation in combined operation with rocket weapons, artillery, airborne troops, and means of active air defense. Without achievement of aerial superiority one cannot think about a swift seizure of the strategic initiative in the beginning period of a war, and of successful development of combat operations on land and sea.[48]

In a general nuclear war the main objectives presumably would be: (1) attacks by Soviet bomber aviation on Western atomic air bases, above all SAC; and (2) by Soviet fighter aviation and antiaircraft conventional and missile artillery on Western air formations that succeed in avoiding destruction on their bases. This action by Soviet long-range bomber aviation, which would require attacks on bases located both in the United States and around the world, would thus be "an independent operation of the air forces." It would continue to implement the strategic concept of destroying the enemy's armed forces, as indicated by another writer in *Military Thought* (in 1955): "Supremacy in the air has the objective not only to resolve the tasks of the air force, but *above all* to create favorable conditions for the operations of the ground forces, and on the coastal sectors for the navy."[49]

Among other important targets of long-range aviation are army and navy bases and concentrations, and interdiction targets such as major rail and road junctions and ports.[50] Finally, as we have noted, selective bombing of military-industrial targets such as aviation and munitions factories would probably complement direct action against the enemy's air and other armed forces.[51]

The continuous Soviet efforts to improve their active air defense program have been intensified in recent years. These efforts were emphasized by Marshal Zhukov in his speech in February 1956, when he noted that "the relative weight of air defense forces in the composition of the armed forces has grown significantly. . . ." As he explained the cause, "the task of defense of the rear of the country has never loomed so large as under contemporary conditions." And, as he further noted:

> Considerable work on the organization of the air defense of the country has been conducted with a calculation of the real threat from the air, especially from long-range rockets, and also the development of jet strategic aviation. At the present time, air defense has contemporary supersonic fighter aviation, high quality anti-aircraft artillery, anti-aircraft rocket weapons, and other means of securing air defense.[52]

Marshal Malinovsky has, since replacing Zhukov as Minister, also stressed the need for still greater attention "to the problems of air defense and anti-missile defense."[53] The Soviet air defense system (PVO) now has guided surface-to-air missiles in addition to great numbers of conventional anti-aircraft artillery guns. The fighter interceptor component of the air defense force has over 3,500 modern interceptors, including increasing numbers of supersonic all-weather fighters of advanced design and capable of firing air-to-air missiles.

Since mid-1954 increased attention has been given to civil defense preparation and training, and a number of manuals and pamphlets on civil defense against atomic attacks have been published. Civil defense is primarily entrusted to the "Local Anti-Air Defense" (MPVO) organization of the Ministry of

190

the Interior (MVD). This arrangement is logical, inasmuch as local police, fire protection, etc., are administered by the MVD, and it represents a continuation of the civil defense system established prior to World War II. The paramilitary youth organization (DOSAAF) and the Soviet Red Cross Society play important roles in civil defense training. Since early 1955 the manuals have explicitly provided for anti-atomic defense training.

Throughout the postwar period the Soviets have developed several series of modern fighters for general purposes, and in recent years all-weather interceptors also. Those models that are standardized (like the MiG-15, 17, 19, and 21) have been procured in very large quantities. Similarly jet light bombers (such as the IL-28) and attack bombers have been provided in substantial numbers to meet the requirements of tactical close support and interdiction in support of the ground forces. Two-thirds of Soviet aircraft strength continues to be assigned to support of the surface forces. These indications underline the significance of doctrinal expressions of the importance of combined arms operations.

In conclusion, we see that the role of air power in Soviet strategy is distinguished by a number of characteristics differing from our own. Soviet recognition of the implications of nuclear weapons was delayed during Stalin's time. It has since developed and may further change in the future. Crucial importance is attributed to nuclear strikes to destroy the enemy's nuclear delivery capabilities in a general war. Destruction of the enemy's economy and population, of the sources of his war-making capacity, is not considered the basis for a strategic concept ensuring victory, although in a total war this is certainly seen as one extremely important element complementing the over-all counter-force campaign against the enemy's military forces of all arms wherever located. In this counter-force strategy, the ground forces play a very important role and hence are assigned substantial tactical air support. Air defense, including fighter aviation, is similarly given considerable importance. Air power has not become the corner-stone of Soviet military strategy, but it has been recognized as a key element of increased importance in the nuclear era and has been provided with the resources to develop what the Soviets consider to be the necessary capabilities to perform its missions.

Notes to Chapter 8

1. For a fuller survey of the Stalinist period and early changes, see Garthoff, *Soviet Military Doctrine,* 1953, pp. 321-360, and Garthoff "Soviet Attitudes Toward Modern Air Power," *Military Affairs,* Vol. XIX, No. 2, Summer 1955, pp. 76-80.

2. Maj. Gen. of Aviation Ye. Tatarchenko, "Some Problems of the Development of Air Power," *Vestnik vozdushnogo flota,* No. 5-6, May-June 1946, pp. 60 and 64.

3. Maj. Gen. P. Korkodinov, "Operational Art of the Red Army," *Morskoi sbornik,* No. 6, June 1946, p. 11.

4. Major K. Laktionov, "Fundamental Tendencies in the Development of Aviation in the Course of the Second World War and in the Post-war Period," *Morskoi sbornik,* No. 11-12, November-December 1946, p. 108.

5. *Ibid.,* p. 125.

6. Marshal of Aviation N. Skripko, "Long Range Aviation," *Krasnaia zvezda,* August 11, 1946.

7. Lt. Col. V. Chalikov, "On the Role of Strategic Aviation," *Voennaia mysl',* No. 9, September 1946, p. 81.

8. Col. A. Volkov, "Fighter Aviation in Contemporary War," *Voennaia mysl',* No. 4, April 1949, p. 40.

9. Col. Gen. of Aviation A. Nikitin, "Soviet Aviation," *Voennaia mysl',* No. 2, February 1949, p. 62. See also Lt. Gen. of Aviation N. Zhuravlev, "Air Forces," *Bol'shaia Sovetskaia Entsiklopediia,* 2nd ed., Vol. 8, 1951, pp. 431-32.

10. Lt. Gen. of Aviation A. Golovanov, "Long-Range Aviation (ADD)," *Krasnaia zvezda,* November 12, 1942.

11. Col. N. Denisov, *Boevaia slava sovetskoi aviatsii,* Moscow, 2nd ed., [July 8] 1953, p. 120.

12. Col. Gen. of Aviation V. Sudets, "Stalinist Aviation," *Izvestiia,* August 18, 1946. See also Marshal of Aviation K. Vershinin, "The Military Air Power of the Socialist Fatherland," *Vestnik vozdushnogo flota,* No. 8-9, August-September 1946, p. 4; and Marshal of Aviation N. Skripko, *Krasnaia zvezda,* August 11, 1946.

13. Marshal of Aviation N. Skripko, *Krasnaia zvezda*, August 11, 1946.

14. Col. Gen. of Aviation S. Rudenko, "The Soviet Air Forces," *Krasnaia zvezda*, February 10, 1950.

15. Col. V. Pallo, "Soviet Bomber Aviation," *Vestnik vozdushnogo flota*, No. 7, July 1954, pp. 72-73.

16. See "Aviation," *Bol'shaia Sovetskaia Entsiklopediia*, 2nd ed., Vol. 1, 1949, p. 105 and Eng. Majs. R. Vinogradov and V. Zaitsev, "Multimotor Aviation of Our Country," *Vestnik vozdushnogo flota*, No. 12, December 1949, *passim;* Col. Gen. of Aviation S. Rudenko, *Krasnaia zvezda*, February 10, 1950; Lt. Gen. of Aviation F. Agal'tsov, *Krasnaia zvezda*, July 16, 1950; Lt. Gen. of Aviation P. Batitsky, *Izvestiia*, July 8, 1951; Majors V. Vorob'ev and A. Kliuchnik, *Vestnik vozdushnogo flota*, No. 4, April 1952, p. 28; Marshal of Aviation P. Zhigarev, *Pravda*, August 9, 1953; Col. Gen. of Aviation S. Rudenko, *Krasnaia zvezda*, June 20, 1954; editorial, *Vestnik vozdushnogo flota*, No. 4, April 1955, pp. 5-6; Lt. Gen. S. Krasil'nikov, "Military Strategy," *Bol'shaia Sovetskaia Entsiklopediia*, 2nd ed., Vol. 41, [April 21] 1956, p. 70; and "Tactics (Air Force)," *Bol'shaia Sovetskaia Entsiklopediia*, Vol. 41, [April 21] 1956, p. 542.

17. Col. Gen. P. Kurochkin, *Voennaia mysl'*, No. 5, May 1955, p. 19.

18. General H. H. Arnold, *Global Mission*, New York, Harper & Brothers, 1949, p. 469.

19. "Aviation," *Bol'shaia Sovetskaia Entsiklopediia*, 2nd ed., Vol. 1, 1949, p. 99

20. Former Russian Staff Officer (anonymous), writing in the *Manchester Guardian*, June 23, 1950.

21. Cited by Asher Lee, in *The Soviet Air Force*, New York, Harper & Brothers, 1950, p. 177.

22. Engineer N. Mekonoshin, "Aircraft of Strategic Aviation," *Krasnaia zvezda*, August 31, 1955.

23. Editorial, *Voennaia mysl'*, No. 2, February 1955, p. 12.

24. Marshal G. Zhukov, *Pravda*, February 13, 1955, and *Pravda*, February 20, 1956.

25. Marshal G. Zhukov, *Krasnaia zvezda*, March 23, 1957.

26. Col. Yu. Pshenianik, *Sovetskaia aviatsiia*, March 17, 1957.

27. I. I. Savitsky and P. M. Kirillov, *Protivovitriana oborona* (Air Defense) Handbook for DOSAAF Air Defense Instructors, Kiev, [October] 1953, pp. 10-11; and see also *Posobie dlia doprizyvnika* (Handbook for Preconscriptionists), 2nd ed., Voenizdat, Moscow, [January] 1955, p. 52.

28. Lt. Gen. A. Tsvetkov, *Voennaia mysl'*, No. 3, March 1955, p. 49.

29. Col. E. Chalik, *Voennaia mysl'*, No. 9, September 1954, p. 32.

30. Col. N. Denisov, *Boevaia slava sovetskoi aviatsii*, 1953, p. 67.

31. Col. I. Maryganov, *Peredovoi kharakter sovetskoi voennoi nauki*, 1953, p. 32.

32. Lt. Gen. S. Krasil'nikov, in *Marksizm-leninizm o voine i armii*, [November 28] 1956, pp. 156-57. See also Marshal A. Vasilevsky, *Voennye znaniia*, No. 1, January 1957, p. 4.

33. Maj. Gen. V. Khlopov, *Voennaia mysl'*, No. 1, January 1954, pp. 83 and 84.

34. Editorial, *Voennaia mysl'*, No. 4, April 1955, pp. 21-22.

35. Marshal G. Zhukov, *Pravda*, February 20, 1956.

36. The address had been made by General LeMay to the Armed Forces Chemical Association on May 21, 1954, and published in the *Armed Forces Chemical Journal*, July-August 1954, pp. 14-16. The Soviet version appeared in *Vestnik vozdushnogo flota*, No. 6, June 1955, pp. 91-94. See also the review and summary of Thomas Finletter's *Power and Policy* (New York, 1954) : Col. A. Mikhailov, "On the Role of Strategic Aviation in Contemporary War," *Voennaia mysl'*, No. 9, September 1955, pp. 73-77; "Montgomery on the Character of Future War," *Voennaia mysl'*, No. 3, March 1955, pp. 76-84, a translation of the Field Marshal's article published in *U. S. News and World Report*, December 17, 1954, and originally read at California Institute of Technology on November 28, 1954; and D. O. Smith, *Voennaia doktrina SShA* (U.S. Military Doctrine), translated from the American edition, Moscow, 1956, 272 pp.

37. *Kampanii voiny na tikhom okeane* (Campaigns of the War in the Pacific), Moscow, 1949, 512 pp. (Forward by Admiral of the Fleet I. S. Isakov). See pp. 6-7 for the explanation of the alleged purpose of the USSBS.

38. Marshal of Aviation S. Rudenko, *Krasnaia zvezda*, July 3, 1955.

39. Marshal G. Zhukov, *Pravda*, February 20, 1956.

40. Chief Marshal of Aviation P. Zhigarev, *Pravda*, June 24, 1956.

41. "Statement of the Soviet Government Concerning President Eisenhower's Address of December 8, 1953," *Izvestiia*, December 22, 1953. See also "A General in Retirement," *Izvestiia*, January 19, 1954.

42. Lt. Col. P. Safonov, *Vestnik vozdushnogo flota*, No. 9, September 1954, p. 79.

43. For an excellent summation of prewar doctrine, see Col. B. M. Lozovoi-Shevchenko, *Bor'ba za aviatsiei na ee aerodromakh* (The Struggle with Aviation on its Airfields) , Voenizdat, Moscow, 1941, *passim*, and especially pp. 4 and 35. For postwar restatements, see Col. Gen. of Aviation A. Nikitin, *Voennaia mysl'*, No. 2, February 1949, p. 65; Col. A. Volkov, "Fighter Aviation in Contemporary War," *Voennaia mysl'*, No. 4, April 1949, pp. 35 and 39; "Aviation," in the *Bol'shaia Sovetskaia Entsiklopediia*, 2nd ed., Vol. 1, [December 15] 1949, p. 105; and "Operational Air Supremacy," *Bol'shaia Sovetskaia Entsiklopediia*, 2nd ed., Vol. 31, [February 5] 1955, p. 51.

44. V. D. Moskalev, *et al.*, *Uchebnoe posobie po MPVO* (Handbook for Civil Defense) , DOSAAF, Moscow, [June 16] 1956, p. 46; *Osnovy voennogo dela* (Fundamentals of Military Affairs) , 2nd ed., DOSAAF, Moscow, [March 2] 1955, p. 45; Col. N. Vlasov, "Fighters in the Second World War," *Voennaia mysl'*, No. 6, June, 1946, p. 29; and Col. A. Volkov, *Voennaia mysl'*, No. 4, April 1949, p. 39.

45. Lt. Col. L. Korets, *Sovetskaia aviatsiia*, July 16, 1957, and Col. A. Kravchenko, *Sovetskaia aviatsiia*, August 15, 1957. For the earlier view, see E. G. Bor-Ramensky, "The Collapse of the Hitlerite Air Offensive Against Moscow

in 1941," *Istoricheskie zapiski*, No. 51, [July 17] 1955, p. 234; Col. N. Denisov, *Boevaia slava*, 1953, pp. 176-77; Col. A. Volkov, *Voennaia mysl'*, No. 4, April 1949, p. 40; Lt. Gen. of Aviation N. Zhuravlev, *Vestnik vozdushnogo flota*, No. 5-6, May-June 1946, p. 11; and Col. A. Vasil'ev, *Vestnik vozdushnogo flota*, No. 5-6, May-June 1946, pp. 21 and 29.

46. Lt. Gen. A. Tsvetkov, "Operations, Their Essence and Significance in Contemporary Armed Conflict," *Voennaia mysl'*, No. 3, March 1955, pp. 48-49.

47. "Strategic Supremacy in the Air," *Bol'shaia Sovetskaia Entsiklopediia*, 2nd ed., Vol. 41, [April 21] 1956, p. 65.

48. Col. Yu. Pshenianik, "On the Role of Aviation in Contemporary War," *Sovetskaia aviatsiia*, March 17, 1957.

49. Cal. V. Kolechitsky, *Voennaia mysl'*, No. 10, October 1955, p. 77.

50. Maj. Gen. Isaev, *New Times*, March 26, 1955, p. 8.

51. *Ibid.* See also Col. N. Denisov, *Boevaia slava*, 1953, p. 67; Lt. Gen. of Aviation N. Zhuravlev, *Vestnik vozdushnogo flota*, No. 5-6, May-June 1946, p. 15; and "Aviation," *Bol'shaia Sovetskaia Entsiklopediia*, 2nd ed., Vol. 1, 1949, p. 105.

52. Marshal G. Zhukov, *Pravda*, February 20, 1956.

53. Marshal R. Malinovsky, *Krasnaia zvezda*, November 27, 1957.

CHAPTER 9

SEA POWER IN SOVIET STRATEGY

What is the role of sea power in contemporary Soviet strategy? Has the advent of intercontinental ballistic missiles and thermo-nuclear weapons made the navy obsolete, in Soviet eyes? In answering these questions we can avail ourselves of recent Soviet writings on naval affairs, as well as surveying the evidence provided by what the Soviets are actually doing in terms of naval construction and deployment.

Soviet naval objectives and missions, forces and capabilities, and doctrine, must of course be understood in terms of Soviet military strategy as a whole. Current Soviet strategic views reflect two important considerations: (1) continued Soviet attention to major continental theater campaigns on the Eurasian periphery; and (2) new attention to the problems of inter-continental warfare against the United States. The Soviet Navy has, in the past, been developed very largely in terms of its role as a supplement to the ground forces in continental land campaigns. Both stated doctrine and practice confirmed this view also in the Stalinist postwar period.[1] The Soviets continue now to regard major campaigns—land, supported by sea and air—as one important element in future nuclear war. Accordingly, the Soviet Navy is gearing itself for its subordinate contribution to the winning of European-Scandinavian-Middle East-Far East combined operations, with or without the use of nuclear weapons. But the significant belated Soviet shift of attention in the last five years to the crucial new problems of intercontinental strategy has also been reflected in the development of Soviet naval doctrine and capabilities.

THE INFLUENCE OF ATOMIC WARFARE

The weapons of intercontinental warfare are presently two: strategic air and missile power, and strategic sea power. The phrase "strategic sea power" may sound strange to Western world ears, because for us sea power has *always* been strategic. American forces fighting in the South Pacific, and in Europe in two wars, were fighting intercontinentally. But to the Soviets intercontinental warfare is a new experience. No longer is the enemy center of power within the range of a massive combined infantry-tank-tactical air team. If Eurasia were taken, the Free World island outposts off Eurasia and in Africa would still be available for striking the Soviet heartland, and the United States would remain relatively secure from occupation. To be sure, the power of air assaults with thermonuclear weapons could devastate much of the United States (as well as the Soviet Union). But in the Soviet view this would not ensure the ultimately decisive victorious seizure of the enemy territory, nor even fully neutralize it as a base for direct attacks on the Soviet Union. Hence sea power also joins with long-range air forces and missiles both as a weapon for naval warfare and for intercontinental striking missions. We know the new view from the then authoritative Marshal Zhukov, who in 1956 said: "In the construction of the navy we [the Soviets] proceed from the conception that *combat in naval theaters in future war assumes more significance than it had in the recent war*."[2] Admiral Vladimirsky, in 1955, made clear that precisely the emergence of new weapons and technology "requires us to examine carefully anew the role of the navy."[3] In particular, as another Soviet military theoretician stated (also in 1955), nuclear energy in all its various military uses "significantly increases the power of the navy and *widens the framework of the employment of the navy.*"[4]

The Soviet Navy has, throughout its existence, alternated between being a separate service with cabinet representation and being subordinate to the Army. From 1950, when renewed postwar attention to the Navy began, until Stalin's death in 1953, the Soviet Navy was an independent ministry. Since 1953 it has been one element (although still more autonomous than the air forces) in the unified Ministry of Defense. As we have noted, beginning in 1955 a new redefinition of the role of the Navy was undertaken. Admiral of the Fleet Kuznetsov, Commander-in-Chief of the Navy from 1939 to 1947, and again from 1951 to 1955, was relieved to make way for a conversion of the Navy's role. Admiral Gorshkov is presently the Commander-in-Chief.

What are the lines along which the Soviet Navy is being refashioned for the atomic age, and for intercontinental warfare in particular?

In the first place, there is the preparation of the entire Navy for defense against nuclear weapons. It may be useful to cite one authoritative statement of this recognition, from the pen of Senior Naval Captain Shavtsov, writing in the General Staff organ *Military Thought* (in 1955):

> The employment of the atomic weapon in combat operations at sea makes necessary raising the requirements for all means of operational security, and especially for reconnaissance and air defense. In addition, it requires the organization of atomic defense of ships, aviation, and other naval forces in the theater. Without a well-organized atomic defense, under contemporary conditions, one cannot win or maintain mastery of the sea.[5]

The Soviet Navy has also put this into practice, and has actively conducted atomic defense training, as well as publishing various articles on the subject for the guidance and instruction of naval officers.[6]

198

Secondly, as Admiral Vladimirsky noted in 1956, "the advent of atomic weapons has already led to important changes in naval tactics."[7] Perhaps the most important of these changes noted in Soviet writings have been the recognition of the need for dispersal and of the importance of tactical surprise.[8]

Finally, we come to the most significant strategical development: the attempt to establish *strategic missions and capabilities for the Soviet Navy in the era of nuclear warfare*. Soviet naval strategy now calls for two new missions: (1) neutralization of the enemy's naval and maritime transport capabilities; and (2) strategic striking power for employment against the enemy's military forces, bases and ports, and military industry. One other important mission is still in the early stages of consideration, but would seem to loom large as a likely area of increased future Soviet naval interest: large-scale amphibious operations over long ranges, and the use of sea transport (including large submarines and seaplanes) for this purpose.

THE SURFACE FLEET

In developing capabilities for offensive operations against the enemy fleets and home targets, the Soviets have stressed two weapons systems: (1) submarines, particularly with missile-launchers, for nuclear attacks; and (2) missile-launching cruisers. Defensively, missiles and naval aviation are regarded as important. As the above implies, the Soviets have decided that large surface vessels—battleships, heavy cruisers, and aircraft carriers—are obsolete in the nuclear era. This decision was doubtless facilitated by the virtual absence of Soviet warships in these categories. Until recently the Soviets maintained two old battleships (a third, the ex-Italian *Novorossisk*, sank after striking a mine in 1955) and three old cruisers, but these obsolete units have by now probably all been retired. The Soviets have never had an operational aircraft carrier. The Soviets do, however, have a strong surface fleet of modern design consisting of approximately 27 cruisers, of which at least 16 are of postwar construction, and about 140-150 sea-going destroyers, of which some 125 are postwar.[9]

It has been reported, though still unconfirmed, that one reason for the dismissal of Admiral of the Fleet Kuznetsov in 1955 was his continued strong support for the program of con-struction of a fleet of conventional gun-bearing light cruisers, rather than agreeing to the conversion of Soviet cruisers to missile armament.[10] Khrushchev has been quoted as saying at a Moscow diplomatic party that "Kuznetsov was trying to fight the next war with the weapons of the last," and on another occasion he said to General Twining that "admirals are always looking backward and living in the past." On his visit to England, Khrushchev said that cruisers were good for carrying political leaders on visits, and their guns for "firing salutes," but not for much else.[11] Probably some of the present Soviet cruisers, and any future ones, will be converted or constructed as guided-missile cruisers. Indeed, one or more such vessels may already exist.

Admiral Vladimirsky has frankly stated that the Soviets be-lieve large surface vessels to be obsolete because of new weapons potentialities. "It has become clear that to construct large vessels—battleships, heavy cruisers—is unprofitable. . . ."

> Further, the powerful might of guided missiles, which with the aid of various systems can be guided precisely to the target, significantly reduces the role of large ships in naval combat, since even relatively small ships armed with missile weapons can successfully conduct combat operations against the very largest battleships and cruisers armed with conventional ar-tillery.[12]

Captain Shavtsov also points out that: "*The most favorable targets for atomic blows under contemporary conditions are large naval vessels.*"[13]

Aircraft carriers, the modern "capital ship" and in the West successor to the battleship, are totally absent from the Soviet Navy. Moreover, as Admiral Burke has confirmed, there are no indications that the Soviets intend to build carriers.[14] Evi-

200

dently the Soviets consider the vulnerability of any large surface vessel to be too great and the striking power insufficient. Soviet discussions comment on the carrier's "risk of being annihilated," and state that it is necessary "to note the great vulnerability of aircraft carriers to various contemporary weapons." [15]

In the prewar period, some naval circles favored strongly the construction of aircraft carriers.[16] If the war had not interrupted the large naval construction program begun in 1938, the Soviets might have developed a carrier arm. Even now, the Soviets concede that the carrier weapons system is capable of "significantly increasing the operating radius of aviation."[17] There are articles discussing U.S. Navy carriers, with the primary purpose of familiarizing Soviet naval men with the enemy's views and capabilities.[18] But the Soviets have definitely concluded that because of its vulnerability to modern weapons the aircraft carrier is an unacceptable weapons system.

Another Soviet criticism of aircraft carriers is primarily propagandistic. They argue that carriers, because of their vulnerability, are useful only for a first-strike mission—and therefore are only of value to an aggressor. Marshal Zhukov, in fact, used this argument to justify American and British interest in carriers and Soviet lack of interest.[19]

Despite the Soviet rejection of the aircraft carrier, they have an awareness of the need for naval aviation and air superiority in naval theaters of operation. Captain Shavtsov has noted: "One cannot speak of mastery of the sea under contemporary conditions without mastery of the air," and "Atomic weapons have significantly increased the potentialities of aviation in the struggle for mastery of the sea."[20] This restatement of the importance of naval aviation for the nuclear era merely underscores the previous Soviet view.[21] Moreover, the Soviet Naval Air Force of some 3,500 aircraft is equipped with modern jet fighters and light bombers—although it is entirely shore-based.[22] One of the substitutes for aircraft carriers which the Soviets foresee is the use of atomic-propelled aircraft for long-range sea patrol and attack missions. One military theoretician, writing in the authoritative *Military Thought* in 1955, specifically said: "The use of atomic propulsion for naval aviation makes possible dealing blows on the enemy and in support of the fleet *from land bases, without the use of aircraft carriers.*"[23] The Soviets have followed U.S. Navy development of the *Seamaster* and *Tradewind,* and have also displayed considerable interest in nuclear-propelled seaplanes.[24]

Thus we see that to support attack missions and gain supremacy of the seas the Soviets are not relying on aircraft carriers or large surface vessels, but (for the future) on missile-launching cruisers, modern light cruisers and destroyers, and naval aviation to the extent of its range from land bases (presently only with conventional turbojet fighters and naval bombers). There is, of course, one other key element in the Soviet offensive naval force: submarines.

The Subsurface Fleet

Submarines have traditionally played both a "tactical" role of killing enemy combat ships, and a "strategic" role of interdiction and blockade of the enemy's sea communications lines. Since about the beginning of 1954 the Soviets have also shown an awareness of the value of submarines in the nuclear era as a delivery system for *intercontinental* strikes.[25] The Soviet interest in submarines was already well developed by the time of the recent war, and in the postwar period the construction of conventional torpedo-firing submarines was the major part of the naval program (along with conventionally gunned light cruisers). The Soviet submarine fleet presently numbers thrice that of the United States, and over nine times that of Germany in 1939. Approximately 250 of the total of over 500 submarines in service are modern, long-range vessels.[26]

Submarines have a dominant role in Soviet naval strategy, and great importance in Soviet over-all military strategy, due to their suitability for two key tasks. One is the strategic interdiction mission; the other is the intercontinental striking mission. The role of the interdiction mission may appear to many Americans as one of decreased importance for a future thermonuclear war. But the Soviets continue to regard even future general war as likely to involve significant long campaigns in the Eurasian peripheral theaters, in particular Europe. From this perspective, the interdiction of Western sea communications with North America is of major importance. Rear Admiral Andreev, in an article in 1957, has thus declared: "Contemporary wars are conducted with large armies and . . . under combat conditions such armed forces require constant reinforcement of men, weapons, ammunition, fuel, food, equipment, etc." American troops abroad, and all the NATO allies, states Admiral Andreev, are so dependent upon transoceanic supply that we "cannot conduct wide-scale combat operations" without it. In fact, he states, "the essence of the matter is that for the imperialist states *the very possibility of conducting war* depends upon the support of uninterrupted operation of sea and ocean communications," so that such communications "can have a serious influence on the course and outcome of a war."[27] Thus, in the particular circumstances of the NATO forces, the Soviets are bound to devote substantial efforts to the strategic interdiction mission.

The reasons for Soviet interest in submarines for intercontinental attacks on strategic targets of the enemy need no elaboration.

The Soviets see two methods for submarines to make strategic strikes both against enemy sea forces and communications and against enemy land targets. One is the use of torpedoes with nuclear warheads; the other is the launching of guided or ballistic missiles with nuclear or thermonuclear warheads.

The Soviets have, ever since the end of 1953, referred on many occasions to the possibilities of employing torpedoes with atomic warheads.[28] Admiral Vladimirsky (as early as 1955, and again in 1957) has noted the obviously great increase in the effectiveness of nuclear armed torpedoes for use against enemy ships, since a vessel need not even be hit in order to be sunk.[29]

Moreover, Admiral Vladimirsky has explicitly pointed to the possibility of delivery of mines and underwater torpedos with nuclear warheads *into the harbors* of major enemy ports and naval bases.[30]

Missile-Launching Submarines

The ballistic or guided missile with atomic warhead is the second new weapon of the submarine fleet for naval engagements and strategic strikes. A number of Soviet naval writers have, since 1955, described the possible use of submarine-launched missiles for attacks on naval bases and other strategic targets on land. To cite but one authoritative reference, again we read in a statement by Admiral Vladimirsky: "Submarines armed with guided missiles having atomic warheads can conduct powerful surprise blows on industrial centers, seaports, and enemy bases and thus fulfill tasks *on a strategic scale*."[31] Vladimirsky noted in particular (taking into account limitations of accuracy of submarine-launched missiles): ". . . Such targets are strong coastal objectives having a large area." Other articles have extended the possibilty to include also targets "deep in the enemy's territory."[32]

Most Soviet discussions refer to guided missiles; a few refer to ballistic rocket missiles, presumably a later stage in development. Similarly, a few sources have revealed the Soviet interest in subsurface launched missiles. Rear Admiral Pavlovich noted in 1957 that precisely "the possibility of using submarines for action against industrial and administrative centers of the enemy by long-range guided missiles has . . . above all, raised the need for creating structures to permit submarines to launch their missiles without surfacing."[33] The Soviets have also shown an interest in the development of underwater containers holding ballistic rockets—containers which could be towed by a submarine and anchored at selected locations for timed or remote-control launching of the missiles.[34] Discussions of the future development of this weapons system also envisage the

204

particular value of nuclear propulsion for the submarines, which would be prepared for launching atomic missiles against strategic targets.[35] The Soviets have evaluated the invulnerability of the submarine-missile weapons system as relatively good. (Nonetheless, in discussions of combatting the enemy's missile-launching submarines or surface vessels, the Soviets stress the need for "preemptive blows" on the launching vessels.[36]) Captain Shavtsov, cited earlier in this chapter, stated as early as 1955: "Submarines, in our view, are the least vulnerable to atomic weapons. In the first place, they are difficult to detect not only at sea, but even in bases, since in case of atomic threat to a base they can submerge. In the second place, in dispersion at base and still more in operations at sea, the destruction of more than a single vessel is very unlikely. . . ." He concluded that a single submarine was "not such a tempting target for an atomic blow."[37] This may not tell us the size of the Soviet stockpile of nuclear weapons in mid-1955, but it surely suggests that the working-level military planners had not at that time been led to believe that "nuclear plenty" had arrived. Since that time the Soviets have recognized more fully the implications of "atomic plenty" and of the announced United States development of an atomic depth charge for antisubmarine operations. The Soviets themselves have (in 1957) observed that an atomic depth charge would destroy a submarine at 600 meters distance.[38] But the Soviet evaluation of the utility of a submarine-launched missile capability for strategic nuclear strikes, of course, remains undiminished by this changed view of the attractiveness of single vessels for atomic attack.

AMPHIBIOUS OPERATIONS

We have now surveyed the two new missions, and the lines of development of the corresponding capabilities: (1) for neutralization of the enemy's sea communicatons; and (2) for contributing to the strategic assault on the enemy's home bases. As we noted, there is a third mission of great potential importance, although to date little explored. Amphibious operations have never been well developed in Soviet practice, either in training or in combat. The landings made in World War II were all either small-scale, or large river crossings, and frequently against negligible opposition.

Soviet naval writers have recently begun to investigate problems of seaborne landing operations, and operations to counter attempted enemy amphibious assaults, with the use by both sides of nuclear weapons. The concentration of transports and accompanying naval vessels for a large landing is recognized as a valuable possible target for atomic attack, and must therefore be accomplished "with a calculation so that a single atomic explosion will remove the least quantity of forces and weapons from action." [39] From the standpoint of the defender, it is similarly held that "the employment of atomic weapons in counter-landing operations creates exceptionally favorable conditions for the achievement of its objective in short time." [40]

"Strategic landings," in the Soviet definition, "are usually made with the objective of invasion of the enemy's territory and the creation of a new front." [41] The scale of effort visualized by the Soviets for such strategic landings might comprise one or several field armies. Airborne troops, as well as amphibious forces, may join to effect a strategic landing. [42] The Soviets have begun to display some interest themselves in strategic landing operations, and although they have a "naval infantry" (marines), to date they have not developed major amphibious forces. It is possible that the future will see an increased Soviet effort to develop such a capability.

DEFENSIVE MISSIONS

Let us turn now to the *defensive* missions of the Soviet Navy. Defense of the Soviet coastal areas, including air defense, is in general a mission of the Navy. Both the numerous smaller surface units of the four Soviet fleets (Baltic, Black Sea, Northern and Pacific) and the naval shore establishment have this as their primary function. Admiral Levchenko, a deputy commander-in-chief of the Navy, devoted an entire article late in 1956 to the role of Soviet naval artillerymen with the fleets and on shore, stressing their equipment both with conventional guns, and with "rocket and missile weapons, and methods of their employment on land and at sea."[43] A subsequent article (in late 1956) declared specifically that coastal artillery "is at the present time being equipped with guided missiles."[44] Thus the missile promises to become an important defensive, as well offensive, weapon of the Soviet Navy. The present relatively short-range Soviet Naval Air Force is, of course, largely limited to a defensive role. Defense of the Soviet border areas will necessarily remain a major preoccupation of the Soviet Navy in view of the strong enemy (Western) naval striking forces which it would have to attempt to ward off and destroy in a war. Defense of the Soviet sea communications would be a secondary mission in the light of the relatively small scale of such communication lines. One field in which the Russians have long excelled is mine warfare, and even Soviet cruisers are outfitted for minelaying. The experience of the U.S. Navy at Wonsan harbor in 1950 bears witness to the effectiveness of current Soviet minelaying techinques. The possibility of nu-clear-charged mines would be a serious obstacle to Western naval actions in Soviet waters, and even in our own home waters, since the mines can be laid by submarines and aircraft.

Thus we see that the new Soviet Navy will consist primarily of light cruisers and destroyers (presently with conventional guns, probably later with missile armament), submarines armed with torpedoes and missiles bearing atomic warheads, jet defensive and supporting naval aviation, later long-range nuclear-propelled strategic striking bombers, and defensive gun and rocket coastal and anti-aircraft artillery. The Soviets may or may not develop amphibious forces of strategic significance.

We have surveyed the development of Soviet naval doctrine and strategy for the nuclear age. What, precisely, would be the actual employment of Soviet naval forces in a future war?

SOVIET WARTIME NAVAL STRATEGY

The major part of the Soviet Navy would be assigned to actions in conjunction with land and air forces on the Scandinavian, European, Balkan-Middle Eastern, and Far Eastern fronts. The Soviet Navy is, due to geographical considerations, necessarily divided among four separated seas which generally correspond to these four land theaters. The largest Soviet sea force is the Baltic Fleet, with about eight modern cruisers and a large share of all the other components of the Soviet Navy including submarines. The Black Sea Fleet has about a half-dozen modern cruisers. Both of these fleets are located on inland seas, the accesses to which are, at least initially, controlled by the NATO powers. These Soviet forces are, however, stronger than those of the other states which maintain naval strength there (Sweden in the Baltic, and Turkey in the Black Sea). The Northern Fleet, with about six modern cruisers and several score of long-range submarines, faces no close enemy force in peacetime. The Far Eastern Fleet, with about six modern cruisers and a large submarine arm, is a potent local force, but no match for American naval forces in the Far East (to say nothing of the whole U.S. Pacific Fleet). It has been reinforced in recent years by transfers of three cruisers, several destroyers, and a large number of submarines.

Let us scan briefly the possible Soviet naval objectives at the outbreak of a war.

The Scandinavian Straits are very vulnerable to relatively rapid closure by Soviet land forces (with air and naval support, probably including airborne and seaborne assaults), and it thus becomes quite unlikely that the U.S. and U.K. would commit naval forces (other than submarines) to the Baltic to contest control of a sea likely to be entirely bounded by Soviet-controlled shores. This is, of course, speculation; if the Western powers were to decide to defend Scandinavia with large forces, naval surface (and probably air) units would certainly be included in the force. Conversely, if the Soviets did not assault Scandinavia initially, the picture would depend upon Swedish neutrality or participation, and Western decisions concerning measures for the defense of Denmark and possibly concerning offensive action in the Baltic Sea.

In the Black Sea, the Turkish Navy, despite the acquisition of some modern destroyers and several modern U.S. submarines, would not be in a position alone to launch effective offensive action against the Soviet Black Sea Fleet or coasts. However, the Turkish Straits are less vulnerable to early Soviet seizure by land than those of Scandinavia, and might well be used to reinforce the Turkish Navy by U.S. or U.K. naval forces (doubtless including suport from one or more carriers located in the Mediterranean) which could give the Black Sea Fleet a serious challenge, and probably destroy it or drive it into Crimean and Ukrainian ports.

The Northern Fleet, in the White and Barents seas, would doubtless participate in any Soviet action in Scandinavia, and rapidly transfer at least part of its forces (especially its submarine arm) to the North Atlantic. Again, the form and extent of action which the West decides to undertake in this subtheater will decide the limits of its operations.

The Far Eastern Fleet, weakest in major surface vessels but strong in submarine and coastal craft, would probably assume the strategic defensive. If committed to the open sea, it would be risked against the superior U.S. naval forces.

In summary of the immediate consequence of initial fleet distribution, we see that the Baltic and Black Sea fleets would probably seek to clear those seas and, in conjunction with land and air forces, seek to deny the entries to those seas to Western naval forces. Initially they would assume the offensive to secure a more stable defensive position. The Northern and Far Eastern fleets would by their presence require any Western naval assault in those regions to be major in scope, and could harrass normal sea lanes of the North Atlantic and North Pacific, respectively. With the important exception of their submarine arms, they could, however, readily be restricted to coastal waters if the Western powers were to assign the necessary naval forces for this purpose. We shall return to probable wartime strategic employment of the Soviet naval forces later; before concluding this preliminary discussion of the significance of separation of the Soviet Navy into four fleets, we should look briefly at the degree of possible transfer among these fleets in wartime. The Black Sea has no egress, save through the Western-controlled Dardanelles, Gibraltar, and Suez straits, except for possible transfer of small vessels via inland rivers and canals to the Baltic. The White Sea Canal permits transfer of vessels up to and possibly including cruisers between the Baltic and Northern fleets. The Northern and Far Eastern fleets may use the Northern Sea Route during part of the year, but this would involve considerable time and great risk, and would probably only be done on a small emergency scale. Thus practical flexibility is restricted to cruisers and smaller vessels between the Baltic and White seas (until, of course, such time as the Soviets might have secured all of Scandinavia, when the North Atlantic might be used to connect these fleets).

In addition to the fact that the Soviet fleets are separated from one another, the Soviet Union (with three-fourths of its frontier—some 60,000 kilometers—littoral) has a long, thinly defended coast. The Arctic and Pacific coasts are naturally least accessible, but nevertheless the most vulnerable; the Black Sea follows (so long as the Turkish Straits are secure); then the Arctic and White Sea (and in wartime, the North Atlantic); and last the Baltic Sea is relatively least vulnerable. Yet the Soviets have placed primary stress upon fortifying the Baltic coasts, due to the greater proximity of the Baltic Sea to the Soviet centers of power.

The Soviet bases are relatively few and in some cases isolated. Let us turn first to the Far East. The chief Soviet naval bases are widely separated: Vladivostok, Sovetskaia Gavan, Nikolaevsk, and Petropavlovsk. Vladivostok is, of course, well hemmed in on the Sea of Japan. It shares the offensive advantage and corresponding defensive vulnerability of proximity to the Japanese main islands. Sovetskaia Gavan and Nikolaevsk (and inland, Khabarovsk) are both protected and blocked by Sakhalin and the Kurile Islands. The Kuriles are a valuable offensive forward base and defensive shield. Petropavlovsk on Kamchatka, only 700 miles from Kiska in the Aleutians, is a fine base except for its isolation and dependence upon long air and sea lines of communication and supply. Although the Soviets have in the past displayed great interest in the Manchurian and Chinese ports on the Yellow Sea, they probably would not station a major part of their Far Eastern naval forces in this region so long as they do not control South Korea and the Tsushima Straits.

In the event of war, the Soviets would probably assume the strategic defensive in the Far East (which would not be contradicted by probable Chinese actions in Southeast Asia and on the Korean peninsula). The Soviets might attack either Japan or Alaska with airborne troops, but from the sea they could assault only Hokkaido. Except for its submarine arm, the Soviet Far Eastern Fleet would probably be bottled up rather quickly in the seas of Japan and Okhotsk.

Action by either side in the Arctic Ocean or Kara Sea can not be predicted beyond noting the probability of very limited action. In the region of the White and Barents seas and the North Atlantic several possibilities are open. The Soviet Northern Fleet has four bases: Murmansk-Poliarnoe, Arkhangelsk, Severodvinsk, and Pechenga (Petsamo). The Soviets would probably grant high priority to the securing of naval bases (especially for submarines) on the Norwegian coast, and (especially for air and missile bases) on Spitzbergen. The Northern Fleet would be assigned this mission, in coordination with land thrusts through Finland and Denmark and probably with airborne assault of Spitzbergen. If these objectives could be secured, either Iceland and Greenland, or the United Kingdom, would become the objectives of the Northern and Baltic fleets, now operating under a united command for the North Atlantic. The success of such a strategy would depend upon the outcome of the land thrusts into Denmark, Norway, and Finland (possibly Sweden would be bypassed until the others were vanquished), and upon the extent of sea power the Western powers would choose to commit to the defense of Scandinavia. Spitzbergen and Iceland, with possible air and missile bases potentially threatening both adversaries, are of particular strategic significance.

In the Baltic Sea the absolute control of the Gulf of Finland would swiftly be extended to the Gulf of Bothnia and probably to the whole of the Baltic (with the above-mentioned possibility that Sweden might initially be spared, assuming she remained neutral). Denmark would be overrun by a land thrust supported by airborne and seaborne landings on the islands, and Norway assaulted from the north by land and sea, from the south by airborne and possibly seaborne forces, and in the later stages by land through Sweden. A strategic plan on this order explains the otherwise relatively large proportion of surface vessels assigned to the Baltic Fleet. The Baltic Fleet has a large number of excellent bases, including Leningrad, Kronstadt, Tallinn, Ventspils, Libau, Memel, Kaliningrad (Königsberg), Kolberg, Baltisk (Pillau), Swinemunde, and Rostock. The major portion of motor torpedo boats, landing craft, and other vessels likely to be used for amphibious and seaborne assault—as well as the majority of their "naval infantry"—is in the Baltic. Similarly, missile stations on the East German coast face Scandinavia.

The Black Sea Fleet would presumably have the objective of protecting the sea flanks of land thrusts toward the Straits and from the Caucasus, and of seeking to deny the Straits to Western naval forces. Their adequacy for this task would depend, of course, primarily upon the opposition met from the West. If the Black Sea Fleet should succeed, and a land

212

thrust secure the Straits, it would become the Soviet Mediterranean Fleet, and at a later phase of the war share the mission
of assaulting Crete, Cyprus, Suez and such other objectives as
only the progress of the war could portend. Soviet interest in
the eastern Mediterranean and Red Sea areas has already been
made apparent in the great stress the Soviets (like their Tsarist
predecessor in this matter) have placed upon opening the
Straits to themselves and closing it to others. In 1945 at Potsdam, and later by diplomatic pressure upon Turkey, the Soviets
unsuccessfully sought peaceful acquisition of this objective. Also
at Potsdam in 1945, the Soviets sought a role in administering
the former Italian colonies of Libya and Eritrea. Soviet plans
for penetration of the Mediterranean suffered severely with
the defection of Yugoslavia in 1949, but recent gains in Syria
and Egypt have opened new possibilities. At present the sole
base in the Mediterranean available to the Soviets is the Al-
banian base at Valona.

The Soviet Black Sea Fleet has a number of good operating
bases on the northern coasts, principally Odessa, Nikolaev,
Kherson, Eupatoriia, Sevastopol, Feodosiia, Kerch, and Novo-
rossiisk; several lesser ones on the eastern coast (Tuapse, Sochi,
Sukhumi, Poti, and Batumi) ; and the two satellite parts of
Varna and Constanta on the western coast. (The Turks have
only one good base on the southern coast, Sinope).

In this discussion examination of the capabilities and objectives of the submarine arm of the Soviet fleets has been de-
ferred, because of the unique ability of this force to operate
virtually without support from the other naval arms, and to
gain access to the high seas despite the Western naval strength
which denies this as a serious possibility to the Soviet surface
fleets. Unlike the other arms, a substantial portion of the
Soviet submarine forces would from the outset undertake offensive operations (although, basically, attacks on enemy sea lanes
remain strategically defensive). Due to limitations of range,
a large number of Soviet submarines could only be used for
coastal area defense missions. It may be presumed that the

West would exert serious efforts to close the Skagerrak-Kattegat, Kiel Canal and Dardanelles Straits to submarines of the Baltic and Black Sea fleets. The Soviets would nonetheless still have significant numbers of modern long-range submarines operating from the Barents Sea (and probably soon from Norway) and the Far Eastern Soviet and Chinese bases, which would be aggressively used against Western naval forces and vital lines of supply.

Finally, we come to the naval contribution to the intercontinental strategic striking mission. The problems of avoiding detection of submarines before the strike, and of attaining accuracy, would probably limit the role of missile-launching submarines to a supplement to the basic air and missile strikes. Nonetheless, it could be an important component in the overall Soviet war plan. Admiral Burke has said this capability "could constitute a serious threat to our ports and to our coastal cities," noting that over half the major cities of the United States lie within 100 miles of the coasts.[45]

In this discussion our concern has been largely with Soviet naval objectives and capabilities in the initial phases of a major war. Soviet aims and capabilities must be considered in terms of Western aims and capabilities. Finally, they depend largely on the outcome of the strategic thermonuclear offensive and counteroffensive between the United States and Soviet Union. It is not possible here to attempt to speculate on the outcome of contested objectives. Still, we may assume that if the war had not ended in the initial thermonuclear exchange, the Western naval forces would seek to deny the Soviet Navy access to the open sea in the White and Barents seas and in the Far East, perhaps invade the Black Sea, and possibly even invade the Baltic Sea. In any case the Soviet fleets would all be forced into the strategic defensive. Flank support to land drives on the borders of the island seas and on the Scandinavian Cape, possible amphibious operations in the same theaters and in northern Japan, and possible harrassment of Western maritime and naval forces by surface units in the North and Far East

214

are the only offensive opportunities for the surface fleets. The major part of the surface and air units would be concerned with defending the exposed Soviet coasts. Only submarine operations would be significant in the great oceans.

Thus the first phase. There would doubtless be intermediary phases (if the first were to succeed) which we shall not attempt to examine here because the situations would be too speculative. But let us for a moment turn to what may be termed "the ultimate phase," if unfortunately it should ever be reached. This would be a situation of Soviet control of Eurasia, except perhaps for certain island strongholds such as Spitzbergen, Iceland, England, Central Africa (an island for this purpose), Australia, and Japan. This situation would indeed be exceedingly dangerous to the West, but it would also remain a critical problem to the Soviets, and we can not doubt they are even now well aware of this. The fact of intercontinental warfare is overwhelming. The problem of effectively closing with the enemy would be truly enormous for both adversaries, but especially so for the Soviets. The Soviets are placing great effort into developing their strategic air and missile capability and submarine strength, but it is not conceivable that they could hope to match the West on the surface at sea, even granting capture of significant portions of European navies. To be sure, the problem which the West would face in trying to defeat the Soviets in such a situation would be almost as difficult. Hence, the West might be vulnerable to peace overtures which the Soviets could advance in order to consolidate their power and, with the resources of two continents, they could begin to gird for the later final clash after having built the necessary naval and other intercontinental capabilities to *seize* as well as to devastate the United States.

The discussion above has been entirely concerned with the role of the Soviet Navy in a major war. The Soviets may also have in mind the role their naval forces could play in limited and local wars. If there were a limitation on the use of nuclear weapons, for example, the role of the Navy for interdiction of

215

sea communications would become crucially important, even though the strategic striking role might fade away. In a local war units of the appropriate fleet might either be loaned as "volunteers" or openly committed to local engagements. In such a war the absence of carriers might be strongly felt. But in general the Soviets presume that the type of modern surface and submarine fleet which they are building, and the development required by geographic-strategic circumstances, would serve both for limited and local wars and for general nuclear war.

THE NAVAL CHALLENGE

Sea power is essential to the Soviets particularly because it is essential to us, the enemy. Reflecting this fact, the submarine capability for disruption of the opponents' sea communications is particularly strong. Also, the surface, air, and coastal components are predominantly geared to defensive actions against possible Western naval assaults. But, in addition, a new strategic striking mission is now leading to the acquisition of capabilities (above all missile-launchng submarines) for intercontinental strikes.

This is the challenge. Admiral Gorshkov, the Commander-in-Chief of the Soviet Navy, made clear the significance attached by the Soviets to the role of sea power when he stated a little over two years ago:

> The Central Committee of the Party and the Soviet government devote great attention to the development and perfection of the navy, which plays an important role in the composition of our armed forces. Combat in naval theaters assumes immeasurably greater significance in contemporary war than formerly.[46]

Sea power has *not* become the main element in Soviet strategy, nor can it. Theater forces, predominantly land with strong air support, remain the main component for the mission of gaining the Eurasian continent. So it is that Soviets continue to regard the main role of the Navy as cooperation in support of the land forces. In making this judgment the Soviets recognize that (to quote a naval officer writing in *Soviet Fleet* in 1957) : "The place and role of the Navy in the system of the armed forces cannot, of course, once and for all be taken as unchangeable." But the next sentence of this naval statement reads: "However, the main task of the Navy has been and *will remain* cooperation with the Soviet Army. . . ."[47]

Sea power has been granted an important, though not dominant, role in all of the major missions of the Soviet armed forces: the strategic offensive, the home defense, and the "tactical" or theater offensive. Its significance should not be neglected.

Notes to Chapter 9

1. See Garthoff, *Soviet Military Doctrine*, 1953, Chapter 21, for a review of wartime and postwar doctrine to 1953.

2. Marshal G. Zhukov, *Pravda*, February 20, 1956. Also Admiral S. Gorshkov, *Sovetskii flot*, February 23, 1956.

3. Admiral L. Vladimirsky, "New Technology on Ships," *Komsomol'skaia pravda*, July 23, 1955.

4. Lt. Col. M. Gvozdev, "Some Means of the Use of Atomic Energy for Power for Military Purposes," *Voennaia mysl'*, No. 9, September 1955, p. 31.

5. Capt. 1st Rank D. Shavtsov, "On Mastery of the Sea," *Voennaia mysl'*, No. 7, July 1955, p. 17.

6. A series of five articles under the supertitle "Atomic Explosion at Sea" was published in the naval paper *Sovetskii flot*, November 18, 23, and 28, and December 7 and 10, 1954. Other articles on "Atomic Defense of Ships" appeared in *Sovetskii flot* on January 4, 1955, and January 10, 1956.

7. Admiral L. Vladimirsky, *Sovetskii flot*, September 21, 1956; and see Admiral S. Gorshkov, *Sovetskii flot*, February 23, 1956.

8. D. A. Vershinin, *et al.*, "Tactics of the Naval Forces," *Bol'shaia Sovetskaia Entsiklopediia*, 2nd ed., Vol. 41, [April 21] 1956, pp. 544-45.

9. This estimated strength is based on various reliable reports; see the official NATO release, cited in *U. S. News and World Report*, July 20, 1956; Adm. Arleigh Burke, Chief of Naval Operations, cited in "Soviet Control of Seas on

Increase," Washington *Post and Times Herald,* February 1, 1956; Hanson Baldwin, "The Soviet's Forces—IV, A Study of the Navy," New York *Times,* March 29, 1956; "Soviet Navy Held Second in Power," New York *Times,* December 15, 1955; Col. L. D. Hittle, "The Rise of Russian Sea Power," *Marine Corps Gazette,* August 1955, pp. 20-22; Hanson W. Baldwin, "The Soviet Navy," *Foreign Affairs,* July 1955, pp. 587-604; and Hanson W. Baldwin, "Ivan Goes to Sea," *Saturday Evening Post,* November 2, 1957, pp. 112 and 114.

10. "Sinking of Soviet Cruiser by Mine in '55 Is Reported," New York *Times,* April 25, 1956.

11. *Ibid.; Aviation Week,* July 2, 1956, p. 26; and Elie Abel, "Russian Arms Cut Laid to Emphasis on Nuclear Power," New York *Times,* May 17, 1956.

12. Admiral L. Vladimirsky, *Komsomol'skaia pravda,* July 23, 1955.

13. Capt. 1st Rank D. Shavtsov, *Voennaia mysl',* No. 7, July 1955, p. 15.

14. Cited in "Soviet Navy Held Second in Power," New York *Times,* December 15, 1955.

15. Rear Adm. A. Sagoian, *Sovetskii flot,* May 17, 1956; and Eng. Lt. Cols. A. Ashenkov and I. Kudriashev, *Krasnaia zvezda,* December 15, 1955; see also Admiral V. Platonov, *Sovetskii flot,* December 14, 1956; Admiral L. Vladimirsky, *Krasnaia zvezda,* February 15, 1957; Col. N. Tsarev, *Sovetskii flot,* March 5, 1957; and Rear Admiral N. A. Pitersky, *Znai flot* (Know Your Fleet), DOSAAF, Moscow, [April 27] 1956, pp. 116-17.

16. For example, see the article by L. Gordon and N. Mal'tsev, "On the Question of Aircraft Carriers," *Morskoi Sbornik,* No. 4, April 1940, esp. p. 40.

17. Capt. 1st Rank D. Shavtsov, *Voennaia mysl',* No. 7, July 1955, p. 15. See also Eng. Col. A. Ashenkov and Eng. Lt. Col. I. Kudriashev, "Aircraft Carriers," in *Sovremennaia voennaia tekhnika,* [August 1] 1956, pp. 120-24.

18. For early comments, see Capt. Lt. I. A. Razumnyi, "Carrier Formations of the U. S. Navy in the War in the Pacific," *Morskoi sbornik,* No. 7, July 1946, pp. 61-86; and Major K. V. Laktionov, *Morskoi sbornik,* No. 11-12, November-December 1946, p. 125. For recent discussions, see Lt. Col. I. Kudanov, "Guided Missiles of the U.S. Navy," *Sovetskii flot,* June 5, 1955; Capt. 1st Rank D. Shavtsov, *Voennaia mysl',* No. 7, July, 1955, p. 15; Eng. Lt. Cols. A. Ashenkov and I. Kudriashev, "Aircraft Carriers," *Krasnaia zvezda,* December 15, 1955; Capt. 2nd Rank A. Aleshin, "The Organization of Anti-Ship Defense According to American Views," *Sovetskii flot,* January 20, 1956; and Rear Adm. A. Sagoian and Capt 1st Rank Z. Slepenkov, "American Views on the Employment of Aircraft Carriers," *Sovetskii flot,* May 17, 1956.

19. Marshal G. K. Zhukov, in *Krasnaia zvezda,* March 23, 1957.

20. Capt. 1st Rank D. Shavstov, *Voennaia mysl'* No. 7, July 1955, pp. 9 and 16.

21. For example, see Maj. Gen. of Aviation A. Shuginin, "Naval Aviation in the Fatherland War," *Vestnik vozdushnogo flota,* No. 7, July 1946, p. 16. Shuginin is now Chief of Staff of the Naval Air Force, and a lieutenant general.

22. Burke, cited in Washington *Post and Times Herald,* February 1, 1956; H. Baldwin, in New York *Times,* March 29, 1956; Hittle, in *Marine Corps Gazette,* August 1955, pp. 20-22.

23. Lt. Col. M. Gvozdev, *Voennaia mysl'*, No. 9, September 1955, p. 32.

24. For example, see Major G. Smirnov, "For Aggression at Sea: The Main Directions of Development of Flying Boats in the U.S.A.," *Sovetskii flot*, April 12, 1957.

25. For an early example, see the article by an anonymous Retired General, "Where the U.S. 'Policy of Strength' is Leading," *Izvestiia*, January 19, 1954.

26. See footnote 9 above.

27. Rear Admiral V. Andreev, "Sea and Ocean Communications in Contemporary War," *Krasnaia zvezda*, April 25, 1957.

28. "Statement of the Soviet Government Concerning President Eisenhower's Address of December 8, 1953," *Pravda*, December 22, 1953; Col. S. N. Kozlov, *Vooruzhenie armii*, 1954, p. 11; Prof. Maj. Gen. B. Olisov, "Atomic Weapons and Atomic Defense," *Krasnaia zvezda*, August 3, 1954; Eng. B. Liapunov, *Raketa* (Rockets) Voenizdat, Moscow, 1954, p. 127; "The Atomic Weapon," *Bol'shaia Sovetskaia Entsiklopediia*, 2nd ed., Vol. 31, [February 5] 1955, p. 243; Eng. Lt. Col. M. Arkhipov, in *Sovremennaia voennaia tekhnika*, [August 1] 1956, p. 6; Admiral V. Platonov, "Contemporary Views on the Conduct of Combat Operations at Sea," *Sovetskii flot*, December 14, 1956; Admiral L. Vladimirsky, "Contemporary Military Ship Construction," *Krasnaia zvezda*, February 15, 1957; Eng. B. V. Liapunov, *Rasskazy o raketakh* (Stories about Rockets), Gosenergizdat, Moscow-Leningrad, 1955, p. 8; and Capt. 1st Rank D. Shavtsov, *Voennaia mysl'*, No. 7, July 1955, p. 15.

29. Admiral L. Vladimirsky, *Komsomol'skaia pravda*, July 23, 1955; and Vladimirsky, *Krasnaia zvezda*, February 15, 1957.

30. *Ibid.*

31. Admiral L. Vladimirsky, *Sovetskii flot*, September 21, 1956. See also Capt. 2nd Rank I. Chernyshev, *Voennye znaniia*, No. 6, June 1957, p. 12; and Capt. 1st Rank D. Shavtsov, *Voennaia mysl'*, No. 7, July 1955, p. 16; Vladimirsky, *Komsomol'skaia pravda*, July 23, 1955; Vladimirsky, *Krasnaia zvezda*, February 15, 1957; Rear Adm. A. Kruchenykh, *Sovetskii flot*, March 23, 1957; and Maj. Gen. of Eng. Tech. Service G. Pokrovsky, *Voennaia mysl'*, No. 3, March 1955, p. 24.

32. Eng. Lt. Col. A. Ashenkov, "Contemporary Submarines," *Krasnaia zvezda*, May 11, 1956, and see Rear Adm. A. Kruchenykh, *Sovetskii flot*, November 15, 1957.

33. Prof. Rear Adm. N. Pavlovich, "The Naval Art and the Development of the Combat Technology of the Fleet," *Sovetskii flot*, March 6, 1957. See also Eng. Lt. Cols. M. Arkhipov and V. Yansiukevich, *Sovetskii flot*, December 4, 1957.

34. See Col. N. Aleksandrov, "An Underwater Container with a Rocket Weapon," *Sovetskii flot*, February 20, 1957; I. A. Bykhovsky, *Atomnye podvodnye lodki* (Atomic Submarines), Sudpromgiz, Leningrad, [July 25] 1957, pp. 61-63; and Lt. Col. G. Pol'sky, "Underwater Firing of Guided Missiles," *Voennye znaniia*, No. 9, September 1957, p. 17.

219

35. See Eng. Lt. Col. A. Ashenkov, *Krasnaia zvezda*, May 11, 1956; and Lt. Col. M. Gvozdev, *Voennaia mysl'*, No. 9, September 1955, p. 30.

36. Rear Adm. A. Kruchenykh, *Sovetskii flot*, March 23, 1957.

37. Capt. 1st Rank D. Shavtsov, *Voennaia mysl'*, No. 7, July 1955, p. 16.

38. Adm. L. Vladimirsky, *Krasnaia zvezda*, February 15, 1957.

39. Capt. 2nd Rank N. V'iunenko, "Some Questions of the Organization and Conduct of Naval Landing Operations," *Voennaia mysl'*, No. 2, February 1955, p. 33.

40. Lt. Col. M. Romanov, "Some Questions of Contemporary Counter-Landing Operations," *Voennaia mysl'*, No. 10, October 1955, p. 3.

41. V'iunenko, *Voennaia mysl'*, No. 2, February 1955, p. 28.

42. *Ibid.*, p. 27.

43. Adm. G. Levchenko, *Sovetskii flot*, November 18, 1956.

44. N. Gretsky, "Coast Artillery," *Voennye znaniia*, No. 12, December 1956, p. 13.

45. Adm. Arleigh Burke, cited in the New York *Times*, November 13, 1955.

46. Adm. S. Gorshkov, *Sovetskii flot*, February 23, 1956.

47. Capt. 1st Rank N. Nikolaev, "The Role of the Navy in the System of the Armed Forces of the U.S.S.R.," *Sovetskii flot*, May 29, 1957.

CHAPTER 10

MISSILES IN SOVIET STRATEGY

The Soviet announcement in August 1957 of their successful tests of an Intercontinental Ballistic Missile (ICBM) called the world's attention to the Soviet missile program. The launching of the first artificial satellite of the earth in October 1957 dramatically underscored the earlier Soviet announcement on the rocket. Both were but the latest and most publicized of many indications of the extensive and advanced character of Soviet rocket and missile development. What is the role of missiles—in particular, of long-range ballistic missiles, the IRBM and ICBM—in Soviet military strategy?

THE ROLE OF MISSILES

Long-range ballistic rockets are, as the Soviets recognize, "intended for firing against strategic targets disposed in the deep rear of the enemy. . . ."[1]

More specifically, as we shall see, enemy air bases and missile-launching bases are indicated to be in the category of strategic targets considered particularly appropriate for rocket attack. The strategic role of missiles is, thus, to an extent merely assignment of an additional capability to implement the strategic concept of achieving military victory by destroying the enemy's military forces located at distant and intercontinental

221

ranges. But there is also a peculiar role of long-range missiles extending beyond that of other weapons systems. It is this distinctive mission which makes it useful to consider the role of missiles in Soviet strategy separately from land, air, and sea power (each of which, as we have seen, employs appropriate guided missiles and rockets in defensive and offensive forms as a part of their now "conventional" armament). *Deterrence* is the mission to which the Soviet leaders have "assigned" long-range ballistic rockets (and also, apparently, part of the submarine missile-launching capability). Soviet commentaries on their ICBM, including remarks of Khrushchev, have reflected clearly this Soviet concern for a "deterrent" against the United States, and their reliance on ballistic rockets as such a deterrent.[2] There are, of course, no hard and fast separations of missions, and in a very real sense *all* the Soviet armed forces serve in part as a deterrent. Likewise, the military forces in general, but the long-range ballistic missiles in particular, serve as the basis for actions to deter and to pressure *others,* that is, for *blackmail.* This *offensive* political use of the new missile capability thus complements the *defensive* value of the weapons for deterrence. But the reasons behind the special role for long-range ballistic rockets in these non-hostilities "cold war" missions lie in the peculiar advantages—and limitations—of the weapon system. Both for this reason, and to delimit more clearly the role of long-range missiles from that of long-range aviation, it is desirable to note the Soviet views on the relative advantages of each.

ROCKETS VS. BOMBERS

In a number of public statements in the fall of 1957, most notably those of Khrushchev and Marshal of Aviation Vershinin, the Soviets claimed that ballistic rockets make bombers "obsolete." Khrushchev used the term "obsolete," and declared that: "The present period is something of a turning point.

Missiles

Military specialists believe that airplanes, bombers and fighters, are in their decline. Bombers have such speeds and altitudes that they are vulnerable to attack by contemporary rockets."[3] He also declared: "Fighter and bomber airplanes can now be put into museums."[4]

Marshal of Aviation Vershinin more soberly presented the military evaluation which Khrushchev characteristically exaggerated. Vershinin, after noting the abilities of the ICBM to strike any point on the globe, declared: "Under contemporary conditions, of course, bombers also are being built. The U.S.A. especially is basing itself on that form of weapon. But rocket weapons now impugn the expediency of development of bomber aviation, since rocket weapons are more reliable and more certain." In particular, Vershinin points out: "It is almost out of the question that rockets would not reach their targets. Contemporary means of air defense are ineffective in combatting these rockets."[5]

The theme that bombers are vulnerable to air defenses, while ballistic rockets are not, runs through the various military and political commentaries which have followed the Soviet ICBM development and announcement.[6] In part, of course, this view is disseminated because of the advantage to Soviet propaganda of claiming superiority in a weapon which, it is said, makes obsolete the weapon in which the United States is admittedly stronger. In fact, it is probable that the *actual* evaluation of the Soviet military leadership is less extreme. For there has been a definite recognition by competent Soviet military technicians and specialists of the continuing importance for some time of manned and unmanned bombers as well as ballistic missiles.

Beyond the statements stressing deterrence, the Soviets have revealed their evaluation of the specific military advantages—and limitations—of ballistic missiles. Thus, for example, Lt. Colonel Tiurnin noted (in early 1957) four particular advantages of guided and ballistic missiles over bomber aviation: (1) the possibility of using mobile launchers, (2) the all-

223

weather capability of guided missiles, (3) the opportunity for the use of missiles even under conditions of hostile general air superiority, and (4) the possibility of launching surprise blows from concealed launching points.[7] In the general Soviet view, at least as expressed prior to the definite Soviet acquisition of the ICBM (and hence as uncolored by the present propaganda emphasis on the rockets), the role of bombers will decline for certain missions but remain for others. The ICBM and IRBM will assume the burden of attacks on stationary strategic targets such as cities and industrial complexes, and operational targets such as known enemy air bases. Thus Major General of the Engineering Technical Services G. I. Pokrovsky, an authoritative military technologist, as early as March 1955, wrote in the semi-classified General Staff organ *Military Thought* that "the destruction of targets, the coordinates of which are known in advance, will more and more be accomplished by pilotless weapons armed with atomic and thermonuclear warheads."[8] Again, in the fall of 1956, General Pokrovsky spoke of this new important role for ballistic rockets in particular. But he also noted that for some important missions the ballistic missiles were not suitable, and that guided missiles and conventional bombers would continue to be necessary for these roles. In his words: "Long-range rockets can only destroy targets, the coordinates of which are known in advance. They cannot destroy mobile targets. For this, self-seeking guided missiles or piloted weapons are needed, since a man can pilot or guide by remote control, observing combat targets beyond the battlefield with the aid of television."[9] General Pokrovsky has subsequently (in 1957) reiterated that the future employment of ballistic missiles will be against "targets previously known and precisely located on the map."[10]

Bomber aviation, and guided missiles or pilotless bombers, will in the Soviet view thus continue to have important roles. Again, Major General Pokrovsky has stressed this in a commentary made *after* the Soviet ICBM.[11] The main role of bombers will probably be to find and attack targets not previously identified or precisely located: the traditional mission of armed reconnaissance. And, probably still considered valid, in manned bomber systems, "aviation guided missiles [air-to-surface missiles] can be employed for operations against strategically important targets having strong air defenses."[12]

On the whole, however, the role of long-range bombers will probably be what it has been in the past; to serve as the far-reaching military arm to be employed, in conjunction with all other arms of the military forces, against the armed forces of the enemy.

In discussing the current Soviet evaluation of the relative roles of the ICBM and bomber aviation, it may be useful to note that the apparently continuing Soviet evaluation was first made in the immediate postwar period, prior to the virtual ban on discussion of missiles which prevailed from 1947 until late 1953. Major General of Aviation Tatarchenko was the first to raise the question, in an article in the official Air Forces' journal, in 1946. He posed the issue flatly: "Can long-range rockets replace bomber aviation?" And he answered:

> An underestimation of this new mighty means of warfare [missiles] would be a fatal mistake. To even a moderately educated person it must be clear that this new weapon in 1944-1945 appeared in an extremely primitive early form. One can hardly doubt that it will in the future develop significantly further. *But does that mean that long-range rocket bombs will completely replace the bomber in the air? Of course not!* As the battleship did not replace the cruiser, nor the mine-layer, nor the cutter, nor even the rowboat, similarly even the most grandiose development of rockets will not eliminate the necessity for any class of aircraft, least of all high-speed giant aircraft, bomber and transport.
>
> High-speed giant aircraft are the foundation of strategic aviation. Missions of this form of aviation are extremely varied and cannot be accomplished with rocket bombs alone. *Rocket missiles are a means for destroying stationary targets which occupy considerable area. The realm of use of rocket missiles is fairly specific. Strategic aviation resolves many times more universal missions.*[13]

While these may have been Tatarchenko's own ideas, there are indications that these views in general probably represented the attitude of the Soviet Long-Range Air Force staff at that time. Marshal of Aviation Skripko, then Deputy Commander of the Long-Range Air Force, stated in *Red Star* later in 1946: "It is entirely obvious that with the contemporary level of technology the operation of formations of long-range aircraft with well-trained crews will without doubt be more effective than the dispatch of 'blind missiles' alone. Strategic aviation will develop along with the appearance of new weapons."[14] In part, of course, the Soviets may not have foreseen the potentialities of rockets in 1946 (though Tatarchenko was one of the very few who at least attempted to!). Even as late as the fall of 1954, Engineer Lt. Colonel Safonov noted in the Air Force's journal, without giving any sign of disagreement, that foreign sources had said that "even in 1960" ballistic missiles "will have a range not exceeding 500-600 km." and cruise-type guided missiles "not over 1000 km." range.[15] The fact that this statement was so obviously a gross understatement is curious and interesting, especially in view of its appearance in late 1954. Colonel Safonov then concluded with a statement which would appear to be at variance with Western calculations of the implications of high-yield weapons for requirements of accuracy, unless gross errors indeed are expected: "An atomic missile, as a big expensive weapon, must be delivered accurately on the target."[16] But still more curious was the appearance as late as January 1957 of a repetition of the idea that "nuclear, and especially hydrogen, weapons" are so expensive that they must be accurately delivered.[17] Nonetheless, Soviet advances, both in rocketry and in nuclear weapons design, had evidently led them by late 1957 to conclude that for stationary, known targets ballistic missiles are sufficiently accurate to be the most expedient weapon. Bomber aviation will continue, even after ballistic rockets are available in sufficient operational quantities, to play an important role in attacking untriangulated, mobile, and fleeting targets, particularly the enemy's military forces.

FUTURE PROSPECTS FOR BALLISTIC MISSILES

The confidence of recent Soviet statements, made in the flush of their achievement of the ICBM prior to the United States, may seem in itself to answer the question. As Major General Pokrovsky put it as early as 1956: "The future without doubt, belongs to long-range ballistic rockets. . . ."[18] For, as he explained, "one can suppose that after some time the practical accuracy of long-range rockets will approximate the accuracy of bombing from high altitudes from high-speed aircraft. Such rockets, obviously, will quickly supplant long-range aviation."[19] But General Pokrovsky, himself a "missile enthusiast," has more recently cautioned also that the ICBM is not in any sense an "ultimate weapon," that possible means of defense against it will exist, and that manned airplanes and guided missiles will be necessary to evade enemy defenses.[20] A German Communist military commentator who also has been a "missile enthusiast," Egbert von Frankenberg, similarly stated (in 1956) that the ICBM "can, in certain circumstances, cause havoc, but its accuracy in hitting the target depends upon many uncertain factors."[21] Thus it is useful to examine Soviet views on future improvement and development of ballistic missiles.

One line of further development, which the Soviets do not discuss in any detail, is the gradual perfection of rockets themselves. New developments in highly heat-resistant metals and ceramics will permit greater speeds of re-entry into the earth's atmosphere. Thus the problem of interception, already very great, will become still more difficult. Also, new improved solid propellants will decrease the time required for preparing and firing the ICBM.

One possibility foreseen for the distant future is nuclear propulsion of rocket missiles. As early as September 1945, Lt.

General of Artillery Nesterenko raised this possibility in the authoritative *Military Thought*.[22] Again, in early 1947, Lt. General of Artillery Kuleshov wrote about this possibility of the use of nuclear propulsion to "increase the speed, range, and power of rocket projectiles."[23] There followed a long silence during the period of intensive postwar censorship (1947-53), but since 1954 a number of Soviet sources have written with implicit optimism of the possibility of nuclear propulsion for rockets (among others, Major General Pokrovsky and the engineer B. Liapunov).[24]

One general statement of possible interest, made in 1954, mentioned the potentiality of accuracy and unlimited range of rockets. Professor Kosmodemiansky, writing in a booklet, stated: "Rocket projectiles can be shot to any distance. Contemporary successes of radar and teleguidance make possible the achievement of satisfactory accuracy in hitting the designated target."[25]

It is from these perspectives that the Soviets see the growing role of long-range ballistic missiles gradually replacing many but not all of the missions of piloted bombers. It is also useful to examine in this context Soviet views on the problem and prospects of *defense* against ballistic missiles.

DEFENSE AGAINST LONG-RANGE BALLISTIC MISSILES

As we have noted, since the Soviet announcement in August 1957 of attainment of an ICBM there have been many statements commenting to the effect that: "The advantage of ballistic rockets over strategic bombers consists in that they are practically invulnerable to present means of air defense. By virtue of their speed and altitude they can deal surprise blows on anyone."[26] But these statements do not reflect the full span of Soviet attention to the problem.

In two books which went to press in October and November, 1956, Major General Pokrovsky contributed the first serious

Soviet discussions of problems of defense against ballistic missiles. His comments are sufficiently incisive and well stated to deserve liberal quotation. In the first of these accounts, regarding interception of a ballistic missile once launched, he calls attention to the fact that

> . . . in flight, a long-range rocket has extremely great speed.
> . . . One can suppose that a long-range rocket, launched by the enemy by surprise, will be detected by radar only several tens of seconds before the moment of detonation, and too little time will remain for a normal alarm and shelter of people. Thus a long-range rocket in practice achieves surprise of attack on a distant target. A massed blow of long-range rockets, launched by surprise by an aggressor against a peaceful country will be especially powerful, since the launching pads and rockets on these launchers can be prepared in concealment in peacetime without possibility of their reconnaissance and destruction by the defender.[27]

In the other book he similarly declared that the speed of a ballistic rocket "prevents its interception and destruction by conventional flying means [fighter-interceptors], artillery fire, *or any other means*. It is possible that some counter-weapon will be found, but without doubt for quite some time the probability of destruction of the rockets cannot be very great."[28] In March, 1957, he reiterated these views.[29] But in an article in September, 1957, when the whole weight of jubilant Soviet comment was on the great advantages of ballistic rockets, he cautioned that a defense against the ICBM could and would be developed in the future. Pokrovsky's article marked the first Soviet reference to radar detection of an ICBM. His estimate of 200 miles radar detection, giving 50 seconds warning, provides for a possible defensive rocket interception.[30] And, he noted, a ballistic rocket cannot take evasive action.

A technical officer, Major Kriksunov, contributed an interesting article on "Problems of the Interception of Intercontinental Ballistic Rockets," in which he discussed nuclear warhead requirements for the anti-missile missile. He recommended a "small atomic charge" of 20 KT, and said a CEP (circle of probable error) of 300 meters would be sufficient to destroy the ICBM.[31]

Another technical specialist, Lt. Colonel Nikolaev, in another article devoted to interception of both ballistic and guided missiles, claimed that basically the problem of defense and interception is the same as against piloted bombers. The same weapons system of interceptors and anti-aircraft artillery rockets would serve. But one problem he advances is quite unique. He declared that in possibly detonating the intercepted missile, i.e., in "the explosion of a thermonuclear warhead even at distances of 30 to 40 kilometers from the air defense weapons, the latter will receive significant damage and will be overcome [sic] by radioactive contamination."[32] It is curious that he doesn't also note the similar effect of an intercepted but detonated charge on the *primary* target, but limits his comment to the effect on the air defense installation. This could mean that the Soviet air defenses are so deployed that they might be subject to damage in cases where the primary targets are not.

These comments suggest the line of Soviet thinking on the prospects for defenses against ballistic rockets: in the short run, virtually none; in the longer run, defenses will be found. But the Soviets appreciate fully that the best defense against missiles "must consist in dealing preemptive blows on their launchers,"[33] that is, to hit them before they can be fired. Again, the most valuable Soviet discussion is one by Major General Pokrovsky, who wrote in 1956:

> The most effective defense against such long-range rockets is by means of their destruction in the storage places, in the process of transport, and on the launching platforms where the preparation for each firing takes a rather long time. Unfortunately, one must keep in mind that the launching platforms for long-range rockets do not require very complicated preliminary equipping, and therefore can be deployed in the most unexpected places, where helicopters can quickly

bring the components of the rocket and the necessary equipment for assembly and firing.[34]

And, further, "each rocket can be launched from an individual
launching pad, and moreover these launching platforms can
be constructed relatively quickly, quite dispersed, and well
concealed. Their detection by the enemy prior to the launching
of the rocket can be made difficult, and in any case more
difficult than the detection of airfields. Therefore it will be
very difficult for the enemy to prevent the launching of a
rocket."[35]

Thus we see that the Soviets consider the ICBM and IRBM
to be practically invulnerable to interception, and practically
invulnerable to enemy attack before launching. In short, the
ballistic missile is the logical and best weapons system for the
mission of *deterrence*.

OPERATIONAL CONTROL OF BALLISTIC MISSILES

The vexing problem of assigning missiles to the services—for
operational employment and for research and development
—has plagued our own development program and affects our
strategic planning. What is the Soviet solution to this problem?

In the early postwar period, a number of Army, especially
artillery, generals displayed the greatest interest in rocket development (Major General of Aviation Tatarchenko, whom we
have cited, was indeed virtually the sole Air Force exception).
We have noted Lt. General of Artillery Nesterov's farsighted
interest in nuclear propulsion for an ICBM as early as September 1945. Lt. General Gerasimov predicted in May 1946, in
the official Ground Forces' journal, that "the significance of
rocket artillery, which is difficult to detect and capable of firing
projectiles with sufficient accuracy to destroy targets located
hundreds *and possibly thousands of kilometers away*, will grow
. . . ."[36] In January 1947, Lt. General of Artillery P. N. Kuleshov, in his article on "Rocket Artillery and its Future,"

stated that "a great future opens for rocket artillery, *especially for long-range artillery*," and he further spoke of "rocket artillery of *strategic significance*."[37]

In the postwar research and development program both artillery and Air Force institutions and officers have played important roles. Chief Marshal of Artillery Voronov has been reported to have headed the whole missile program, at least as of several years ago. Marshal of Artillery Yakovlev has also been active in this work. Development of rocket propulsion units, and such work on guided pilotless bombers as has been done, have been directed by the appropriate Air Force agencies, while work on ballistic rockets has apparently been conducted under artillery supervision. The head of the Technical Sciences Section of the U.S.S.R. Academy of Sciences is Academician A. A. Blagonravov—a lieutenant general of the artillery technical services.

The Soviet development program has, according to all available indications such as the accounts of former German scientists who worked on missiles development in the Soviet Union from 1946 to 1953, followed an early and continuing Soviet stress on ballistic rockets. After a few years, relatively little attention was given to non-ballistic guided missiles. This stands in some contrast to the U.S. Air Force emphasis prior to 1953 on guided cruise-type missiles such as the *Snark* and *Navaho*, which promised greater accuracy and payload but at the price of greater vulnerability to the enemy's defenses. This has permitted Communist propaganda to claim an advantage over us, even before the announcment of their priority in successful testing of an ICBM. Thus, for example, the commentary of an East German, Kurt Shulz, who in late 1956 declared that "in recent years it was believed in the United States that guided missiles were superior to ballistic missiles as regards range and accuracy. Accordingly, missiles controlled [guided] by various devices were created in the United States. . . . But all of these techniques have considerable shortcomings. They call for elaborate electronic devices built into the rocket, and for a close-knit radar network for guiding the missile. The main weakness is the high degree of vulnerability of the apparatus to electronic interference of all kinds [ECM]." Shulz continued: "The Americans have only recently realized their mistake and concentrated all their efforts on the making of unguided ballistic rockets. *They are lagging ten years behind the Soviet Union, which took this path from the outset* [e.g., right after the war]." [38] This claim is false, and the purpose solely propaganda. But, as we have noted, there is an underlying element of truth in describing the consistent Soviet stress on ballistic rockets. The Soviets may, however, also have developed a long-range guided missile to perform other missions (such as reconnaissance or "saturation" of warning radar and active air defenses).

By late 1956 several Soviet generals and marshals of artillery were permitted publicly to state (in Colonel General of Artillery Fomin's words) that *"long-range rocket weapons of intermediate and strategic types . . . constitute a form of artillery. Now artillery can be employed . . . also far beyond the limits of the tactical zone of operations of the ground forces."* [39] Colonel General of Artillery Samsonov similarly spoke of long-range rockets as "a variant of rocket-firing guns. Thus we witness a new qualitative leap in the development of *artillery*." [40] And Marshal of Artillery Chistiakov declared that "rocket artillery can be employed for firing atomic projectiles not only in the tactical zone of operations of the ground forces and in their interests, but also *along with* [not as part of] Long-Range Aviation for *strategic* purposes." [41]

In his interview with *Pravda* in September 1957, as we noted earlier, Marshal of Aviation Vershinin stressed the advantages of the ICBM over bombers. This particular comment, and the interview as a whole, has been interpreted by some Western observers as an indication that the Soviet Air Force has been given responsibility for the ICBM. Such an assumption is easily made in terms of our own tradition. However, while this is possible, Vershinin's interview is certainly not a real or reliable indication. For example, he also speaks of the advantages of submarine-launched missiles—a naval weapon. Moreover, when Vershinin spoke of the great destructiveness of mutual strategic use of thermonuclear-loaded missiles, he commented: "We are not speaking of *an artillery duel* or air bombardment, in the meaning that they had in the recent war." [42] The comparison with World War II air bombings is certainly understandable, but it is difficult indeed to conceive his reference to artillery save in terms of considering the ballistic rocket as modern artillery—the terms used by the artillery generals. In this case, it was a sign of Air Force acknowledgment of its own declining strategic role relative to the ballistic artilleryman. While this interpretation is purely speculative, it might find support in the sudden replacement of Chief Marshal of Aviation Zhigarev in January 1957, by Vershinin. Zhigarev had been reported to be a missile enthusiast, and he may have objected unsuccessfully to a decision late in 1956 to give the ICBM to a special new Long-Range Ballistic Rocket Command dominated by artillerymen.

Ultimate control of the ICBM may well be vested in an autonomous "Strategic Striking Force," probably combining the Long-Range Air Force with the long-range missiles, and possibly including a submarine missile-launching component as well. If the strategic air force is not included, it is likely that an artillery marshal will be given the command. If the ballistic rocket artillery and long-range bomber forces are both included, it would be logical to expect a Marshal of the Soviet Union to assume the command, with a marshal of artillery in charge of the rockets, and a marshal of aviation in command of the bombers (and possibly of the guided cruise-type missiles, if such are developed, as pilotless bombers). This would parallel the earlier decision to place the joint Air Defense Forces under, first, a series of artillery generals, and as the importance of the command grew, under a Marshal of the Soviet Union (S. S. Biriuzov).

As we have seen, the Army, the Navy, the Air Force, and the Air Defense Forces each has been assigned the missiles and rockets required by its missions, including missiles up to and probably including the IRBM for both the ground forces and the Navy. The Long-Range or Strategic Ballistic Missile Force, whether entirely separate or associated with the Long-Range Air Force, will doubtless become a most important autonomous command directly subordinate to the Minister of Defense. Its primary missions—deterrence of the West from war, and pressure short of war—are of the greatest political sensitivity and require close coordination with the juncture of military and political strategic policy-making. This is the special role of missiles in Soviet strategy

Notes to Chapter 10

1. Col. I. Metreveli, "Guided Missiles," *Voennye znaniia*, No. 12, December 1955, p. 14.

2. See, for example, Khrushchev's comments reported in the New York *Times,* October 8, 1957

3. Khrushchev, in an interview with Mr. Reston, cited in the New York *Times,* October 10, 1957.

4. Khrushchev, at a reception in Moscow, cited in the Washington *Post and Times Herald,* October 8, 1957.

5. Marshal of Aviation K. A. Vershinin, *Pravda,* September 8, 1957, and *Krasnaia zvezda,* September 10, 1957.

6. To note but a few, see the official announcement itself, *Tass* and *Radio Moscow,* August 26, 1957, and *Pravda,* August 27, 1957; L. Rovinsky in *Novoe vremiia,* No. 37, September 12, 1957, p. 15; and Engineer Major V. Kruchinin, in *Krasnaia zvezda,* September 3, 1957.

7. Eng. Lt. Col. V. Tiurnin, "Guided Missiles with Atomic Warheads," *Krasnaia zvezda,* January 11, 1957.

8. Maj. Gen. of Eng. Tech. Service G. I. Pokrovsky, *Voennaia mysl',* No. 3, March 1955, p. 23. Also, see V. D. Moskalev, *Uchebnoe posobie po MPVO,* (Civil Defense Handbook) , 1956, p. 11.

9. Pokrovsky, *Nauka i tekhnika v sovremennykh voinakh,* Voenizdat, Moscow, [October 8] 1956, p. 78.

10. Pokrovsky, *Voennye znaniia,* No. 3, March 1, 1957, p. 37.

11. Pokrovsky, *Sovetskii patriot,* September 11, 1957.

12. Dr. Prof. Maj. Gen. of Eng. Tech. Service V. Pugachev and Eng. Major V. Marisov, "Guided Missiles: Structure and Means of Employment," *Krasnaia*

zvezda, February 15, 1955. See also Eng. Col. G. Metreveli, "Guided Missiles," *Voennye znaniia*, No. 12, December 1955, pp. 14-15.

13. Maj. Gen. of Aviation Ye. I. Tatarchenko, "Some Problems of the Development of Air Power," *Vestnik Vozdushnogo Flota*, No. 5-6, May-June 1946, p. 63.

14. Marshal of Aviation N. Skripko, "Long Range Aviation," *Krasnaia zvezda*, August 11, 1946.

15. Eng. Lt. Col. P. Safonov, *Vestnik vozdushnogo flota*, No. 9, September 1954, p. 78.

16. *Ibid.*, p. 79.

17. Col. B. Aleksandrov, "Aircraft, Carriers of Atomic Weapons," *Krylia rodiny*, No. 1, January 1957, p. 30.

18. Maj. Gen. G. Pokrovsky, *Marksizm-leninizm o voine i armii*, Moscow, [November 28] 1956, p. 254.

19. *Ibid.*, p. 255.

20. Pokrovsky, *Sovetskii patriot*, September 11, 1957.

21. E. von Frankenberg, *Radio Berlin*, East Germany, January 28, 1956.

22. Lt. Gen. of Artillery A. Nesterenko, "On the Role of Rocket Artillery," *Voennaia mysl'*, No. 9, September 1945, p. 31.

23. Lt. Gen. of Artillery P. N. Kuleshov, "Rocket Artillery and Its Future," *Za oboronu*, No. 1-2, January 1947, p. 24.

24. Maj. Gen. G. Pokrovsky, in *Marksizm-leninizm o voine, armii, i voennoi nauke* (Marxism-Leninism on War, the Army, and Military Science), Voenizdat, Moscow, [February 3] 1955, p. 170; B. V. Liapunov, *Rasskazy o raketakh* (Stories About Rockets), Gosenergizdat, Moscow-Leningrad, 1955, pp. 71-73; M. K. Tikhonravov and B. V. Liapunov, "Rockets," *Bol'shaia Sovetskaia Entsiklopediia*, 2nd ed., Vol. 35, 1955, pp. 667-68; P. G. Perel'man, "Atomic Propulsion," *Nauka i zhizn'*, No. 1, January 1956, pp. 26 ff.

25. Dr. Prof. A. A. Kosmodemiansky, *Znamenitiyi deital' nauki K. E. Tsiolkovsky* (The Notable Scientist K. E. Tsiolkovsky), 2nd ed., Voenizdat, Moscow, 1954, p. 127.

26. N. Varvarov, "Intercontinental Ballistic Missiles," *Sovetskii flot*, August 30, 1957.

27. Pokrovsky, *Nauka i tekhnika v sovremennykh voinakh*, [October 8] 1956, p. 51.

28. Pokrovsky, in *Marksizm-leninizm o voine i armii*, [November 28] 1956, p. 255.

29. Pokrovsky, in *Voennye znaniia*, No. 3, March 1, 1957, p. 37.

30. Pokrovsky, *Sovetskii patriot*, September 11, 1957.

31. Eng. Maj. V. Kriksunov, *Sovetskaia aviatsiia*, April 25, 1957.

32. Eng. Lt. Col. M. Nikolaev, "Problems of Interception of Intercontinental Pilotless Aircraft," *Sovetskaia aviatsiia*, March 21, 1957.

33. Rear Admiral A. Kruchenykh, in *Sovetskii flot*, March 23, 1957. The con-

text of his statement was naval ballistic missiles, but the reference is also applicable to the ICBM.

34. Pokrovsky, *Marksizm-leninizm o voine i armii,* [November 28] 1956, p. 201.

35. Pokrovsky, *Nauka i tekhnika v sovremennykh voinakh,* [October 8] 1956, p. 51. See also the same view expressed by N. Varvarov, in *Sovetskii flot,* August 30, 1957.

36. Lt. Gen. M. Gerasimov, "On Certain Problems of the Training of Troops," *Voennyi vestnik,* No. 10, May 1946, p. 29.

37. Lt. Gen. of Artillery P. N. Kuleshov, "Rocket Artillery and Its Future," *Za oboronu,* Nos. 1-2, January 1947, p. 24.

38. Kurt Shulz, *Radio Berlin,* East Germany, December 7, 1956.

39. Col. Gen. of Artillery N. S. Fomin, *Sovetskaia rossiia,* November 18, 1956.

40. Col. Gen. of Artillery F. A. Samsonov, *Radio Moscow,* November 17, 1956.

41. Marshal of Artillery M. N. Chistiakov, *Krasnaia zvezda,* November 18, 1956.

42. Marshal of Aviation K. Vershinin, *Pravda,* September 8, 1957.

IV

CHAPTER 11

A LOOK INTO THE FUTURE:

SOVIET STRATEGY IN 1970 AND BEYOND

Discussion of Soviet strategy in the period of 1970 requires three presuppositions. In the first place, it is assumed that no *major* Soviet-American war has occurred in the interim, though significant limited wars may have occurred. Secondly, it assumes that that no real settlement of differences and agreement on major disarmament has been reached. Finally, it assumes that the Soviet Union has not suffered an internal revolution.

Why 1970? The preceding chapters of this book have analyzed Soviet military doctrine and strategy as they exist in 1958. The impact of this military weapons system and doctrine will necessarily continue for a number of years. Important modifications and innovations may occur in the 1960's, but the length of time needed for changing from a new concept to a new strategy limits substantially the possibility of drastic change for about a decade—that is, if the strategy is to be implemented by appropriate capabilities. The main lines of development in the 1960's have been spelled out in the preceding discussions: we can see the perfection of ballistic rockets, submarine-launched missiles, air defense missiles, nuclear-propelled aircraft and rockets, and finally the various means for transforming the Army's weapons and transportation means for the nuclear battlefield of the future.

The present chapter is, to the author's knowledge, the first attempt made to forecast (though not to "predict" precisely) the Soviet strategy and weapons systems of ten to fifteen years from now. Tremendous changes will mark the 1970's. War will, literally, be "out of this world" as even outer space becomes a new potential battleground.

STRATEGIC OBJECTIVES

The world of 1970 may have seen important shifts in the balance of power in various parts of the globe. Until quite recently this fact alone would have rendered almost impossible a projection of any strategy. But in the future even massive shifts may sometimes occur without altering the fundamental military significance of some key strategic facts. Most probably, the Soviet Union will have achieved certain gains in its position, and also will have suffered some failures and setbacks. No prediction of the net balance is either possible or necessary. Eastern Europe may have been lost to the Communists; or Western Europe may have been weakened and partly won by the Soviets. The Near East and Africa may have matured without falling under the Soviet spell or subversion, or they may have been substantially eroded away from neutralism and the West by Soviet efforts. A serious possibility in Asia is a growing estrangement of Communist China from the Soviet Union. Alternatively, the Soviet-Chinese Bloc may remain closely united. It may have gained in Korea, Japan and Southeast Asia, or it may have suffered reverses in territory presently occupied. A balance of Soviet losses—or gains—in Europe, the Near East, and the Far East would be important, but it would probably not alter basically the fundamental Soviet objective: to preserve and improve the Soviet position by all measures short of general war.

If there has been a substantial *stability* of the presently prevailing balance of power in the world, the Soviets may well have turned their energies increasingly to internal problems.

A Look into the Future

The intensity of the Soviet drive for expansion of influence may have declined, though the objective will probably remain. Opportunities for advance will never be neglected. But the drive for expansion may subside in the face of prolonged stalemate. Emphasis on military forces to preserve mutual deterrence will then predominate.

If the Soviets have succeeded in substantially *gaining* in Eurasia and Eurafrica, they will presumably be more confident that their wave of gradual victory will continue to sweep on toward the last redoubt of opposition, North America. A train of successes in cold war and cold peace will counsel continued avoidance of war, but military strategy will face with greater urgency the requirements of neutralization and seizure of America in the last-gasp struggle by weakened "imperialism." The Soviets will probably anticipate, whether correctly or not, an increasing danger of American initiation of a preventive war to stop the Red Tide.

If the Soviets have *lost* heavily, the increasing internal instability of the Soviet regime may tempt some elements of the leadership for reasons of personal or regime survival to initiate a "preventive war" of desperation. The degree of Western pressure might mitigate or stimulate such tendencies. But the strategic requirements for neutralizing the United States would be dominant, accompanied by serious attention to building the necessary elements of military power for defense and offense on the periphery of the Soviet bloc.

Thus the political-military situation will importantly affect the emphases in Soviet military strategic planning and establishment of force levels. But in all three cases important military requirements will exist in common.

ORGANIZATION, COMMAND, AND STRATEGIC PLANNING

In addition to the influence on Soviet strategy of developments defining the geostrategic arena, an important element

243

in strategic planning will be the new blood in the High Command. By 1970 the High Command will be composed of men who were but battalion, company and even platoon commanders in World War II, and military theoretical development will be largely in the hands of staff colonels who entered military service *after* World War II. (By contrast, today's marshals were battalion and regimental commanders in the Russian Civil War). The implications of this change will probably be great, and they cannot all be foreseen. Most important, the technological acuteness of these new senior military men will be very high. The role of the military in the Soviet political system, while difficult to judge, will probably be at least sufficiently important in military strategic matters to insure the adoption of the new weapons systems which will emerge.

The organization of the armed forces will gradually evolve further along the lines of *missions* rather than geophysical mediums of conflict: (1) *strategic deterrent forces* (ICBM, suboceanic launched missiles, and others to be discussed); (2) *theater forces* (ground, airborne, air support, naval coastal support); (3) *strategic offensive forces* (bombers and guided missiles, strategic airborne and amphibious forces); and (4) *strategic defensive forces* (anti-ICBM, air defense, and others). The elements of the Navy and Air Forces will thus tend to diffuse into these various missions; the Army will continue to dominate the second and will come to contribute to the third as long-range invasion forces are formed. The new missile force (the first listed) will rise to great importance, to priority status if the balance of power is largely stalemated. Both the strategic offensive and defensive forces will further develop. The surface navy, the traditional infantry, the interdiction and aerial superiority air forces, and the conventional bomber aviation arms will all tend substantially to fade away.

It is the new weapons systems and capabilities of the four basic arms of the future military establishment which will determine the potentialities and characteristics of Soviet strategy in the 1970's. The new weapons systems briefly sketched below

244

are generally projections of ideas now being explored by the Soviets, which may succeed by that time.

THE STRATEGIC DETERRENT FORCES

The greatest changes will occur in the now just emerging strategic deterrent force. The ICBM, in its earliest operational form, will by the early 1960's have largely assumed this mission from the bomber aviation (which had been the only available marginal substitute during the 1950's). But a series of new weapons emerging in the 1960's will add substantially to the variety and potency of this new force. First, there will be advanced ICBM's, as new highly heat-resistant materials and new fuels—including nuclear—permit more advanced models to achieve still higher speeds of re-entry into the earth's atmosphere, and thus to reduce interceptibility.

A second series of deterrent weapons will be the suboceanic-launched rockets. One category developing in the 1960's will be the subsurface-launched IRBM fired from especially prepared submarines. But other potentialities also will be utilized by the 1970's. For one, subsurface containers can be delivered and anchored by submarine at sea, and later fired by remote control. These weapons would not have great accuracy, but they would be exceedingly difficult to detect. Hence they are well suited to deterrence, though not to "counter-force" destruction of military objectives. Their deterrent value would derive from the fact that large thermonuclear warheads would wreak great havoc, and could in fact depend for their main effect on radioactive fallout. If launched in the Pacific, the prevailing winds could carry this deadly radioactive fallout over the entire United States. Also, as the geography of the oceanic floor becomes known (and the Soviets are now very active in oceanographic mapping, especially in the Pacific Ocean) the suboceanic terrain can be used for "fixing" locations accurately enough for aiming ballistic missiles. Undersea permanent *manned* missile stations are even possible.

245

A third element in the strategic deterrent capability will be the accurate mapping (for ICBM target purposes) of the entire globe by means of infra-red, photographic, television and other devices in satellites used for reconnaissance missions. This will be the first military utilization of the *sputnik,* and by 1970 it will already be "conventional."

A fourth element of strategic deterrence will probably be advanced "ABC weapons"—weapons of (atomic) radiological warfare (RW), bacteriological warfare (BW), and chemical warfare (CW). Such weapons exist today, but will surely be more potent and more readily deliverable in military significant doses by 1970. They can, for example, also be released from suboceanic containers in the Pacific to "ride" the prevailing winds covering the United States. Soviet research on cosmic rays, now actively in progress, may yield potentialities for a real harnessing of the sun's power in a "death-ray" weapon.

The fifth and most novel form of deterrent weapon will be the IPBM—the "InterPlanetary Ballistic Missile." Space platforms—in 1970 unmanned, and later possibly manned—can be placed to orbit around the earth like an ordinary *sputnik,* or can be established on the moon. In either case, they may be armed with ballistic rockets which can later be fired at specific target areas on the earth. More simply, armed rockets may themselves be sent up as satellites to cruise around the world until fired by prearranged signal.

These are all realistic possible weapons for 1970 and the years soon following. Moreover, the Soviets have already developed an interest in submarine-launched missiles, oceanic containers with ballistic missiles, radiological warfare, and reconnaissance and rocket-launching satellites.

THE THEATER FORCES

The theater forces will be essentially the Army of the future, one at least as different from that of today as the present one is from that of World War II. Conventional infantry will have been replaced by fully mechanized and largely "airbornized" soldiers. Conventional artillery will remain, but the major weapons of artillery will be rockets, ranging from less than one to more than a thousand miles in range of fire, and from high-explosive to high-yield thermonuclear shells. Mobility will transform both the infantry and artillery into armored forces, and the tank forces will thus tend to merge or absorb them. New tanks may even fire nuclear shells, and tanks may be developed which can fly. The greater operational mobility required for future nuclear war of maneuver will be gained by the widespread use of varied vertical-takeoff aircraft, aerodynes and helicopters. Not only will the new Army take to the air, it will take to the ground. New vehicles for *subterranean* movement, or at least rapid burrowing for temporary protection, will have appeared. New means of communications, including television, and night vision aids, will permit rapid reconnaissance and movement. Such tactical aviation as remains will be even more closely integrated into the Army. In addition to the use of nuclear shells, rockets, and bombs, there may be "battlefield" use of paralyzing gases and rays, and of radiological weapons.

The purpose of the theater forces would be the rapid subjection of all the Eastern hemisphere. "Nuclear neutralization" by massive destruction might be employed against key enemy areas of great resistance (such as Great Britain), but on the whole the Soviets would expect to conquer, rather than pulverize, Eurasia and Africa. For this purpose of conquest, the large theater forces would have to be maintained.

THE STRATEGIC OFFENSIVE FORCES

The feature distinguishing strategic offensive forces from the weapons systems of strategic deterrence is the purpose. In the event of war, that is the failure or considered abandonment of deterrence, the weapons of destruction which had until that time served a deterrent purpose would be used for attack. But additional capabilities would be needed. For one thing, attack on enemy offensive forces requires more accurate delivery than do weapons of terror for deterrence. The enemy's own deterrent and offensive forces will be "hardened" against mere drops of multi-megaton bombs and rockets in the vicinity, and the time for radioactive fallout to take effect is critical. Hence great precision of accuracy is required, and in 1970 this may still mean largely the use of supersonic, possibly nuclear-propelled, manned bombers and glide rockets, and unmanned guided missiles, in addition to the ICBM.

Destruction is not, however, the only means of neutralization of the enemy. In addition to these various long-range nuclear strikes, the Soviets will seek to *seize territory* in order to deny any possibility of continued resistance and to consolidate gains. Thus the strategic offensive forces must include powerful *invasion* capabilities if the Soviets ever hope completely to suppress the United States. By 1970 there will probably be strong forces for transoceanic invasion in giant transport submarines, and in nuclear-powered and conventional transport aircraft, and during the 1970's perhaps by transport rocket as well.

THE STRATEGIC DEFENSIVE FORCES

Air defense, in the old-fashioned form of the 1950's, would still exist, but the stress would have shifted to more perfect systems to meet the ICBM and IPBM threat.

One new means of "civil defense" would be the extensive decentralization of the economic system—begun in 1957—and coordinated with decentralized political (Party) controls and military districts. Thus nuclear devastation of the traditional control center, Moscow, would no longer threaten the serious disruption it would have meant in the 1940's and 1950's, and even the 1960's.

A Look into the Future

The development of active defenses would follow two courses. First, during the 1960's the anti-aircraft guided missiles would be largely replaced by anti-rocket and anti-missile missiles as the threat largely shifted from cruise-type manned or unmanned bombers to the ICBM. By 1970 barrage-type missiles with great altitude capabilities might be used to create clouds of small artificial meteorites to "intercept" hostile ballistic missiles even before or as they re-enter the earth's atmosphere, as new means of long-range detection of actual firings would become operational. Perhaps a major form of defense would be jamming from space platforms of the enemy's initial firing-guidance radar. Such jamming might even include techniques for turning the enemy's rockets back to fall on the country from which they were originally fired.

Strategic defense would be an extremely important element both in the deterrence picture and in preparation for countering strategic attacks.

CONCLUDING COMMENTS

This brief glance into the future is useful simply to see that Soviet strategy today and in the years ahead is developing and taking full advantage of new scientific, technological, and weapons potentialities. The *strategic concept* gives every sign of continuing essentially unchanged into the future. The new political strategic concept of deterrence plus pressure is accompanied by military preparation for any kinds of wars which the Soviets may choose or be compelled to fight. The main requirement is that flexibility in strategic decision must be preserved so that in the choice between various possibilities in any situation the Soviets can select the most advantageous and least costly of alternatives. This requires a large and balanced military establishment, which the Soviets maintain.

This is the challenge of Soviet strategy in the nuclear age.

V

CHAPTER 12

SOURCE MATERIALS ON SOVIET STRATEGY:

A BIBLIOGRAPHIC AND INTERPRETIVE GUIDE

The major source of information on various Soviet doctrinal and strategic beliefs is their military writings. Some of these are official documents of the Ministry of Defense, and virtually all are "semi-official" by virtue of being accepted for publication. One may well question the sincerity and veracity of information published in the pages of a controlled press. But in the case of views published in the Soviet military press, there are several particular features which assist us to evaluate the material. In the first instance, some of the views expressed are not consciously presented, but are implicit and reflect important ways of thinking—and ideas without such reflection having been intended. Such expressions are not subject to censorship, because neither author nor censor appreciates the significance of the statements. Much of the Soviet military press is more or less publicly available; for example, the service newspapers and most of the service journals are, while not usually available for foreign subscription, not "security classified" by the Soviets. But some sources, including the chief military-theoretical journal, *Military Thought*, are specifically limited to Soviet officers, with distribution tightly restricted and controlled. The fact that views appearing in this organ and other non-publicly available Soviet sources correspond with and endorse those published in the open military press shows that, while some things are of course omitted from the general military press, those matters actually discussed are seriously presented. But this is not surprising. Military writings (periodical and other) are recognized by the Soviets as a main guide for the development of doctrine and for the instruction of professional military cadres at all levels. Most important, recent Soviet military history, the structure and capabilities of the present Soviet military establishment, and Soviet military training are all fully consonant with the strategic concept and implementing doctrines which their expressed military theory expounds.

The present discussion will review (1) the Soviet military periodical press, (2) recent (1953 through 1957) important and useful general Soviet books on military doctrine, and (3) the problem of using sources other than published Soviet military writings.

THE MILITARY PERIODICAL PRESS

The function of the military periodical press in the Soviet Union is, in its essentials, the same as in all other countries: to stimulate new ideas, and to inform and educate the readers in officially accepted doctrine. In the Soviet system, the latter element is particularly pronounced, and it involves substantial effort at political indoctrination. But the treatment of questions on military science and the military art is above all intended to *teach* Soviet officers the accepted doctrine. Different journals are intended to serve for various components of the military establishment, and for various levels of the military structure.

There are three official daily newspapers, and a large number of lesser unit newspapers for various military districts and fleets.

Krasnaia zvezda (Red Star) is the newspaper of the Ministry of Defense for the Army. It has been published since 1924. Although not so stated on the masthead, it is in fact issued under the supervision of the Chief Political Administration of the Ministry of Defense. Most articles are propaganda exhortations, "news" on political and military training, and general tactical-technical discussions. Ground forces matters are most extensively covered, but naval and air subjects also are treated. Only occasionally, perhaps on an average of once a month, the editorials and lead articles are of real interest in terms of their doctrinal content.

Sovetskii flot (The Soviet Fleet) is the corresponding organ of the Soviet Navy. Its predecessor, published from 1938 until 1953, was *Krasnyi flot* (Red Fleet). The present paper was resumed after a lapse of about one and one-half years, in October 1954. Its content is parallel with that of *Red Star* except that naval matters of course predominate in doctrinal, tactical, and technical discussions. The doctrinal content of this newspaper is perhaps a little higher than that of *Red Star*.

Sovetskaia aviatsiia (Soviet Aviation) is the organ of the Soviet Air Forces. It has been published only since December 1956. (A predecessor, *Stalinskii sokol*, Stalinist Hawk, was published from 1941 until 1953). Again, its content is parallel to that of *Red Star* and *Soviet Fleet,* with a natural emphasis on matters concerning aviation.

Sovetskii patriot (Soviet Patriot) is not strictly a military newspaper; it is the organ of DOSAAF, the paramilitary youth organization. Issued twice weekly, this paper does occasionally contain articles of interest, especially on air defense and civil defense, since DOSAAF has an active role in training volunteers—and the population—for civil defense work.

These four central newspapers are all regularly received in the United States, where virtually complete files exist. The various local unit newspapers are only irregularly obtained, and only scattered files are available, but their doctrinal value is very low.

Now let us turn to the military periodical magazines. The few main ones are among the most valuable sources of material on Soviet military thinking.

Voennaia mysl' (Military Thought) is the chief theoretical journal, and has been published monthly since 1937 by the General Staff. Since 1941 it has not been available for general or foreign subscription, and since 1947 it has been marked: "For Generals, Admirals, and Officers of the Soviet Army and Navy Only." In actual circulation it is further limited, but it is generally available to officers down through the level of field grade (regimental staffs and battalion commanders). Articles in this journal cover a wide span of important strategic and tactical problems, and are written by the leading military authorities and theoreticians of the Soviet Union. The best works of students at the higher war colleges, the Voroshilov General Staff College and the Frunze Command and Staff College, are sometimes published in it. Unlike most of the other military journals, its articles are not indexed in the weekly *Letopis zhurnalnykh statei* (Calendar of Periodical Articles) nor in the subject file index of military articles in the Lenin Library. Also, while occasionally selected articles from *Military Thought* are printed in book collections of articles published openly by the Military Publishing House, they are never so identified. Articles reprinted from it, *with* identification are used in security-classified books which are used by the Voroshilov and Frunze academies. This journal is, in fact, so far as we know, the most important general medium for expression of Soviet military doctrinal and strategic thinking. And, as is evident from the previous discussion (especially in Chapter 4), it has played an important role in provoking some significant modifications in Soviet military doctrine in the last few years. *Military Thought* is thus a particularly important source for learning about Soviet military thinking. It was widely used in preparing the present book. The chief editor is Lieutenant General N. A. Radetsky, and the editorial board is a distinguished panel of Soviet generals, marshals, and admirals. Unfortunately, full files of this journal are not available here, for obvious reasons.

Voennyi vestnik (The Military Herald) is a monthly publication of the ground forces, in being since 1921. Tactical and ground forces' technical and ordnance matters are the chief subjects covered. It is a very useful source of information on the ground forces tactical doctrine, but only very occasionally do articles on strategic thinking appear there. It is regularly received in the United States.

Vestnik vozdushnogo flota, (The Herald of the Air Fleet) has been published by the Air Forces since 1917 (monthly since 1945). Air tactics and aviation technical developments are featured, and only rarely do articles on strategic doctrine appear. It is regularly received.

Vestnik protivo-vozdushnoi oborony (The Herald of the Air Defense Forces) has been issued monthly since 1929 by the Air Defense Forces. Recent issues have not been available to the author, but it probably continues to carry little beyond tactical-technical discussions on active air defenses.

Morskoi sbornik (The Naval Journal) has been published since 1917. Again, while recent issues have not been available, this journal doubtless continues to present articles on tactical-technical naval subjects. It is the most useful of the various "service journals" (not including *Military Thought)* because it also carries important articles on naval strategy. And, like *Military Thought,* it is not indexed or cited in open publications or libraries.

Tankist (The Tankman), *Artilleriiskii zhurnal* (The Artillery Journal), *Voennyi sviazist* (The Military Signals Man), *Tyl' i snabzhenie vooruzhennykh sil* (The Rear and Supply of the Armed Forces), and *Voenno-inzhenernyi zhurnal* (The Military Engineering Journal) are the other main service journals, each specializing in its field, and very rarely containing articles with expressions of strategic views. Full files of these journals are not available.

Propagandist i agitator is an important publication of the Chief Political Administration of the Ministry of Defense, intended for the guidance of the senior political officers in the armed forces. It is issued twice each month. Usually it presents articles relating to political indoctrination of the military

257

cadres, but sometimes it includes valuable articles on military science to orient the senior political officer on the latest professional military thinking. It is restricted in its distribution and not indexed elsewhere. For lower levels of the political administration the *Bloknot agitatora vooruzhennykh sil* (Handbook for the Armed Forces' Agitator), issued three times monthly, conveys materials for actual use in political indoctrination lectures. In June 1957 a new monthly called *Partiino-politicheskaya rabota v sovetskoi armii i voenno-morskom flote* (Party-Political Work in the Soviet Army and Navy) began publication. It is intended for the Party organizations in the armed forces.

In addition to these official service journals, there are several popular magazines devoted to military affairs.

Sovetskii voin (The Soviet Warrior) and *Sovetskii moriak* (The Soviet Seaman) are popular "literary" journals published twice monthly by the Chief Political Administration especially for enlisted personnel. They are devoid of military science interest.

Voennye znaniia (Military Knowledge) and *Kryl'ia rodiny* (Wings of the Motherland) are published by the paramilitary DOSAAF. While generally limited to introductory treatment of military affairs, these magazines are of interest, and occasionally contain useful articles on more general military matters. They are regularly received and available.

The general public press, especially articles and interviews published in *Pravda* or *Izvestiia,* on occasion treats military matters. Ordinarily these articles are intended for a propaganda purpose, but the rare statements dealing with strategic matters usually reflect accepted doctrine.

BOOKS AND MANUALS

The Soviets annually publish several hundred books, manuals, and pamphlets on various aspects of military affairs. Most of these are published by the Military Publishing House

(Voenizdat), a subsidiary of the Ministry of Defense. By far the vast majority of these are routine popular accounts of individual military historic campaigns, weapons, tactics, and presentations of political-military propaganda.

For the present bibliography, the author has selected those books published in the five years from 1953 through 1957 that are most useful for understanding Soviet strategy, military doctrine, and military science. The listing is divided into four categories: (A) Military Theory, (B) Military History, (C) General Military Affairs Guides and Manuals, and (D) Weapons Developments. In all, 75 sources are listed, as selected out of the total of over 1,000 publications located and read. The author conducted his research not only with access to all American libraries, but also in various libraries in Moscow. Since full official bibliographical listings were available, there were no omissions excepting of course works security-classified by the Soviet authorities, and even in this category some were by rare fortune accessible in Moscow.

For the entire Soviet period prior to 1953, the author is embarrassed to have no choice but to recommend his own bibliography contained in *Soviet Military Doctrine* (The Free Press; Glencoe, Illinois, 1953; pp. 507-565) which, while not complete, is by far the most comprehensive one available.

In the listings which follow, the dozen most useful and important works are marked by an asterisk. The similarity and even identity of titles of some theoretical works should be ignored; they are not new editions, but entirely different works.

A. *Military Theory*

* 1. Levanov, Col. I. N., Col. B. A. Belyi, and Col. A. P. Novoselov, editors, *Marksizm-leninizm o voine i armii* (Marxism-Leninism on War and the Army), Voenizdat, Moscow, [May 20] 1957, 287 pp.
  This work was issued as the main theoretical volume in a new Officers' Library being published for the guidance of Soviet officers by the Ministry of Defense. It was pre-

259

pared by a collective effort of seven professors at the Lenin Military Political Academy. The most recent and thorough Soviet study of military theory.

2. Mil'shtein, Maj. Gen. M. A. and Col. A. K. Slobodenko, *Voennye ideologi kapitalisticheskikh stran o kharaktere i sposobakh vedeniia sovremennoi voiny* (Military Ideologues of the Capitalist Countries on the Means of Conducting Contemporary War), Znanie, Moscow, [April 22] 1957, 64 pp.

* 3. *Marksizm-leninizm o voine i armii* (Marxism-Leninism on War and the Army), A Collection of Articles, Voenizdat, Moscow, [November 28] 1956, 287 pp.
An important book, composed largely of articles which had appeared in the authoritative *Military Thought*.

4. Chuvikov, Col. P. A., *Marksizm-leninizm o voine i armii* (Marxism-Leninism on War and the Army), Voenizdat, Moscow, 2nd ed., [September 14] 1956, 160 pp.
This book has been unfavorably reviewed for its failure to keep pace with doctrinal evolution.

5. Skovorodin, Lt. Col. M. D., *Taktika kak sostavnaia chast' voennogo iskusstva* (Tactics as a Component of the Military Art), Voenizdat, Moscow, [February 8] 1956, 96 pp.
This interesting book is an elaboration of a theoretical view originally published by the author in *Military Thought*, February 1954.

* 6. Skopin, V. I., *Militarizm* (Militarism), Voenizdat, Moscow, [August 3] 1956, 584 pp.
This is an unusual and fascinating book. It is written by one of the few non-military Soviet specialists on military affairs (though "under the scientific editorship" of Professor Maj. Gen. N. V. Pukhovsky). The book has been in preparation for over twenty years, and is presented in the style of a "capital work" definitive for its subject. It is offered by the publisher "for military and civilian readers," and has been favorably endorsed in reviews in both the military and civilian press.

7. Pukhovsky, Prof. [Maj. Gen.] N. V., *O vozmozhnosti predotvrashcheniia voin v sovremennuiu epokhu* (On the Possibilities for Averting War in the Contemporary Epoch), Znanie, Moscow, [November 27] 1956, 32 pp.
This work, unique in its theme, was originally a public lecture, here distributed in 127,500 copies. The author's

military rank and connection are not given with the booklet.

* 8. *Marksizm-leninizm o voine, armii, i voennoi nauke* (Marxism-Leninism on War, the Army, and Military Science), A Collection of Articles, Voenizdat, Moscow, [February 3] 1955, 220 pp.
Like its successors in 1956 and 1957, listed above as items 1 and 3, this is a collection of writings, mostly from *Military Thought* and the *Military Herald*. It is quite useful, standing at the watershed between the earlier doctrine and the later modified doctrine.

9. Pukhovsky, Maj. Gen. N. V., *Voina i politika* (War and Politics), Voenizdat, Moscow, 1955.
Unfortunately, this book has not been available. The author is a distinguished military professor.

10. Petrov, Col. V. N., *Prochnost' tyla kak postoianno-deistvuiushchii faktor* (Stability of the Rear as a Permanently Operating Factor), Voenizdat, Moscow, 1955.

11. Derevianko, Lt. Col. P. M., *Krizis amerikanskoi voenno-teoreticheskoi mysl'i* (The Crisis of American Military Theoretical Thought), Voenizdat, Moscow, 1955.

*12. Lagovsky, Col. A. N., *Strategiia i ekonomika* (Strategy and Economics), Voenizdat, Moscow, [September 20] 1957, 200 pp.
This is a most useful indication of Soviet thinking on the economic needs and consequences of nuclear war.

13. Popov, Col. Gen. V. S., *Vnesapnost' i neozhidannost' v istorii voin* (Surprise and the Unexpected in the History of Wars), Voenizdat, Moscow, [June 10] 1955, 206 pp.
The author unfortunately wrote this book at the very time the Soviet evaluation of the role of surprise was in transition, and the book was criticized by Marshal of the Tank Troops P. Rotmistrov in a review in the *Military Herald,* November 1955.

*14. *O sovetskoi voennoi nauke* (On Soviet Military Science), A Collection of Articles, Voenizdat, Moscow, [June 30] 1954, 208 pp.
This was the first of the series of collective theoretical works, a device adopted only after "Stalinist" military science dissolved into Soviet military science in 1953. It is a very useful source for gaining insight into early post-

Stalin military thinking. The authors are mostly colonels in staff and academic positions, and most of the articles appeared earlier in *Military Thought* and *Military Herald*.

15. Taranchuk, Col. M. V., *Postoianno-deistvuiushchie faktory, reshchaiushchie sud'bu voiny* (The Permanently Operating Factors Which Decide the Fate of Wars), Voenizdat, Moscow, 1954, 136 pp.

16. Kozlov, Col. S. N., *Vooruzhenie armii—odin iz postoianno-deistvuiushchikh faktorov, reshaiushchikh sud'bu voiny* (The Armament of the Army—One of the Permanently Operating Factors Which Decide the Fate of War), Voenizdat, Moscow, [March 30] 1954, 48 pp.

17. Khomenko, Col. E. A., *O voinakh spravedlivykh i nespravedlivykh* (On Just and Unjust Wars), Voenizdat, Moscow, [June 26] 1954, 96 pp.
A military-theoretical propaganda piece, by an instructor at the Lenin Military-Political Academy.

*18. Maryganov, Col. I. V., *Peredovoi kharakter sovetskoi voennoi nauki* (The Advanced Character of Soviet Military Science), Voenizdat, Moscow, [October 30] 1953, 151 pp.
An excellent picture of Soviet military thinking in the early post-Stalin period before extensive changes had occurred. Written "under the scientific editorship" of Lt. Gen. S. N. Krasil'nikov.

19. Pukhovsky, Maj. Gen. N. V., *O sovetskoi voennoi nauke* (On Soviet Military Science), Voenizdat, Moscow, [November 16] 1953, 86 pp.
This interesting work was the first to attack the "cult of the individual" of Stalin.

20. Kashirin, Col. P. A., *Rol' moral'nogo faktora v sovremennykh voinakh* (The Role of the Morale Factor in Contemporary Wars), Voenizdat, Moscow, 1953, 144 pp.
Written by an author who has made a "career" out of writing, or rewriting, articles and booklets on the role of morale.

21. Osipov, Col. Z., *Zabota Kommunisticheskoi partii ob ukreplenii aktivnoi oborony SSSR* (The Solicitude of the Communist Party for Strengthening the Active Defense of the U.S.S.R.), Voenizdat, Moscow, [October 24] 1953, 72 pp.

Written by a prominent officer in the political administration.

22. Kuz'min, Col. G. V., *Istochniki pobed Sovetskikh Vooruzhennykh Sil* (The Sources of the Victories of the Soviet
Armed Forces), Znanie, Moscow, [December 9] 1953, 32 pp.
Originally a public lecture, and printed here in 200,000
copies.

23. Denisov, Col. N., *Boevaia slava Sovetskoi Aviatsii* (The
Combat Glory of Soviet Aviation), Voenizdat, Moscow,
2nd ed., [July 8] 1953, 264 pp.
A popular account, but with a good reflection of official
thinking in 1953 on the role of air power in war.

B. *Military History*

(Note: There are dozens of books and brochures on various
campaigns and battles, some of them good monographs.
But they are excluded from the listing below because our
present interest is in the general military-theoretical value
to be derived from the more useful general studies.)

* 1. *Sbornik materialov po istorii sovetskogo voennogo iskusstva v Velikoi Otechestvennoi voine, 1941-1945 gg.* (A
Collection of Materials on the History of Soviet Military
Art in the Great Fatherland War, 1941-1945), Frunze
Military Academy, Voenizdat, Moscow, [August 10, 1955]
1956, 510 pp.
This volume was prepared by a group of generals and
colonels on the staff of the Frunze Academy under the
editorship of Lt. Gen. V. F. Vorob'ev, as the fourth in
a series of special texts for the military colleges. This
work is security-classified by the Soviet authorities. It
contains many articles taken from *Military Thought* (and
so identified), *Military Herald*, and other publications,
as well as sections from unpublished lectures and documents. A very valuable source.

* 2. *Vashneishie operatsii Velikoi Otechestvennoi voiny 1941-
1945 gg.* (The Most Important Operations of the Great
Fatherland War, 1941-1945), Voenizdat, Moscow, [January
30] 1956, 623 pp.
A useful collection of articles and contributions by a
number of generals and colonels, edited by Col. P. A.

263

Zhilin. Archives and staff records were used in its preparation.

3. *Sovetskye Vooruzhennye Sily v Velikoi Otechestvennoi voine 1941-1945 gg.* (The Soviet Armed Forces in the Great Fatherland War, 1941-1945), Voenizdat, Moscow, 1956, 112 pp.

   This book was prepared for use in political courses in the Soviet armed forces. Unfortunately it is not available.

4. *Deistviia voenno-morskogo flota v Velikoi Otechestvennoi voine* (The Operations of the Navy in the Great Fatherland War), Voenizdat, Moscow, [January 5] 1956, 420 pp.

   A useful collection of articles on the Soviet Navy in World War II.

* 5. *Sbornik materialov po istorii voennogo iskusstva v Velikoi Otechestvennoi voine* (A Collection of Materials for the History of the Military Art in the Great Fatherland War), Series 4, Voroshilov Military Academy, Voenizdat, Moscow, 1955, Vol. 1, 304 pp; Vol. 2, 468 pp; Vol. 3, 378 pp; Vol. 4, 495 pp; and a Supplement of Maps, 36 pp.

   This is an extremely valuable collection of the best articles from *Military Thought* and other published and unpublished sources on the war period. Prepared under the editorship of Prof. Lt. Gen. A. I. Gotovtsev, this is the most complete and comprehensive military history to date. It is security-classified by the Soviet authorities. The four volumes of Series 4 are a continuation of the earlier issued Series 1 through 3 on The History of the Military Art.

6. *Aviatsiia nashei Rodiny* (Aviation of Our Motherland), A Collection of Articles from *Herald of the Air Fleet,* Voenizdat, Moscow, [May 16] 1955, 566 pp.

   Prepared under the editorship of Col. I. F. Shipilov, this collection presents the articles which have appeared in past years on Soviet aviation development, war history, and technological advance.

7. *Ocherki istorii Velikoi Otechestvennoi voiny 1941-1945 gg.* (Essays on the History of the Great Fatherland War, 1941-1945), Academy of Sciences of the U.S.S.R., Moscow, [September 20] 1955, 534 pp.

   This is the best-known recent Soviet military history. It was the subject of strong debate on the pages of *Problems of History* in 1956, and was criticized for insufficient attention to overcoming the cult of Stalin as directed at the Twentieth Party Congress—although, as the editors noted in rebuttal, the book was published months earlier. The authors are a group of military historians on the General Staff, headed by Col. B. S. Tel'pukhovsky.

8. Strokov, Col. A. A., *Istoriia voennogo iskusstva* (History of the Military Art), Voenizdat, Moscow, Vol. 1, [October 17] 1955, 662 pp.
Colonel Strokov is professor and head of the department of military art at the Lenin Military Political Academy. This volume deals only with ancient times, but includes introductory discussion of current views.

9. Razin, Maj. Gen. E. A., *Istoriia voennogo iskusstva* (History of the Military Art), Voenizdat, Moscow, Vol. 1, [June 17] 1955, 559 pp.
This volume covers exactly the same field as the one noted above. Professor Razin is at the Frunze Academy.

10. Golikov, Col. S., *Vydaiushchiesia pobedy Sovetskoi Armii v Velikoi Otechestvennoi voine* (The Outstanding Victories of the Soviet Army in the Great Fatherland War), Gospolitizdat, Leningrad, 2nd ed., 1954, 310 pp.

11. Somin, N. I., *Vtoraia mirovaia voina 1939-1945 gg.* (The Second World War, 1939-1945), The Higher Party School of the Central Committee of the CPSU, Moscow, 1954, 72 pp.

12. Burdzhalov, E. N., *Velikaia Otechestvennaia voina Sovetskogo Soiuza 1941-1945 gg.* (The Great Fatherland War of the Soviet Union, 1941-1945), The Higher Party School of the Central Committee of the CPSU, Moscow, [May 29] 1953, 164 pp.

13. Vorob'ev, Col. F. D. and Col. V. M. Kravtsov, *Pobedy Sovetskikh Vooryzhennykh Sil v Velikoi Otechestvennoi voine 1941-1945, kratkii ocherk* (The Victories of the Soviet Armed Forces in the Great Fatherland War, 1941-1945; A Short Outline), Voenizdat, Moscow, 2nd ed., [March 16] 1954, 432 pp.

14. *Istoriia voenno-morskogo iskusstva* (A History of the Naval Art), Voenizdat, Moscow, 1953, 3 volumes.
An official publication of the Main Naval Staff. Intended for naval schools.

15. *Voennoe iskusstvo kapitalisticheskogo obshchestva 1789-*

265

Soviet Strategy in the Nuclear Age

1917 gg. (The Military Art of the Capitalist Societies, 1789 to 1917), A Collection for Military Academies, Frunze Academy, Voenizdat, Moscow, 1953, 372 pp.
This is Series 2 in the Frunze Academy works; Series 4 was discussed above as item 5 on our list. This volume is not security-classified by the Soviets, though it is also not available to the public.

C. General Military Affairs Guides and Manuals

1. *Ustav vnutrennei sluzhby Vooruzhennykh Sil Soiuza SSR* (Internal Service Regulations of the Armed Forces of the U.S.S.R.), Voenizdat, Moscow, 1957, 224 pp.
The basic non-combat regulations of the Soviet armed forces.

2. *Stroevoi ustav Vooruzhennykh Sil Soiuza SSR* (The Drill Regulations of the Armed Forces of the U.S.S.R.), Voenizdat, Moscow, 1957, 192 pp.

3. *Ustav garnizonoi i karaul'noi sluzhb Vooruzhennykh Sil Soiuza SSR* (Garrison and Guard Duty Regulations of the Armed Forces of the U.S.S.R.), Voenizdat, Moscow, 1957, 208 pp.

4. *Distsiplinarnyi ustav Vooruzhennykh Sil Soiuza SSR* (Disciplinary Regulations of the Armed Forces of the U.S.S.R.), Voenizdat, Moscow, 1956, 52 pp.

5. *Osnovy voennogo dela* (The Fundamentals of Military Affairs), DOSAAF, Moscow, [March 2] 1955, 344 pp.
The general training and orientation guide for the paramilitary DOSAAF. This edition was still current in late 1957.

6. *Posobie dlia doprizyvnika* (Handbook for the Preconscriptionist), Voenizdat, Moscow, 2nd ed., [January 5] 1955, 352 pp.
A general orientation guide concerning the Soviet armed forces and military affairs.

7. Pobezhimov, Col. I. F., *Ustroistvo Sovetskoi Armii* (The Structure of the Soviet Army), Voenizdat, Moscow, 1954, 142 pp.

8. Kartashev, R. D., *Posobie po voenno-morskomu delu* (A Guide to Naval Affairs), DOSAAF, Moscow, [August 19] 1955, 238 pp.
A general introductory guide and handbook.

Bibliographic and Interpretive Guide

D. *Weapons Developments*

(Note: A number of the books listed below are popular informational works, but in lieu of other sources they also serve as a reference source for military men interested in doctrinal implications of weapons technology. Many popular works of lesser interest have not been included.)

* 1. *Sovremennaia voennaia tekhnika* (Contemporary Military Technology), Voenizdat, Moscow, [November 17, 1956] 1957, 276 pp.
   This work is a compilation, by Maj. Gen. V. P. Moskovsky and Eng. Col. P. T. Astashenkov, of three dozen articles on nuclear weapons, radar, aviation, tanks, artillery, and new scientific developments, which appeared earlier in *Red Star*.

* 2. Pokrovsky, Maj. Gen. Eng. Tech. Service G. I., *Nauka i tekhnika v sovremennykh voinakh* (Science and Technology in Contemporary Wars), Voenizdat, Moscow, [October 8] 1956, 88 pp.
   An extremely important book describing the strategic implications of new military technological developments.

3. Mal'shinsky, A., *Khimicheskoe oruzhie inostrannykh armii i protivokhimicheskaia zashchita* (Chemical Weapons of Foreign Armies and Means of Anti-Chemical Defense), DOSAAF, Moscow, [April 27] 1957, 95 pp.

4. Kokosov, B. V., *Protivoatomnaia, protivokhimicheskaia, protivobakteriologicheskaia zashchita soldata v boiu* (Anti-Atomic, Anti-Chemical, and Anti-Bacteriological Defense of the Soldier in Combat), Voenizdat, Moscow, [February 16] 1957, 128 pp.

5. Sinitsyn, V. P., *et al.*, *Mestnaia protivovozdushnaia oborona* (Civil Defense), Textbook for Middle and Pedagogical Schools, Ministry of Education, Moscow, 2nd ed., [February 1] 1956, 151 pp.

6. *Uchebnoe posobie po MPVO* (Textbook on Civil Defense), DOSAAF, Moscow, [June 16] 1956, 223 pp.
   The official defense guide.

7. Kirillov, P. M., *DOSAAFovtsu o MPVO* (For the DOSAAF Member, on Civil Defense), DOSAAF, Moscow, [October 3] 1956, 112 pp.

8. Traskin, K. A., *Radiolokatsionnaia tekhnika i ee primenenie* (Radar and Its Use), Voenizdat, Moscow, 1956, 158 pp.

9. Petrov, V. P., *Upravliaemye snariady i rakety* (Guided Missiles and Rockets), DOSAAF, Moscow, [April 2] 1957, 119 pp.
   Instructional, with illustrations of types from American-published materials.

10. Liapunov, Eng. B. V., *Upravliaemye reaktivnye snariady* (Guided Missiles), Voendizdat, Moscow, 1955.

11. Pokrovsky, Maj. Gen. Eng. Tech. Service G. I., *Rol' nauki i tekhniki v sovremennoi voine* (The Role of Science and Technology in Contemporary War), Znanie, Moscow, [October 2] 1957, 24 pp.

12. Gil'zin, K. A., *Ot rakety do kozmicheskogo korablia* (From Rockets to Space Ships), Oborongiz, Moscow, [February 18] 1955, 112 pp.

13. *Sredstva i sposoby zashchity ot atomnogo oruzhiia* (Ways and Means of Defense Against Atomic Weapons), Voenizdat, Moscow, 2nd ed., [January 25] 1956, 125 pp.
    A collection of articles, expanded from an earlier edition in 1954. A useful review of Soviet thinking on defensive measures.

14. Arkhipov, Eng, Lt. Col. M. P., *Osnovy ustroistvo atomnogo oruzhiia i protivoatomnaia zashchita* (Fundamentals of the Structure of Atomic Weapons, and Anti-Atomic Defense), DOSAAF, Moscow, [July 14] 1956, 87 pp.

15. Naumenko, Eng. Lt. Col. I. A., *Atomnoe oruzhie i protivoatomnaia zashchita* (The Atomic Weapon and Anti-Atomic Defense), Uzhgorod, 1956, 36 pp.

16. Vorob'ev, Ye I. and U. Ya. Margolis, *Atomnaia energiia i protivoatomnaia zashchita* (Atomic Energy and Anti-Atomic Defense), Institute of Health Education, Moscow, 1956, 78 pp.

17. Zapol'sky, G. N., *Atomnoe oruzhie i protivoatomnaia zashchita naseleniia* (The Atomic Weapon and Defense of the Population), DOSAAF, Moscow, 1956, 47 pp.

18. Syrnev, V. P. and N. P. Petrov, *Radioaktivnye izlucheniia i ikh izmereniia* (Radioactive Rays and Their Measurement), Voenizdat, Moscow, 1956, 256 pp.

19. Naumenko, Eng. Lt. Col. I. A. and I. G. Petrovsky, *Udar-*

naia volna atomnogo vzryva (The Shock Wave of an Atomic Explosion), Voenizdat, Moscow, 1956, 160 pp.

20. Arkhipov, Eng. Lt. Col. M., *Svetovoe izlucheniia atomnogo vzryva* (The Light Rays of an Atomic Explosion), Voenizdat, Moscow, 1956, 210 pp.

21. Gvozdev, Lt. Col. M. M. and Col. V. A. Yakovkin, *Atomnoe oruzhie i protivoatomnaia zashchita* (Atomic Weapons and Anti-Atomic Defense), DOSAAF, Moscow, 1956.

22. Ivanov, I., *Yadernye izlucheniia atomnogo vzryva* (Nuclear Rays of an Atomic Explosion), Voenizdat, Moscow, 1956, 214 pp.

23. Lebedeva, Yu. A. and A. S. Zubkin, *Chto nado znat' ob otravliaiushchikh i radioaktivnykh veshchestvakh* (What One Should Know about Poisonous and Radioactive Substances), DOSAAF, Moscow, 1956, 64 pp.

24. Moiseev, V. M., *Boevye radioaktivnye veshchestva i mery zashchity ot nikh* (Combat Radioactive Substances and Means of Defense against Them), Kuibyshev, 1956, 19 pp.

25. Kuznetsov, G. F., *Porazhaiushche svoistva atomnogo oruzhiia i mery zashchity* (The Destructive Characteristics of Atomic Weapons and Means of Defense), Kuibyshev, 1956, 24 pp.

26. Krylov, V. I., *Atomnoe oruzhie vzryvnogo deistviia i sredstva protivoatomnoi zashchity* (Atomic Weapons' Explosive Effects, and Means of Defense), Latgosizdat, Riga, 1956, 60 pp.

27. *Programma zaniatii s naseleniium po protivoatomnoi zashchite v kruzhkakh pervichnykh organizatsiakh DOSAAF* (Program of Anti-Atomic Defense Instruction of the Population through Primary Groups of the DOSAAF Organization), DOSAAF, Moscow, 1955, 12 pp.
    This is a basic civil defense directive, adopted in August 1955.

28. *Atomnyi vzryv na more* (Atomic Explosion at Sea), A Collection of Articles, Voenizdat, Moscow, 1955, 104 pp.
    Not available, but based on available articles which appeared in a series in *Sovetskii flot*.

29. *Pamiatka soldatu i serzhantu po zachchite ot atomnogo oruzhiia* (Soldiers' and Sergeants' Manual on Defense against Atomic Weapons), Voenizdat, Moscow, 1954, 46 pp.
    This was the first official Ministry of Defense manual on atomic defense.

A Note on Soviet Security

The availability of several Soviet security-classified sources, materials which are not intended to be seen by the general public or foreigners, is very valuable not only for their specific content, but also because they provide a check on the reliability of data in parallel open publications. The chief such sources are the available issues of the periodical *Military Thought,* and several higher War College studies listed above, to which the author gained access in the Soviet Union. These sources go further into some sensitive matters than do the openly published materials, but in no case did the open materials display any discrepancy or divergence from the secret ones. This confirms and underlines the conclusion that the open sources are, to the extent they do treat strategic matters, a generally reliable source.

Other Sources

The problem of seeking out, and using, sources other than Soviet-published materials is difficult. Secondary sources, Western commentaries, are rarely of use for extending beyond published Soviet sources.* One infrequent exception is the official release of information by responsible Western governmental authorities, as in published NATO reviews of the Soviet military strength, etc. Another category, not really "secondary" or "primary," is the body of writings by former Soviet officers. Some of these have been very good, particularly concerning the Soviet secret police and intelligence. None in recent years have been in a position to contribute usefully to our knowl-

* One deserving exception is the fine analysis contributed in various articles by N. Galay, in the *Bulletin of the Institute for the Study of the USSR* (in Munich), although his work has sometimes been hampered by lack of access to important Soviet published sources.

edge of Soviet strategic thinking. Nonetheless, official Western releases and responsible former Soviet sources are useful supplementary sources for information on such subjects as Soviet training practices, military force levels and deployment, etc.

A word might be in order on the *technique* of analysis of Soviet sources other than those actually dealing with doctrine. To note one example, the ranks, relative standing, and assignment of senior Soviet military men can be gleaned from various reports in the Soviet press. Sometimes clues appear in such personnel changes. Let us take a hypothetical example: Admiral N. is made chief of the operations section of the naval main staff. Now if we know that Admiral N.'s whole career had been in submarine operations, it would be a clue and indication—though by itself not proof—that the Soviets were placing increased emphasis within their Navy on their submarine arm. If, in addition, it is reliably reported that the rate of construction of submarines has increased, and that of major surface vessels declined, the changed operational emphasis would be confirmed. If, in the light of these developments, we were also to see that the Soviet military theoreticians declared in their writings that submarines now play a new role of greater importance as missile launchers, we could accept this statement as plausible explanation for the increased emphasis. Further attention could then be directed toward all discussions of submarine-launched missiles, and toward learning about the actual progress of submarine-launched missiles. If significant indications were found, the published statements could be accepted as expressing Soviet doctrine. This is but one simplified illustration.

Although published statements *can* be falsified and deceptive, the writings in Soviet military journals on doctrinal and strategic views have proved remarkably accurate. To be sure, they are less complete and precise than we would like, but they are genuine. The use of deception and falsification in the realm of doctrine has been virtually absent. (Even concrete claims of new weapons advances have been quite accurate, although here the possibility for deception is greater). In the case of doctrine, the main point is that the Soviets simply cannot afford to mislead their own officer corps merely in order to try to mislead us.

Another rare source of information on Soviet strategic thinking is discussion with knowledgeable Soviet officers. The opportunity for such contact is, of course, quite limited even for official representatives, though the mutual contacts of military attachés is the most usual form of such exchange. For other researchers and analysts the opportunity is, if present at all, ordinarily very slight indeed. In preparing this book, the author has been particularly fortunate in being able to discuss unofficially many relevant questions with a number of Soviet officers of the various services. Such conversations, both in the Soviet Union and abroad, were conducted with officers ranging in rank from lieutenant to major general. While these conversations were ordinarily of but limited value for learning about Soviet strategy *per se*, they were a useful guide to gauging the degree of actual belief on the part of the officers in their stated doctrine. The correlation was very great; these discussions confirmed the serious nature of the military press as a stimulus and reflection of military thinking—at least at the upper-middle and lower levels of the officer corps. It is not prudent, since all such discussions were entirely unofficial, to refer to any of these talks in detail. Moreover, since in themselves they represent "raw" and uncollated data, the author has not used these sources as direct evidence of Soviet strategic thinking. But as a general background, they proved useful indeed.

These, then, are the main sources of data for our analysis of Soviet military thinking. It should also be noted that there is the possibility, within limits, of tentatively estimating future Soviet views on the basis of projection of their known past and present approaches. Such estimates can be of great value, though, of course, they require constant review.

Bibliographic and Interpretive Guide

A CONCLUDING COMMENT ON METHODOLOGY

The major source of information about Soviet military strategic thinking is thus the relevant fraction of their military writings. The most important additional source is the status of Soviet military organization and data concerning relative strengths of the various components of the military establishment. Military capabilities alone do not tell us sufficiently the strategic concept and doctrine which will govern their employment in war. But taken together with expressed doctrine, and interpreted, they are a valuable contributing source. Other sources provide helpful supplementary data, but not the primary material required for analysis.

The method of analysis briefly alluded to above has in the past proved accurate and useful. The alternative sometimes proposed or even attempted is to *assume* that the Soviets operate in "the most rational way," a phrase which really means in the way the *analyst* thinks is optimum for achieving results in implementation of the analyst's own implicit strategic concept. This can readily be seen to be an inferior substitute for discovering, even if imperfectly, what the Soviets themselves think to be the best means for meeting the requirements of their strategic concept. Yet if this latter approach is adopted, even objectively conclusive evidence of a Soviet view can be ignored as "irrational." And the acceptance of Soviet written doctrine and other indications which *support* the analyst's "model" of rationality, while *rejecting* all other evidence from the same sources which doesn't fit the preconception, is in cold fact arbitrary or worse. It should be unnecessary even to mention such a fallacious approach, but unfortunately some who have failed to comprehend the need for understanding a different strategic concept have been led by perplexity to the "model rationality" approach.

Thus the methodology of the present study has been, on the foundation of the author's earlier historical study of the de-

273

velopment of Soviet military doctrine from 1917 to 1953, to examine carefully all available sources of information in order to establish the Soviet strategic concept and implementing doctrines. The analysis has revealed a complex but integrated pattern of continuity and change as Soviet military thought has evolved from a backward state at the time of Stalin's death to a well-balanced and challenging posture today.

INDEX

AAA (Anti-Aircraft Artillery), 189, 190, 248
"Absolute Weapon," 76-79
Academy of Sciences, 232, 264
Advance, 5, 14, 98, 102, 103, 155-156, 160-161
Adventurism, 5, 37, 76, 86, 101
 American, 122, 130, 131, 135
Aerodyne, 247
Africa, 106, 197, 215, 242, 243, 247
Air Defense, 44, 45, 46, 50, 52, 53-54, 81, 106-107, 158, 163, 172, 190, 198, 230, 234, 248-249, 255
Air Defense Districts, 54
Air Defense Forces; see Air Defense
Air Forces, 41, 45, 46, 49, 50, 52-56, 57, 81-82, 170-192
Air Main Staff, 43, 53, 179
Air Power, 10, 77, 78, 79
 U.S., 119-132, 170-172
 see also Air Forces, Strategic Air Power, Tactical Air Power
Air Superiority, 188-189, 244
Air Transport, 46, 161-162, 199, 248
Airborne Forces, 44, 45, 53, 57, 81, 82, 161-162, 171, 189, 206, 208, 211, 244, 247
 U. S., 131
Aircraft, 12, 65, 161-162, 174, 177-178
 Strength in, 57, 190, 201
 see also names of individual aircraft
Aircraft Carriers, 37, 52, 65, 86, 187, 199-201
Airfields:
 Vulnerabilities of, 162-163, 188-189, 231

Alliances:
 As beginnings of wars, 133
 Of western countries, 12, 130, 132, 133-135, 137
Amphibious Operations and Forces, 52, 199, 205-206, 207, 214, 244
Annihilation, 9, 13 71, 72, 87, 155
Anti-Missile Defense, 190, 220-231, 248-249
Antonov, O. K., 162
Arctic Ocean, 210, 211
Armored Forces, 160-161
 see also Tank Troops
Army, 149-166
 see also Airborne Forces, Artillery, Ground Forces, Infantry, Tank Troops, etc.
Army Group, 49, 53
Arnold, Gen. H. H., 177
Artillery, 44, 45, 49, 54, 57, 78, 82, 158, 161, 163, 165, 247
 Atomic gun, 157, 163-164
 Long-range rockets, 231-234
 Naval, 207
Artillery Journal, 257
Asia, 99, 106, 137, 151, 211, 243
 see also Eurasia
Atlantic Theater, 51, 133, 210, 212
Atomic Blackmail, 135, 222
Atomic Defense, 78, 157-159, 160
 Studies on, 267-269
 see also Nuclear Warfare
Atomic Power Stations, 162
Atomic Warfare; see Nuclear Warfare
Atomic Weapons; see Nuclear Weapons
A-VDV, 53

275

276

Index

Index

Maneuver:
  Tactics, 158-160
Maneuvers, 69, 156, 167 n.15
Manpower, 57, 91, 150-151, 164
Margelov, Lt. Gen. V., 46
Marines (Naval Infantry), 52
Maritime Communications:
  Soviet, 207
  Western, 203, 205, 216
Marshall, Brig. Gen. S. L. A., 137
Marxism-Leninism:
  On war, 7, 67, 87-88, 98
  Works on, 259-261
  see also Ideology
Maslennikov, Gen. of the Army I. I., 54
"Massive Retaliation," 15, 100, 110
Mediterranean Theater, 52, 106, 133, 209, 213
Meretskov, Marshal K. A., 46
Methodology, 271-274
Mi-6 (Helicopter), 161
Miasishchev, Maj. Gen. V. M., 178
Middle (and Near) East, 135, 154, 196, 242
MiG-15 (Fighter Aircraft), 191
MiG-17 (Fighter Aircraft), 191
MiG-19 (Fighter Aircraft), 191
MiG-21 (Fighter Aircraft), 191
Mikhailov, N. A., 36
Mikoyan, A. I., 17 n.
Military Appropriations, 23, 91
  Of the capitalist powers, 118, 121, 126-127, 129, 184
Military Art; see Military Science, Military Doctrine
Military Commissar; see Political Officers
Military Council, 42, 43, 45, 46, 48, 52
Military Districts, 36, 45, 48-50, 51, 53, 248
Military Doctrine, 7-8, 11-13, 14, 27, 38, 39, 41,, 58, 61-91, 106, 114, 160, 170-171, 241, 254, 256
Military Engineering Journal, 257
Military Herald, 256
Military History, 26, 36, 39, 62-63, 64, 65, 69-70, 254
  Books on, 259, 263-266
Military Knowledge, 258
Military Leadership, 8, 18-39, 244
Military Operations, 9, 88-89, 136, 152, 155-166, 203
Military Press, 253-259

Military Publishing House, 256, 258-259
Military Science, 17 n., 38, 61, 62, 64, 66-69, 71, 82-84, 173, 176, 254
  Bourgeois, 122-123, 126-127
  Laws of, 61-91
  Societies for study of, 66
Military Signal Man, 257
Military Theory:
  Books on, 259-263
  see also Military Science
Military Thought, 8, 62, 63, 66, 68, 69, 70, 71, 85, 88, 253-256, 270
Mine Warfare, 207
Missiles, 10, 12, 39, 46, 63, 64, 65, 76, 77, 81, 130, 152, 161, 163, 186, 221-235
  Advantages of, 223-224, 228
  Air Defense, 189, 228-231, 234, 241, 248-249
  Air-to-surface, 225
  Books on, 267-269
  Defense against, 228-231, 248-249
  For deterrence, 222, 223, 231, 235, 245
  From satellite vehicles, 246
  Guided (pilotless bombers), 224, 227, 230, 232
  Limitations of, 224-226, 227
  Naval, 207
  Research on, 227, 231-232
  Targets of, 221, 222-226
  see also ICBM, IRBM, individual names of missiles
Mobility, 159-162
  U.S., 131, 247
Mobilization, 49, 89, 137, 153
Molotov, V. M., 19, 21, 28, 32, 33, 34
Morale, 82-84, 88, 154-156
  Building, 47
  Of the West, 119-120, 122-123, 137-138
  Undermining, 9, 71-75, 176
  see also Indoctrination
Moscow:
  As control center, 248
  Battle of (1941-1942), 26, 36, 93 n. 20
  Military District of, 27, 49
Moskalenko, Marshal K. S., 25, 27, 28, 29, 35, 36, 76
Moskva (11-18 Transport Aircraft), 162
MPVO (Local Anti-Air Defense), 190-191

279

Index

281

Index